Adorno and Marx

In a time marked by crises and the rise of right-wing authoritarian populism, **Critical Theory and the Critique of Society** intends to renew the critical theory of capitalist society exemplified by the Frankfurt School and critical Marxism's critiques of social domination, authoritarianism, and social regression by expounding the development of such a notion of critical theory, from its founding thinkers, through its subterranean and parallel strands of development, to its contemporary formulations.

Series editors: **Werner Bonefeld**, University of York, UK and **Chris O'Kane**, University of Texas Rio Grande Valley, USA

Available titles:
Right-wing Culture in Contemporary Capitalism, Mathias Nilges
Adorno and Neoliberalism, Charles Andrew Prusik
Toward a Critical Theory of Nature, Carl Cassegård
Spectacular Logic in Hegel and Debord, Eric-John Russell

Adorno and Marx

Negative Dialectics and the Critique of Political Economy

Edited by
Werner Bonefeld and Chris O'Kane

BLOOMSBURY ACADEMIC
LONDON • NEW YORK • OXFORD • NEW DELHI • SYDNEY

BLOOMSBURY ACADEMIC
Bloomsbury Publishing Plc
50 Bedford Square, London, WC1B 3DP, UK
1385 Broadway, New York, NY 10018, USA
29 Earlsfort Terrace, Dublin 2, Ireland

BLOOMSBURY, BLOOMSBURY ACADEMIC and the Diana logo are trademarks of
Bloomsbury Publishing Plc

First published in Great Britain 2022
This Paperback edition published 2024

Series design by Ben Anslow

ISBN: HB: 978-1-3501-9363-5
         PB: 978-1-3501-9367-3
         ePDF: 978-1-3501-9364-2
         eBook: 978-1-3501-9365-9

Series: Critical Theory and the Critique of Society

Typeset by Integra Software Services Pvt. Ltd.

Contents

Part 3 Subjectivity and Pseudo Practice: On Social Praxis

Appendix

List of Contributors

Fabian Arzuaga currently teaches for the Critical Writing Studies program at the University of Pennsylvania in Philadelphia. His work has appeared in *Foundations* and *Philosophy & Social Criticism*. His book *Marx, Adorno and the Critique of Labor: Individuality in the Age of Surplus Populations* will be published by Bloomsbury.

Charlotte Baumann is Fjodor Lynen-Fellow at the University of Sussex, with an experienced researcher grant from the Humboldt foundation. She has published in the *European Journal of Philosophy*, the *Journal of the History of Philosophy* and the *British Journal of the History of Philosophy* and contributed to the *Oxford Handbook on Adorno*.

Nico Bobka is Lecturer at Frankfurt and Darmstadt University of Applied Sciences. He is currently pursuing a project on Theodor W. Adorno's dialectical critique of ontology and the so-called ontological need at the Free University of Berlin.

Werner Bonefeld is Professor of Politics at the University of York, UK. With Beverley Best and Chris O'Kane he co-edited the *Sage Handbook of Frankfurt School Critical Theory* (Sage, 2018). Recent book publications include *Critical Theory and the Critique of Political Economy* (Bloomsbury 2014) and *The Strong State and the Free Economy* (Rowman & Littlefield, 2017).

Dirk Braunstein is Research Assistant at the Institute for Social Research, University of Frankfurt. He is the author of *Adornos Kritik der politischen Ökonomie* (Transcript, 2011) and the editor of *Die Frankfurter Seminare Theodor W. Adornos. Gesammelte Sitzungsprotokolle 1949-1969*, four volumes (de Gruyter, 2021).

Kirstin Munro is Assistant Professor of Political Science at the University of Texas Rio Grande Valley. Her recent publications include articles *in Capital & Class*, *Critical Sociology* (with Chris O'Kane), *Environment and Planning: E* and *Science*

& Society. Her book *Eco-Conscious Households and Sustainability: Compromise, Conflict and Complicity* will be published by the University of Bristol Press.

Chris O'Kane is Assistant Professor of Political Science at the University of Texas Rio Grande Valley. His work has recently appeared in *Critical Historical Studies*, (with Kirstin Munro) *Critical Sociology, Science & Society* and *Review of Radical Political Economics*. With Beverley Best and Werner Bonefeld he co-edited the *Sage Handbook of Frankfurt School Critical Theory* (Sage, 2018).

Charles Prusik is an instructor of philosophy and ethics at Villanova University. He received his PhD in philosophy in 2017. His research specializes in critical theory and political economy, and he is the author of *Adorno and Neoliberalism: The Critique of Exchange Society* (Bloomsbury, 2020).

Marcel Stoetzler is Senior Lecturer in Sociology at Bangor University, UK. He has published on ('Frankfurt School') Critical Theory, feminist theory, and the theory and history of antisemitism. His publications include the edited volume *Antisemitism and the Constitution of Sociology* (University of Nebraska Press, 2014) and *The State, the Nation and the Jews. Liberalism and the Antisemitism Dispute in Bismarck's Germany* (University of Nebraska Press, 2008).

Adorno and Marx: Negative dialectics and the critique of political economy

Werner Bonefeld and Chris O'Kane

The title of the book summarizes a recent intellectual history of the development of the critique of political economy as a critical social theory which emerged in the context of the new left of the late 1960s and has been elaborated by successive generations of critical scholars in different institutional settings ever since. The influence of the Frankfurt School is of particular importance for its development. It is connected with the Adorno-inspired New Reading of Marx in the then West Germany.[1] In the UK, it surfaced as the 'social form' analysis within the framework of the Conference of Socialist Economists.[2] These new readings of the critique of political economy as a critical social theory developed further in the intersection between the early critical theory of the Frankfurt School – mainly Adorno, Horkheimer and Marcuse – the West-German New Reading of Marx and 'social form' analysis under the rubric of 'Open Marxism'.[3] In the United States, it is associated with the work of, amongst others, Moishe Postone, Patrick Murray and Tony Smith.[4] Contemporary developments of the new readings into a critical theory of money and time, the social relations of nature, surplus citizens, history, economic crisis, state, gender, subjectivity and labour include the works by, for example, Beverley Best, Carl Casegaard, Dimitra Kotouza, Christian Lotz, Christos Memos, Frederick Harry Pitts, Charles Prusik and Marina Vishmidt.[5]

The conception of the critique of political economy as a critical social theory is founded, first and foremost, on the rejection of the traditional Marxist notion of the economic forces as primary and its conception of class struggle as the motor of historical progress. Instead, these new readings conceived of the economy as an inverted form of the capitalistically organized social relations, and of the economic categories as perverted social categories. The economic relations thus express the conceptuality of historically specific social relations. Their conceptuality is therefore socially constituted, that is, economic nature amounts to a social nature. It is the nature of historically specific social relations. This insight emerges from Marx's critique of 'The Fetishism of the Commodity and Its Secret' in *Capital*, Volume One. According to this critique, economic relationships are fundamentally spectral.[6] They amount to an objective illusion.[7] Capitalist society is governed by independent movements of economic things and yet, these things are socially constituted. In the words of Herbert Marcuse, society in the form of the economic object manifests itself 'behind the backs of the individuals; yet it is their work'.[8] Their independent movement is thus both real and illusionary. The social individuals are governed by 'the products of their own hands', and it is through their social practices that they endow the economic things with a consciousness and a will. 'They do this without being aware of it'.[9] The economic object thus expresses definite social relations. Even the simplest elements, 'the commodity for example, is already an inversion and causes relations between people to appear as attributes of things and as relations of people to the social attributes of things'.[10]

Marx argues further that the fetishism of commodities emerges from 'the peculiar social character of the labour that produces them'.[11] What is peculiar to capitalism cannot also have a transhistorical force. For the new readings of the critique of political economy as a critical social theory, therefore, the capitalist labour economy is not a socially specific manifestation of general, transcendental economic forces that exist through a succession of modes of production, as argued in the Marxism of the second and third Internationals, Leninism and social democracy, which continue to be argued to this day in Marxian economics, political economy and democratic socialism.[12] Marxian economics understands itself as a science of economic matter. Its critique of the capitalist labour economy is not a critique of labour economy as such. It is rather a critique of the irrationality and exploitative character of the capitalist labour economy, and it amounts to an argument for a rational socialist labour economy in which the state is the central organizational power of economic planning. That is, for Marxian economics the 'labour theory of value is a macro-economic one'.[13] Marxist economics reconciles the critique of political economy with those same economic categories which Marx's critique of fetishism exposes as inverted social categories and thus as deceitful and *verrückte* (perverted) abstractions of the social relations. As pointed out by Simon Clarke, the Marxist argument about a succession of modes of production took its cue not from Marx but rather from Smith's stages theory of history.[14] Furthermore, Marx's reproach in his critique of the Gotha Programme to the socialists of his time similarly rejects their endorsement of labour as the category of social wealth as an ill-founded idea that takes the social character of capitalist labour as the ontological foundation of wealth in every society.

The new readings of the critique of political economy as a critical social theory rejected traditional versions of historical materialism as legitimating the then state socialist regimes and the organizational form of the Party as the vehicle of socialist transformation.[15] Instead, they developed the 'materialist method' as a critique of the existing social relations, one which, in the words of Adorno, 'dissolves things understood as dogmatic'.[16] Adorno characterized the dialectical materialist view of history as a 'perverter of Marxian motives'.[17] According to Marx, it is 'much easier to discover by analysis the earthly core of the earthly kernel of the misty creations of religion than to do the opposite, i.e. to develop from the actual, given relations of life the forms in which these have been apotheosized. The latter method' he continues, 'is the only materialist one, and therefore the only scientific one'. The former method belongs to the abstract materialism of the natural sciences 'that excludes history and its process'.[18] There is only one reality and that is the reality of the definite socio-historical forms of life. For Adorno's students, Adorno's negative dialectics paved the way from the then prevailing ideas of Marxian economics and political economy as an argument about the rational organization of labour economy in socialism towards the critique of political economy as a critical social theory. Negative dialectics is about the forms of life in reified society. Perhaps Helmut Reichelt comes closest when delineating the importance of Adorno's critical theory for the new readings of Marx. As he sees it, Adorno and Horkheimer 'held on to the theory of inverted sociability'. Their critical theory of capitalism as a negative totality of economic inversion 'was primarily concerned with the genetic explication of society and society was understood as the totality of these inverted forms'.[19] In this reading, and with reference to Alfred Schmidt, the critique of political economy amounts to a 'conceptualised practice' of the social relations[20] in and through 'the forms of life in which these have been apotheosized'.[21] Critically understood, Marx's point about the peculiar social character of labour as the foundation of the fetishism of commodities demystifies the centrality of labour as the 'negative ontology' of the capitalist social relations. Moishe Postone's understanding of the critique of political economy as a critique of labour economy derives from this insight. The practical consequences of this shift from a political economy of labour organization to a critique of political economy are formidable. It cuts from underfoot the idea of state-socialism as an alternative to the capitalist labour economy.

Reichelt makes his point about Adorno's pivotal influence in the development of the new readings in a publication about Jürgen Habermas's attempted reconstruction of historical materialism, which for him amounted to a traditional social theory. The attribute traditional refers to a research objective that seeks to identify the logic of social structures in abstraction from their social relations. In the case of Habermas, the separation of social reality into system world, which is the domain of system theory, and life-world, which is the domain of social action theory, characterized the return to traditional conceptions of society in Frankfurt critical theory. In Marxian economics and political economy, this same theoretical dichotomy pertains between, on the one hand, market and state as separate structural entities, and the social forces, on the other. The perennial question whether the economy determines the state, as allegedly it exclusively does in neoliberalism, or whether the state determines the economy, as allegedly it did during the post-war period of the so-called mass democratic Keynesian welfare state,[22] is considered to be a matter of the balance of the social forces that manifest themselves through the state. For Marxian political economy what matters are the social interests and the moral values and the ethical standards attached to them. Habermas reproaches Marx, Adorno and Horkheimer for their failure to underpin their critical theories with normative commitments towards the ideas of justice, freedom, equality and, most importantly, the idea of reason.[23] Their negative critique of political economy, he suggests, is deficient because it lacks the foundational moral categories on which to improve social institutions for the better. In the context of the crisis of 2008, this theorizing led to two overlapping analyses. First, the crisis was seen as a consequence of an avoidable structural dysfunctionality, which was the consequence of outsourcing, the privatization of social welfare commitments and the so-called financialization of the economy. The economic crisis led to a political crisis, which akin to Habermas's arguments about a 'legitimation crisis' in the 1970s appeared in the form of a crisis of democratic institutions and democratic forms of representation. These crises were seen to have been caused by corrupt neoliberal socio-economic values that had captured the seat of government and used the power of the state to disembed the economy from society. Second, for the sake of the good society, one that makes good of the promise of reason, the democratic forces of social justice, equality and freedom have to recapture the seat of government in order to overcome the unfavourable neoliberal socio-economic reality through a democratic politics of social integration and policies of distributive justice, changing the financial economy into a social (market) economy.[24] The practical humanism of the proposed resolution to human misery is well meaning and welcome. What it amounts to is unclear. As an analysis of the logic that holds sway in the capitalist social relations, it is fruitless.

The argument that Marx and Adorno do not espouse moral categories to found their normative commitments towards a politics of redistributive justice and social equality, reason and freedom, is well founded. In fact, both rejected such undertakings. With reference to Adorno, 'the leftist critics fail to notice' that the normative ideas of justice, freedom and equality are 'themselves… afflicted with the same injustice under which they are conceived and bound up with the world against which they are set'.[25] Just as Marx's critique of the economic categories is about the decipherment of the social relations in the form of the economic object, Adorno's social theory does not identify society in abstraction from the social relations. Both Marx and Adorno understand that the moral categories of society do not express transcendental and eternal norms but that they are rather historically specific and that they thus cannot be 'perceived without reference to the historical elements implicit in [them]'.[26] The liberal values of freedom, equality and justice depict individuals released from feudal social structures, who are granted the autonomy to engage within a system of justice that treats poor and rich, dispossessed workers and 'moneybags' as equal partners of wealth and as equals before the law.[27] The freedom from servitude is the freedom of exchange between formally equal traders in labour power, the one buying labour power to profit from its consumption as a personification of money that yields more money, the other selling it to make a living as a personification of surplus labour time. Thinking means venturing beyond. Yet, nobody can extract themselves from the world in which they live. The arguments about transcendental economic forces and transcendental norms read the existing society back into history and forward into socialism. They then judge the existing relations as irrational in the organization of its own economic matter and as falling foul of its own normative values. The argument that contemporary society does not meet its own normative standard cannot be denied. Labour markets are racialized and gendered, and the relationship between buyers and sellers is a class relationship between 'masters' who want to give as little as possible and workers deprived of the means of living who want to get as much as possible.[28] The labour market is a buyer's market. Yet, what is traded and what does the freedom of trade mean for the dispossessed sellers of labour power? If labour power cannot be traded what can be traded in its stead to make a living? The pauper belongs to the conceptuality of capitalist wealth.

While Adorno has tended to be read as a cultural critic of the administered world and of the consumer industry rather than a Marxist critic of society, this volume counteracts this conception. The appendix publishes a summary of a seminar conducted by Adorno in 1962. It was first published in German as an appendix to Hans-Georg Backhaus's *Dialektik der Wertform*. On its own, although the summary gives insight into Adorno's critical theory, it does not establish Adorno's credentials as a critic of political economy. Its importance is that Backhaus perceived of it as an instruction for study by Adorno to his students, at least to those who took him by his Marxist word.[29] Their development of the critique of political economy as a critical social theory holds with Adorno and Marx that the social forms, including the forms of thought and struggle, are forms of definite social relations, that a certain logic holds sway in them and that the purpose of critique is to decipher the social genesis of that logic. What is cannot be true. Yet, it is true nevertheless. Its truth is the untruth of a world in which 'Monsieur le Capital and Madame la Terre do their ghost-walking as social characters and at the same time directly as mere things'.[30] As a critical social theory the critique of political economy is singular both as a radical departure from traditional Marxist scholarship and as an equally radical departure from traditional readings of Adorno's work.

However, there is no such thing as an Adornian Marxism or a Marxian Adornianism. It would be wrong to identify Adorno with Marx or Marx with Adorno, to merely reconstruct Marx or Adorno, or to advocate for Adorno's Marxism or Marx's Adornoism and leave the matter at that. Rather, it is the intersection between Adorno's critical social theory and Marx's critique of political economy that is productive of the emergence of this entirely novel and still developing conceptualization of a critical theory of economic objectivity beyond Marxian political economy and Adornian critical theory. Adorno's experience of capitalism enabled him to articulate insights about it that Marx's critique could not articulate. Marx knew that '*human individuality*, human *morality* itself, has become both an object of commerce and the material in which money exists. Instead of money, or paper, it is my own personal existence, my flesh and blood, my social virtues and importance, which constituted the material, corporeal form of the *spirit of money*'.[31] Adorno's critical theory presents what this society has become in a post-fascist culture of enchanted disenchantment, in which domination and antagonism have persisted and mutual indifference has transformed into the social coldness and systematic cruelty of a negative totality without remove.[32] Adorno did not establish the new reading. He provided the theoretical impetus and inspiration for it.

Scope and structure

Adorno and Marx: Negative Dialectics and the Critique of Political contributes to the manifold efforts at developing the critique of political economy as a critical social theory. The book's objective is not to bring the various new readings under one heading, nor to create a new school, or defend a new orthodoxy. Rather, our authors develop their arguments from the intellectual history of the new readings of Marx. Plurality in intellectual endeavour wards against the dogmatization of what emerged originally as a critical departure from moribund ideas and orthodoxies (which nonetheless persist). What holds the book's contributions together is the commitment towards the critique of political economy as a critical social theory and therewith the critique of the economic categories as inverted social forms. The contributions to Part I – Adorno and the New Reading of Marx – expound the critique of economic categories by the new readings. Part II – Critique of Political Economy as Negative Dialectic of Society – contains chapters about the critique of political economy as a critique of society. The final part, Part III – Subjectivity and Pseudo Practice: on Social Praxis – explores the consequences of new readings for social practice. "'Woe speaks: Go.'"[33] But how?

Bonefeld's opening chapter to Part I sets the scene of the book. He argues that the critique of capitalist society is subversive in character. It dissolves the dogmatic appearance of society as a manifestation of economic nature, and it does so on the conditions that it thinks against the grain of society. The following chapter by Nico Bobka and Dirk Braunstein examines Adorno's reading of Marx. The authors focus in particular on Adorno's negative dialectic as a critique of society in the form of the economic object. The chapter lays out the theoretical groundwork from which the New Marx Reading emerged and continued to develop. In her chapter about Adorno and the New Reading of Marx, Charlotte Baumann argues that the new readings fall short of Adorno's requirement that the critique of capital has to articulate the suffering that it inflicts. At their best, she argues, the new readings establish the logic that holds sway in economic abstraction, but they do not inquire what this means for people. Her chapter expounds Adorno's argument that the critique of political economy has to make suffering speak. Chris O'Kane and Kirstin Munro critically focus on Moishe Postone's essential contributions to the development of the critique of political economy as a critical social theory. They extend Postone's critique of Marxian economics into a critique of contemporary approaches to democratic socialist political economy, social reproduction theory and unitary theories of capitalism that draw these approaches together.

The second part opens with a chapter by Werner Bonefeld on Economic Objectivity and Negative Dialectics. It expounds negative dialectics as a dialectics of the social world in the form of the economic object, one that is governed by the movement of economic quantities, that is, real economic abstractions. Bonefeld argues that the class antagonism belongs to the conceptuality of the economic categories. He examines the sheer unrest of life as the non-conceptual secret of the economic categories. Fabian Arzuaga's chapter extends the scope of Adorno's thesis of the liquidation of the individual from the liquidation of an anthropological type to the liquidation of existing individuals, or what Marx calls the 'surplus population' via the dynamic of capital accumulation and reproduction. The chapter concludes by considering how Adorno's critique of 'objectively untrue' yet 'real conceptualities' discloses not just what is promised by the concept of the individual but also what can be redeemed from the 'real untruth' of the superfluity and fungibility theorized as the liquidation of the individual. Charles Prusik's chapter turns to Adorno to critique neoliberal society in its ideological appearance as a self-regulating, evolving order that asserts itself as an independent economic logic. The chapter delineates Adorno's critical theory of society by focusing on the related concepts in explanation – exchange society is one concept, the other is real abstraction as the key to grounding the ideological function of economic thought in the neoliberal present. In 'Society Reproduces Itself Despite the Catastrophes that May Eventuate', Chris O'Kane expounds contemporary Marxist and critical theory accounts of the emergence of neoliberalism, the 2008 crisis, its miserable aftermath and the rise of right-wing authoritarian populism. He argues that these accounts fail to grasp the crisis-ridden character of political economy. He draws on Adorno's critique of negative totality and permanent catastrophe to expound what is at stake once the thin crust of bourgeois civilization dissolves.

The final part explores the formidable consequences of a critical theory of the critique of political economy for praxis. In 'Conceptuality and Social Practice', Werner Bonefeld asks what it means to say 'no'. Following Marx and Adorno, the relations of real abstraction belong to definite forms of social practice, and the class antagonism belongs to the concept of capital. The class struggle is not about socialism. It is a struggle to make ends meet. For this struggle to succeed, living labour has to generate profit, which is the condition of employment and therewith wage-based access to the means of subsistence. The class struggle belongs to the conceptuality of capitalist society. What, therefore, does it mean to say 'no'? The final chapter by Marcel Stoetzler assess the veracity and meaning of Adorno's critique of pseudo-practice. Why did Adorno characterize 1968 as a pseudo-practice, what sort of practice is needed to halt the further progress of late capitalism and what can be done?

The **Appendix** contains two chapters. One is a contextualizing introduction to Adorno's 1962 seminar on Marx by Chris O'Kane. It highlights its distinction and emphasizes its importance in the development of the New Reading and the critical theory of economic objectivity. The other is the translation of a transcript of Adorno's 1962 seminar, entitled 'Adorno on Marx and the Basic Concepts of Sociological Theory'. Adorno's teachings during the 1960s influenced a whole generation of scholars to read Marx again and conceive of his critique of political economy as a critical social theory.

Acknowledgements

The work on the volume coincided with the corona pandemic which claimed the lives of so many unnecessarily. We are grateful to our authors for the delivery of their chapters in difficult circumstances. To our editors at Bloomsbury, Liza Thompson and Lucy Russell, we say thank you for your patience. Lars Fischer translated the chapter by Bobka and Braunstein. Verena Erlenbusch-Anderson and Chris O'Kane translated the transcript of Adorno's 1962 seminar.

Notes

1 The main publications are Hans-Georg Backhaus, *Die Dialektik der Wertform* (Freiburg: Ca Ira, 1997) and Helmut Reichelt, *Die Neue Marx Lektüre* (Hamburg: VSA, 2008).

2 Simon Clarke, *Marx, Marginalism and Modern Sociology* (London: Palgrave, 1992).

3 John Holloway, *Change the World without Taking Power* (London: Pluto, 1992). Ana Dinerstein, Alfonso Garcia Vela, Edith Gonzalez and John Holloway (eds.), *Open Marxism: Against the Closing of the World* (London: Pluto, 2020).

4 Moishe Postone, *Time, Labour and Social Domination* (Cambridge: Cambridge University Press, 1993). Patrick Murray, *The Mismeasure of Wealth* (Leiden: Brill, 2016). Tony Smith, *The Logic of Marx's Capital* (Albany, NY: SUNY Press, 1990).

5 Beverley Best, *Marx and the Dynamic of Capital Formation: An Aesthetics of Political Economy* (London: Palgrave, 2010); Carl Casegaard, *Towards a Critical Theory of Nature* (London: Bloomsbury, 2021); Dimitra Kotouza, *Surplus Citizens*

(London: Pluto, 2019); Christian Lotz, *The Capitalist Schema* (London: Lexington Books, 2014); Christos Memos, *Global Economic Crisis as Social Hieroglyphic: Genesis, Constitution and Regressive Progress* (London: Routledge, 2021); Frederick Harry Pitts, *Critiquing Capitalism Today: New Ways to Read Marx* (London: Palgrave, 2018); Charles Prusik, *Adorno and Neoliberalism* (London: Bloomsbury, 2020), Marina Vishmidt, *Speculation as a Mode of Production: Forms of Value Subjectivity in Art and Capital* (Leiden: Brill, 2018).

6   See Eric John Russell, *Spectral Logic in Hegel and Debord* (London: Bloomsbury, 2021).

7   As expounded by Helmut Reichelt, 'Social Reality as Appearance', in *Human Dignity*, translated by Werner Bonefeld, edited by Werner Bonefeld and Kosmas Psychopedis (London: Routledge, 2017), 31–68.

8   Herbert Marcuse, *Negations*, translated by Jeremy J. Shapiro (London: Free Association Press, 1988), 151.

9   Karl Marx, *Capital*, vol. 1 (London: Penguin, 1990), 772, 166–7.

10   Karl Marx, *Theories of Surplus Value*, vol. 3 (London: Lawrence & Wishart, 1972), 508.

11   Marx, *Capital*, 165.

12   See, for example, Guido Starosta, *Marx's Capital, Method and Revolutionary Subjectivity* (Leiden: Brill, 2015).

13   Simon Mohun, 'Value, Value Form and Money', in *Debates in Value Theory*, edited by Simon Mohun (London: Palgrave, 1994), 214–30, here 228.

14   Clarke, Marx, *Marginalism and Modern Sociology*. Simon Clarke, *Keynesianism, Monetarism and the Crisis of the State* (Aldershot: Edward & Elgar, 1988).

15   See Leo Panitch, 'The Revolutionary Party', *Constellations* 24, no. 4 (2017), 528–42, for a recent enunciation of the Party.

16   Theodor W. Adorno, *Negative Dialectics*, translated by E. B. Ashton (London: Routledge, 1990), 196.

17   Ibid., 355.

18   Marx, *Capital*, 494, fn. 4.

19   Helmut Reichelt, 'Jürgen Habermas' Reconstruction of Historical Materialism', in *The Politics of Change*, translated by William Martin and Joseph Fracchia, edited by Werner Bonefeld and Kosmas Psychopedis (London: Palgrave, 2000), 105–47, here 107.

20   Alfred Schmidt, 'Praxis', in *Gesellschaft: Beiträge zur Marxschen Theorie 2* (Frankfurt/Main: Suhrkamp, 1974), 264–308, here 207.

21   Marx, *Capital*, 494, fn. 4.

22   See, for example, Wendy Brown, *Undoing the Demos* (Cambridge, MA: Zone Books, 2015). The sheer formalism of this argument is breath-taking. It highlights the market-based injustices of the present by contrasting it with a past that really

never was. The then bureaucratic domination, exploitation, class struggle, racism and sexism are forgotten and what is forgotten did not happen.

23 Jürgen Habermas, *Zur Rekonstruktion des historischen Materialismus* (Frankfurt/am Main: Suhrkamp, 1976).

24 See, for example, Streek, Fraser, Jaeggi, Panitch and Honneth. Crudely put, their economic argument derives from Polanyi's ideas about market and state relations. In this vision, money and capital retreat once the forces of reason occupy the seat of government and bring them under (national) democratic control.

25 Theodor W. Adorno, 'Spengler Today', *Zeitschrift für Sozialforschung* 9, no. 1 (1941), 305–25, here 319.

26 Theodor W. Adorno, *Introduction to Sociology*, translated by E. Jephcott (Stanford, CA: Stanford University Press, 2000), 77–8.

27 On this, and for the reference to 'moneybags', see Marx, *Capital*, chapter 6. For an exploration of legal form, see Bob Fine, *Democracy and the Rule of Law* (Caldwell, NJ: The Blackburn Press, 2002), chapter 4. Andreas Harms, 'Commodity Form and the Form of Law', in *The Sage Handbook of Frankfurt School Critical Theory*, edited by Beverley Best, Werner Bonefeld and Chris O'Kane (London: Sage, 2018), 852–69. See also Tony Smith *Beyond Liberal Egalitarianism* (Leiden: Brill, 2017).

28 On the use of the term 'master' and for an account of the class struggle couched in these terms, see Adam Smith, *An Inquiry into the Nature and Causes of the Wealth of Nations* (Indianapolis: Liberty Fund, 1976), chapter 8. For an account of the classical understanding of political economy as a science of state, see Werner Bonefeld, *The Strong State and the Free Economy* (London: Rowman & Littlefield, 2017), chapter 3.

29 For a comprehensive exploration of the early critical theory along these lines, see the three volumes of *The Sage Handbook of Frankfurt School Critical Theory*, edited by Beverley Best, Werner Bonefeld and Chris O'Kane (London: Sage, 2018).

30 Karl Marx, *Capital*, vol. 3 (London: Lawrence & Wishart, 1966), 830.

31 Karl Marx, *Comments on James Mills. Collected Works*, vol. 3 (London: Lawrence & Wishart, 1975), 215.

32 On negative totality, see Lars Heitmann, 'Society as "Totality"', in *The Sage Handbook of Frankfurt School Critical Theory*, edited by Beverly Best, Werner Bonefeld and Chris O'Kane (London: Sage, 2018), 589–606.

33 Adorno, *Negative Dialectic*, 203.

Part One

Adorno and the New Reading of Marx

2

Cracking economic abstractions: Bringing critical theory back-in

Werner Bonefeld

Rejecting naturalness: On society

The opposite term to a critical theory of society is not uncritical theory. It is traditional theory, at least according to Max Horkheimer who invoked the notion of a critical theory of society in his seminal essay 'Traditional and Critical Theory' of 1937.[1] If one were to summarize the difference between them, at its best traditional theory analyses the world of real (economic) abstractions to comprehend their political, economic, cultural, psychological, social and historical truth from various standpoints and comparative perspectives.[2] Critical theory scrutinises their untruth. It asks about the social constitution of the (economic) abstractions, and it asks about the historically specific character of the social relations that assume the form of a relationship between seemingly natural economic things.

Critical theory thinks against the flow of the world, at least that is its intension. It does not deny that in the capitalist social relations the individuals are governed by the movement of real economic abstractions. Nor does it deny that their movement manifests itself as if by their own volition behind the backs of the acting subjects. Indeed, it accepts that in capitalist society the social individuals are governed by inescapable economic laws that assert themselves as

Earlier versions of this chapter were presented at the *Critical Theory Conference* in Rome in May 2014, read as the Keynote address to the Fellowship conference of *The Independent Social Research Foundation*, held at the University of York in May 2014, discussed at the Manchester *CSE Trans-Pennine Workshop* in July 2014 and at the workshop *Retours a Marx*, held at the University Paris Nanterre in March 2015, and subsequently published as Bringing Critical theory Back-in at a Time of Misery, *Capital & Class*, 40, no. 2, 233–344. This chapter is a substantially revised and updated version of that earlier publication.

if by the force of nature not just over but also through and by means of them. Its acceptance does not entail affirmation of the economic things. On the contrary, it brushes the (economic) categories against their grain to reveal their origin in the capitalistically organized social relations. It is critique of economic nature as a socially constituted nature. Critical theory is critical on the condition that it dissolves the dogmatic appearance of capitalist society as a natural economic thing. It amounts, as Alfred Sohn-Rethel put it, to an anamnesis of the social origin, or genesis, of real economic abstraction.[3]

Critical theory thus argues that although the social relations vanish in their economic appearance, the inhospitable world of the abstract economic forces remains a human world. In capitalist society the individuals are governed by the products of their own hand. That is, the social world manifests itself behind the backs of the individuals, and yet this manifestation, and their 'enslavement' to it, is their own work.[4] It is not the work of some transhistorically conceived logic of the productive forces that move history forward from one mode of production to another, as the positivist Marxists, characterized by Adorno as 'perverter[s] of Marxian motives', believed it to be the case.[5] For critical theory, historical materialism is not a theory of some abstractly conceived material logic of history. Rather, it is critique of the existing social relations in their form of appearance as relations of economic necessity. It is critique of society 'understood as dogmatic'.[6] The truth of society as a relationship of real economic abstractions is the untruth of the individuals as personification (Marx) or character-mask (Adorno) of their own social world.

For a traditional theory of society, the notion of socio-economic necessity is an affront. It smacks of economic determinism, excludes the ideas of contingency and construction, creation and culture, and suggests dogmatic reduction of society to economic effect. Yet, the traditional science of society is entirely founded on the presumption that labour economy is a natural phenomenon. As a natural phenomenon, society is identified by its structural properties, the study of which characterizes the domains of system theory. The idea of society as system leads to the introduction of the theory of social action to account for the behaviours and conflicts that characterize the subjective properties of human agency in the life-world.[7] In traditional social theory society is seen either as a system of structural properties or as a world of social action, and the perennial question is therefore whether society as a system is dominant or whether society as a world of action is decisive. However, the idea that society exists twice, once as system and then as (acting) subject, does not really reproduce in thought the appearance of society as a split reality of structure and agency. The dualism of thought is more apparent than real. Given the choice between society as (economic) system and society as action, social theory unerringly sides with the mischief of society as a system. Although the independent movement of the economic forces cannot be comprehended as such, its effects can be analysed as instances of social contingency, which establish opportunity structures for the pursuit of distinct social projects at the expense of others. The so-called dialectics between structure and agency gives dialectics a bad name.[8] It presumes what needs to be explained.

The notion that modernity is the civilized manifestation of an unfolding logic of, by themselves, unfathomable socio-economic forces and natural economic properties was articulated with lasting effect by Adam Smith, who viewed what he called 'commercial society' as the final manifestation of a natural human propensity to truck and barter that weaves its way through history on the back of a dynamic of constant increases in the productivity of labour, which leads to an ever greater social division of labour and the establishment of a commercial society of generalized exchange relations. The nature of commercial society is magic. It transforms private vices into public virtues just like that; that is, by means of an invisible hand.[9] Natural economic laws are laws of natural necessity. Nature cannot be changed. It can however be destroyed. Natural laws need to be harnessed to avoid destruction and, therefore, in order to survive one has to adapt to them. The presupposition that labour is the productive means of social wealth in every society at any time shifts the focus of critical inquiry towards an argument about the most effective and just organization of labour economy.[10] Instead of a critique of labour economy as an historically specific form of definite social relations, its social nature is naturalized. Capitalist society appears as natural since it manifests itself in the form of a movement of economic quantities, of price and profit, and this movement is not only entirely uncontrollable by the individuals who comprise society. It is, also, hostile to them. At the blink of an eye the economic movement of society can cut off a whole class of propertyless individuals, society's surplus value producers, from access to the means of subsistence, just like that, indifferent to their needs and regardless of their efforts. Since nobody individually is in control, nobody individually can be blamed. Economic fate replaces the magic of religion within its own concept. In the form of economic fate, magic is disenchanted. It appears in the form of an invisible hand that 'takes care of both the beggar and the king'.[11] The invisible hand is the objective subject of reified society. It cows and feeds on the society from which it springs, demanding submission on the pain of ruin.

A critical theory of society does not reject as mere illusion the natural-invisible character capitalist society. The fetish character of capitalist society is real. However, and in contrast to traditional theory, it does not conceive of capitalist society as a manifestation of some transhistorically unfolding economic nature. The circumstance that Man has to eat does not in any way explain the form, content and force of the capitalist economic categories. History and society, not some presumed economic nature, nor the hunter and gatherers with whom Smith began his natural history towards what he calls commercial society, is the critical starting point of inquiry into capitalist economic nature, its power and force, logic and necessity, and consciousness and will. Conceived as a critical social theory, the critique of political economy rejects the ontological conception of economic things as deceitful. Instead, it argues that the supposition that the economic laws of capitalist labour economy are founded on a natural propensity, and are thus natural, is entirely theological in its grasp of capitalist society. The natural-invisible character of capitalist economy is in its entirety socially constituted and social constitution holds sway in and through its economic appearance as a force of nature that does nothing by itself. It is the acting subjects, who, as personifications of the economic categories, endow the logic of economic matter with a consciousness and a will. It is true, in capitalism, people live by the economic forces to make a living and, by doing so, they bestow them with an independent will, which appears in the form of society as a real economic abstraction. They do so without being aware of it. As a critical social theory, the task of the critique of political economy is to demystify the fetish character of the economic categories. It argues that the natural economic laws find their rational explanation through the understanding of definite forms of human social praxis. This practice not only vanishes in the form of its appearance. It also reappears in it as a practice of human personifications of their own social world.

There is only one world, and that is the world in which we live. To the point of death, therefore, the life of all Men hangs by the forces of capitalist economic nature. The idea that critical theory flouts traditional thinking entails thus more than it bargained for. It 'flouts tradition' only for as long as and to the extent that it retains consciousness of its own entanglement with the perverted world of economic inversion. It maintains this consciousness only for as long as it resists the comfort afforded by traditional theory. Traditional theory thinks about capitalist society as an object of analysis and economic calculation or as an object of normative judgement about its promise of freedom.[12] In contrast, critical theory thinks in and through capitalist society to subvert its natural objectivity, at least that is its critical intension. In this society every individual is a coined individual – a living means and medium for the production of capitalist wealth that, on the pain of ruin, is accumulated for the sake of accumulation.[13] Capital posits value for the sake of surplus value to make money yield more money, or it does not with ruinous consequence.[14] Wealth appears in the form of money that 'by virtue of being value... has acquired the occult ability to add value to itself', laying 'golden eggs'.[15] The freedom of the individual is a capitalized freedom, which is the freedom of a coined individual. The satisfaction of needs is a mere sideshow. The traditional theory of an economic nature that is regulated by an invisible hand identifies the vanished human subject, and her needs, as a metaphysical distraction that gets in the way of the calculation of a movement of economic quantities. In the words of Joan Robinson's despairing indictment of economic thought, 'K is capital, ΔK is investment. Then what is K? Why, capital of course. It must mean something, so let us get on with the analysis, and do not bother about these officious prigs who ask us to say what it means.'[16] Traditional thinking really is about things. In contrast, critical theory's attempt to think in and through things seeks out the vanished subject at the moment of its disappearance. Marx's notion of the critique of fetishism as an effort in deciphering the social constitution of economic things articulates the critical intent of his critique of political economy well: it is to 'develop from the actual, given relations of life the forms in which they have become apotheosized'.[17]

Horkheimer's conception of a critical theory of society, then, condemns as traditional a social theory that does not doubt the natural character of society, takes explanatory refuge in invisible principles and views the unfolding economic nature of society from different standpoints of analysis. From the standpoint of labour, it demands higher wages and better conditions, and rightly so; from the standpoint of capital, it demands enhanced labour productivity as a condition of global competitiveness, which is the condition for the sustained employment of labour; from the standpoint of the ecologist, it demands environmental protections; and from the standpoint of normative ideals of social justice, it demands re-distributive justice and equal opportunity. Then there is the view that capitalist economy manifests an irrational economy of labour and from this the thinking in normative orders derives the demand for a rationalized economy of labour that does not discriminate, exploit and dominate the workers. And the logic of the matter – who conceptualizes that? Traditional theory either presupposes what needs to be explained or explains what is already known, or it judges society on the basis of its own normative projections, and it does so without a concept of society.[18] Critical theory thus rejects positivism and its philosophical equivalent of a science of knowledge, according to which the social facts speak for themselves, falsifying or verifying theoretical suppositions about their character. The economic fact that, say, loss of profitability imperils the prospects of sustained employment is an economic reality, and since Man can only know what is given in the factual experience of reality, nothing more can be gleaned from *the facts*, except that for the sake of sustained employment the profitable application of living labour is of the essence, on a world market scale.

The paradigmatic manifestation of the traditional theory is social mathematics. It sets out to rationalize yesterday's movement of prices as a manifestation of a plurality of consumer-value preferences and, on the basis of this direct and immediate calculus, predicts tomorrow's utility movements of economic quantities. That is, it aggregates yesterday's economic behaviour to measure today's deviation in order to predict tomorrow's price movements, with winning intent – to gauge where to invest and what to sell. Quantities of 'capital' are translated into algebra, which expresses 'utility movements' of wealth in the form of abstract symbols. As an exact science of moving economic quantities, economics articulates society as unaware of itself in the form of calculable magnitudes of abstract wealth, of amounts of money that make more money, and it, society, lives the better the more money it yields. In its more critical manifestation, traditional theory thinks in terms of normative orders. In the face of poverty, it constructs a normative argument for a freedom from want without once asking whether poverty is really just a coincidence of capitalist wealth or whether it is in fact innate to its concept. The freedom of labour is the freedom of trade in labour power – and what, given the normative ideal of social justice, ought this trade have to be like to meet the norms of fairness and social justice? In the meantime, the sellers of labour power continue to struggle to make a living.

In conclusion, a traditional theory does not think in and through society. It thinks about society. The traditional refusal to think out of things has important consequences for anti-capitalist arguments about how the things ought to be (arranged). The following sections examine the elements of traditional anti-capitalism. I argue that it amounts at best to ticket thinking and, at worst, to a theological view. Contrary to the rumour about critical theory, its critique of existing conditions does not entail an impoverished praxis. Rather, it entails the question of praxis – what really does it mean to say 'no' in a society that is not only governed by the movement of economic abstractions but also dependent on them for its social reproduction?

Society as subject

As a critical social theory, the critique of political economy holds that economics is the formula of an inverted and bewitched world. This stance raises the question about the meaning of critique in the critique of political economy. What is criticized? According to Marx, his critique of political economy amounts to a 'critique of economic categories' to reveal their origin in the historically specific social relations of production. He thus argued that 'the' economists deal with un-reflected presuppositions.[19] In their hands, the 'law of capitalist accumulation [is] metamorphosed... into a pretended law of nature'.[20] Time is money. Money is time. For the sake of wealth, that is money as more money, time is of the essence – there is no time to lose. Fundamentally, the profitable investment of capital is not an end in itself. Rather, it is a means of avoiding default and bankruptcy. 'Fanatically intent' on avoiding liquidation through 'the valorization of value', the capitalist, this personification of capital, a mere 'cog', recognizes 'the proletarian' as a 'machine for the production of surplus value'.[21] His 'drive towards self-enrichment' is the condition of preserving his capital, and he can only achieve this 'by means of progressive accumulation', accumulation for the sake of accumulation.[22] Regarding the sellers of labour power, their struggle to make ends meet is dependent upon the successful consumption of their living labour for profit, which is the condition of future sales and therewith sustained access to the means of subsistence. The individuals act under the compulsion of the economic forces of time and money, and that is essentially more money in less time. Their freedom is the freedom of economic compulsion, which is the freedom of preserving capital by means of progressive accumulation, 'ruthlessly [forcing] the human race to produce for production's sake';[23] and it is the freedom of making ends meet on the part of the class of surplus value producers who struggle to dodge 'the freedom to starve'.[24] The class struggle belongs to the concept of capital.

Since the individuals act under the compulsion of abstract economic forces, the point of critique cannot therefore be to 'make the individual responsible for relations whose creature he socially remains, however much he may subjectively raise himself above them'.[25] It is not sufficient to criticize capitalists for their seemingly excessive addiction to profit, nor is it sufficient to criticize bankers for pursuing money for the sake of more money. On the pain of ruin, these behaviours manifest the 'objective necessity' of capitalistically constituted social relations. Neither the capitalist nor the banker, nor indeed the worker, can extricate themselves from the reality in which they live and which asserts itself not only over them but also through them, and by means of them. The critique of the banker, or any other politico-economic operative of a system that asserts itself as an independent force over and through the social individuals, misses the object of critique. As a critical social theory, the critique of political economy is therefore not a critique of the personifications of economic categories. It does not argue that the labour economy is corrupted by the private interests of the capitalist and his political friends. It does not therefore demand political action to set things right, ostensibly in the interest of humanity and for the sake of a rationalized labour economy. Instead, it is a critique of the capitalistically organized social relations of human reproduction that assume the form of a movement of economic things, which objectify themselves in the person to the vanishing point of death.

Nevertheless, while every individual is 'ruled by abstractions', the owners of great wealth experience this rule as a source of great enrichment and power. In this context, Horkheimer and Adorno have argued that the 'rulers' are safe for as long as the 'ruled' struggle under the spell of the inverted world, in which, say, the cause of financial crisis, economic downturn, loss of employment and wage income are attributed to the greedy behaviour of identifiable individuals.[26] A spellbound critique of capitalism demands more of this and less of that. It apportions blame and proclaims to know 'how to set things right'. It identifies the wrong-doer and personalizes what is wrong. Rather than capital, it is the profit-making consciousness of the capitalist and the greed of the speculator that is criticized, rejected and condemned. That is, the critique of the capitalist manifests itself as a demand for a better capitalism, one that works in the interests of the 'workers', or in today parlance, the 'many'. Marx's critique of Proudhon focused on this simple point. Proudhon substituted the critique of capitalism for a critique of the capitalist, seeking to free capital from the capitalist so as to utilize the power of capital for the benefit of a well-ordered society, investing in society and creating employment opportunities for the class of surplus value producers.

The critique of the capitalist leaves the category of capital not only entirely untouched by thought. It also elevates 'capital' as a thing beyond critique. Capital thus appears to be no more than an economic mechanism that can be made to work for this class interest or that class interest – in the end, it is the balance of the class forces that decides for which interest capital functions! Rather than touching the category of capital by thought, it identifies the guilty party, condemns it and demands state action to sort things out and to set things right. It thus attributes miserable social conditions to the activity of some identifiable individuals, who no longer appear as personifications of economic categories but, rather, as the personalized subject of misery. This personalization of the economic categories entails a number of differentiations, most importantly between the productive or indeed creative capitalist as a 'producer' of 'real' wealth employing a hard-working and creative people, and the financial or indeed parasitic capitalist who makes his fortune by speculating in money to the detriment of industry and workers. Here the distinction between a use-value production, on the one hand, and exchange value that manifests itself in the form of money, on the other, appears in the forms of distinct personalities – pitting the creative industrialist against the parasitic banker-cum-speculator. There emerges, then, the idea of a capitalism that is corrupted by the financial interests. Finance turns capitalism into a casino at the expense of national industry, national wealth, national workers and national harmony.

The critique of financial imperialism entails the idea of anti-imperialism as a progressive, liberating force. The reverse of anti-imperialism is national liberation, by which the dominated communities defend themselves against the disintegrating forces of financial globalization and imperial power. The idea of the nation as a subject of liberation is as irrational as the belief in a national destiny and a national homogeneity of purposes, from a national industry via the national interest to a national history. The idea of the nation as the foundation of being and becoming recognizes the term 'cosmopolitanism' as a term of abuse. In its stead, it idolizes the 'spirit of the people' as the imagined foundation of national being and becoming.[27] If indeed it is permissible at all to speak about the national spirit of the people, it is a national spirit not by nature, but by a history of class struggle. By reducing history to nature or by reading nature into history, the struggle for national liberation becomes delusional inasmuch as a people are forced to act 'as if' they really are natural forces that have a national history. That is, a definite form of society manifests itself in the form of a movement of coins and then, under the spell of this coined movement, rebels against the personifications of a world governed by coins. The personalized critique of capital identifies the 'wrongdoer' of the wronged society and calls him a merchant of greed. For the sake of employment and industry, something needs to be done. Something can be done! The personalized critique of capitalist social relations is open to abuse from the outset. It thinks akin to a register of blame and condemns the identified party as a power that hides behind the economic phenomena, sucking the living life out of the national community of a hard working people. This identification of the subject of misery leads to the condemnation of the world market society of capital as a network of money and power that for the sake of financial gain destroys the livelihood of a national people, victims of cosmopolitan peddlers.[28]

Society as object

The headlines of misery have changed from war and terror to what seems like a never-ending global economic crisis, pre- and post-pandemic – yet war and terror continue unabated. In this context, the notion that capitalism produces deplorable situations is a most optimistic point of view. Deplorable situations (*Mißstände*) are not the same as deplorable conditions (*Zustände*). The latter says that poverty is a capitalist condition. Challenging it requires a fundamental change in the social relations of production. In distinction, deplorable situations describe entirely avoidable socio-economic circumstances, be they the result of chance developments, government incompetence, pandemics or hard-nosed class-politics. As such, it can be rectified by well-meaning political interventions and political programmes that benefit society at large. Miserable situations require resolution by political means that hold the economy accountable to the democratic demands of the social majority. Deplorable situations require thus a socio-political activism that challenges *This* misery and *That* outrage, seeking to alleviate *This* inequality and *That* injustice and to rectify *This* and *That*. Critical theory looks beyond the contingent to grasp capitalism's fundamental condition. The activism of the given situation feels the pain of the world, and it might succeed in making capitalist society more equal, inclusive, fair and just. Nevertheless, the 'activism' of the deplorable situation is not only affirmative of existing society. It is also delusional about the character of fairness, justice and equality in capitalism. It is based on the conviction that however bad the situation, it can be rectified for good by this intervention or that policy, by this or that technical means, by this welfare support or that public policy, for the sake of fairness, justice and freedom, the end of suffering and misery, and the overcoming of exploitation, discrimination and inequality. It seeks a capitalism that works in the image of its normative ideal, without a question raised about what lays within it. In this manner, the activism of the situation transforms the protest against a really existing misery that blights the life of a whole class of individuals into a selling point for political gain.

There is, says Adorno, a need for a 'practice that fights barbarism'.[29] Barbarism cannot be fought in a direct and immediate manner – what really does it mean to struggle against money, resist the movement of coins, combat the law of economic value, resist the coined freedom of capitalist profit and fight poverty in a system of social reproduction that contains the pauper in its conception of its wealth.[30] To put this point differently: The humanization of social relations is the purpose and end of the struggle for human emancipation from relations in which Man is a degraded being governed by real economic abstractions. Should the effort at humanizing capitalist society's treatment of its workers succeed, the better for the poor and miserable. Humanized profit making is much preferable to the slaveholder's whip and worse. Humanizing capitalism prevents it from descending into social catastrophe with ease. Its efforts sustain the precarious crust of civility in bourgeoise society. Adorno's revision of Kant's categorical imperative, according to which one should recognize and treat Man never as a means but always as a purpose, is apt: 'Hitler has imposed a new categorical imperative upon humanity in the state of their unfreedom: to arrange their thinking and conduct, so that Auschwitz never repeats itself, so that nothing similar ever happen again.'[31] The effort at humanizing fetters the state of unfreedom with golden chains. However, the effort of humanization presupposes inhuman conditions, and it is thus confronted by the paradox that it presupposes as eternal those same conditions that provoke the effort of humanization in the first place. Inhuman conditions are not just an impediment to humanization but a part and parcel of the concept of humanization. What then does it mean to say 'no'? It is easy to say what is wrong. It is however quite impossible to say what is right in the negative totality of capitalist society.[32]

Adorno captures the difficulty of saying 'no' well when he argues that the 'total movement of society' is 'antagonistic from the outset'.[33] That is to say, 'society stays alive, not despite its antagonism, but by means of it'.[34] Contrary to traditional Marxism, class struggle is not something positive. Rather, it belongs to and characterizes the negative world, and drives it forward. Class struggle for access to the means of life does not express an ontologically privileged position, according to which the working class is the driving force of historical progress.[35] Rather, to be a productive worker 'is a great misfortune'.[36] That is to say, class is not a positive category. It is a negative category. Class is a category of the false society, one that posits a mass of dispossessed labourers as producers of surplus value and one that concentrates the means of life as means of profit at the disposal of a few hands. The critique of class society does not find its positive resolution in the achievement of fair and just exchange relations between the buyers of labour power and the producers of surplus value. The critique of class society finds its positive resolution only in a society in which the progress of 'the muck of ages' has come to an end, in the classless society.[37]

A constructive critique of class society, one that wants to do good for the surplus value producers, is entirely traditional in its account of society. It posits the observable fact of class division, classifies the individuals according to their observed market positions and occupations, takes into account income levels and educational achievements, and calculates with predictive intent the probabilities of conflict and acquiescence. It posits class and affirms what is posited. In its practical dimension, it amounts, argue Horkheimer and Adorno, to 'ticket thinking'.[38] Such thinking is one-dimensional. It rejects the critique of class society by speaking out for the working class, with a claim to power. That is, it demands a shift in the balance of class forces to set things right ostensibly on behalf of the class tied to work, seeking a better deal for the wage-slaves. Ticket thinking proclaims falseness. It does 'not talk about the devil'.[39]

By putting forth a programme of social transformation without thought about the conceptuality of capitalist wealth, ticket thinking 'looks on the bright side' and proclaims falseness.[40] Its falsehood is not untrue. It identifies the existing conditions of misery and makes it seem as if they present a mere pathology of capitalist wealth. This stance articulates an objective illusion. It supposes that all would be well if only government were to stand up to the capitalist interests and their imperialist backers. The illusion says that the profitable accumulation of money that yields more money does not really count; what counts is the satisfaction of human needs. It says that the failure to make a profit entails no threat to social reproduction; what counts is not profit but human beings. It suggests that the life of the class tied to work does not hang by the success of turning her labour into profit as the fundamental condition of achieving wage-based access to the means of life; what counts is goodness. It says that debt is not a mortgage on future surplus value; what counts is consumption. It rejects as absurd that useful things that cannot be turned into profits are burned; what counts is use-value production. It rejects as unfounded the insight that in the capitalistically organized social relations, 'the needs of human beings, the satisfaction of human beings, is never more than a sideshow'.[41] It opposes money as capital, M... M'. Instead, it considers money as means of purchasing commodities (C... M... C) and demands that money be put into the pockets of workers to strengthen their purchasing power, connecting them more firmly to the means of subsistence. The exchange of labour power (C) for money (M) that is then exchanged for means of subsistence (C), C... M... C, is, however, a function of M... C... M'. Profitable employers purchase labour power. Unprofitable employers do not.

Profit-making is the means of avoiding bankruptcy and for the sake of sustained access to the means of subsistence, the sellers of labour power depend on the profitable exploitation of their labour by 'moneybags'. The illusion of the epoch suggests that profits do not matter. What matters is the well-being of workers. The illusion of the epoch confuses the reality of capitalism with its (illusionary) promise of a freedom from want.

The illusion of the epoch identifies what really counts, and yet it leaves the economic categories untouched by thought. It does not recognize the very society that it rejects, abstractly. Only a reified consciousness can declare that it is in possession of the requisite knowledge, political capacity, and technical expertise and know-how not only for resolving capitalist crises but, also, to do so in the interests of the class that works. For the sake of progress, it demands a rationalized labour economy, equitable exchange relations and fair working conditions. 'Abstract negativity' barks in perpetuity and without bite.[42] Instead, it sniffs out the miserable world, from the outside as it were, and puts itself forward as having the capacity, ability, insight and means for organizing capitalist economy for the workers, securing the full-employment of the class that lives by labour. Abstract negativity describes the theology of anti-capitalism. Theologically conceived, anti-capitalism is devoid of Now-Time. Instead, it views the present as transition towards its own future, promising deliverance from misery amidst 'a pile of debris' that 'grows skyward'.[43]

Postscript: Society as struggle

For a critical theory of society, the critical concept of enquiry is not hegemony. It is governmentality. Each individual carries her bond with society in her wallet. Everybody lives for money. For the sake of making a living, she needs to make money. Money does not only make the world go around; its possession also establishes a connection to the means of life. As such, the class struggle is a struggle for money – it governs the mentality of bourgeois society, from the struggle for employment, over wages and conditions, and against redundancy. What a misery? In the face of great social wealth, the propertyless sellers of labour power struggle for fleeting amounts of money to sustain themselves as producers of surplus value. There is a fate far worse than being an exploited worker; and that is to be an unexploitable worker. For the sake of making a living, what is the price of a kidney?

Especially in miserable times, it is important to understand that the struggle for the society of human purposes does not follow some abstract idea. It is a struggle for access to 'crude and material things without which no refined and spiritual things could exist'.[44] What then are the dispossessed surplus value producers struggling for? 'In-itself' they struggle for access to the means of subsistence to satisfy their human needs. They struggle for wages and conditions, and they struggle to defend wage levels and conditions. They struggle against capital's 'were-wolf's hunger for surplus labour' and its destructive conquest for additional atoms of unpaid labour time, and thus against the reduction of their life to a mere time's carcase. They struggle against a life constituting solely of labour-time and thus against a reduction of human life to a living resource. They struggle for respect, education and recognition of human significance, and above all for food, shelter, clothing, warmth, love, affection, knowledge, time for enjoyment and dignity. Their struggle as a class 'in-itself' really is a struggle 'for-itself': for life, human distinction, life-time and, above all, satisfaction of basic human needs. The working class does not struggle for socialism. It struggles to make a living. It struggles for access to the means of life and for comfort. It does all of this in conditions, in which the increase in material wealth that it has produced pushes beyond the limits of its capitalist form of wealth, money that yields more money for the sake of more money. Every so-called trickle-down effect that capitalist accumulation might bring forth presupposes a prior and sustained trickle up in the capitalist accumulation of wealth. And then society 'suddenly finds itself put back into a state of momentary barbarism; it appears as if famine, a universal war of devastation had cut off the supply of every means of subsistence'.[45] The struggle of the dispossessed does not express an ontological privilege. It is 'dictated by hunger'.[46]

The existence of the social individuals as personifications of seemingly self-moving economic forces does not entail the reduction of social consciousness to economic consciousness. It entails the concept of economy as an experienced concept of struggle to overcome misery, and economic consciousness as an experienced consciousness of suffering. For the propertyless sellers of labour power, economic consciousness is an unhappy consciousness. This is the unhappy consciousness of the struggle for access to the means of life. It is this struggle that makes the oppressed class the depository of historical knowledge. Instead of thinking about history, one needs instead to think out of history, out of the battles for freedom, slave insurrections, peasant revolts, the struggles of Les Enragés, working-class strikes, riots, insurrections and revolutions, to appreciate the traditions of the oppressed, recognize the smell of danger and the stench of death, gain a sense of the courage and cunning of struggle, grasp the spirit of sacrifice and comprehend, however fleetingly, the density of a time at which the progress of the muck of ages almost came to a standstill. Class struggle 'supplies a unique experience with the past'.[47] Whether this experience 'turns concrete in the changing forms of repression as resistance to repression or whether it turns concrete in forms of repression', is a matter of experienced history.[48] A definite logic holds sway in real economic abstraction. Its secret history is the sheer unrest of life.

Notes

1   Max Horkheimer, 'Traditional and Critical Theory', in *Critical Theory Selected Essays* (London: Continuum, 2002), 188–243.

2   According to Alfred Sohn-Rethel, *Warenform und Denkform* (Frankfurt: Suhrkamp, 1978), who first advanced the notion of real abstraction, real abstraction amounts to a concrete process. In Adorno's terminology, the objective conceptuality of society comprises a real abstraction of seemingly self-moving economic categories that, although socially constituted in their entirety, impose themselves on the acting subject as if by force of nature. On this see Helmut Reichelt, 'Social Reality as Appearance: Some Notes on Marx's Conception of Reality', in *Human Dignity: Social Autonomy and the Critique of Capitalism*, edited by Werner Bonefeld and Kosmas Psychopedis (London: Routledge, 2017), 31–67. On the Adorno's debt to Sohn-Rethel, see Helmut Reichelt, 'Die Marxsche Kritik ökonomischer Kategorien. Überlegungen zum Problem der Geltung in der dialektischen Darstellungmethode im 'Kapital', in *Emanzipation als Versöhnung: zu Adornos Kritik der Warentausch-Gesellschaft und Perspektiven der Transformation*, edited by Iring Fetscher and Alfred Schmidt (Frankfurt: Verlag Neue Kritik, 2002), 142–90, here 181, fn.5. On real abstraction as a category of a critical social theory, see Frank Engster and Oliver Schlaudt, 'Alfred Sohn-Rethel: Real Abstraction and the Unity of Commodity-Form and Thought Form', in *The Sage Handbook of Frankfurt School Critical Theory*, edited by Beverley Best, Werner Bonefeld and Chris O'Kane (London: Sage, 2018), 284–301.

3   The German original says: 'Historischer Materialismus ist Anamnesis der Genese'. Sohn-Rethel, *Warenform und Denkform*, 139.

4   See Horkheimer, 'Traditional and Critical Theory', 229.

5   Theodor W. Adorno, *Negative Dialectics*, translated by E. B. Ashton (London: Routledge, 1990), 335. One of the more eloquent contemporary representatives of dialectical materialism is Terry Eagleton, *Why Marx was Right* (New Haven: Yale

University Press, 2011). For a seminal critique of historical materialism dogmatically conceived, see Richard Gunn, 'Against Historical Materialism', in *Open Marxism*, vol. 1, edited by Werner Bonefeld, Richard Gunn and Kosmas Psychopedis (London: Pluto Press, 1992), 1–45; and Simon Clarke, 'Althusserian Marxism', in *One Dimensional Marxism*, edited by Simon Clarke, Terry Lovell, Kevin McDonnel, Kevin Robins and Victor Jeleniewski Seidler (London: Allison & Busby, 1980), 7–102.

6   Adorno, *Negative Dialectics*, 196.

7   On system and life world in Habermas's social theory see, Helmut Reichelt, 'Jürgen Habermas' Reconstruction of Historical Materialism', translated by William Martin and Joseph Fracchia, in *The Politics of Change*, edited by Werner Bonefeld and Kosmas Psychopedis (London: Palgrave, 2000), 105–47.

8   On the dialectic of structure and agency, see Werner Bonefeld, 'Crisis of Theory', *Capital & Class* 17, no. 2 (1993): 25–47.

9   On Smith's concept of labour economy, see Simon Clarke's *Marx, Marginalism and Modern Sociology* (London: Palgrave, 1992).

10   Apart from adapting to the demands of capitalist labour economy, one might also hope to achieve a more rational organization of labour economy, progressing the economy of labour from its supposedly irrational manifestation in capitalism to its rationalization by means of public authority in socialism. See David Harvey, 'History versus Theory: A Commentary of Marx's Method in *Capital*', *Historical Materialism* 20, no. 2 (2012): 3–38. Although entirely traditional in its conception, Harvey's understanding of labour economy as an enduring necessity of social wealth is widely shared, including contemporary versions of critical theory, which after decades of neglect rediscovered the economy as a discursive reality since 2008. See, for example, the conversation about between Nancy Frazer and Rahel Jaeggi, *Capitalism: A Conversation in Critical Theory* (Cambridge: Polity, 2018). Like Harvey, they argue for the rational organization of labour economy by means of state and for the sake of reason. For a critique of the contemporary linkage between (Habermasian) critical theory and Marxism economics, see Chris O'Kane, 'Society Maintains Itself Despite All the Catastrophes that May Eventuate: Critical Theory, Negative Totality, and Crisis', *Constellations* 25, no. 2 (2018): 287–301. See Moishe Postone, *Time, Labour, and Social Domination* (Cambridge: Cambridge University Press, 1994) for a seminal a critique of Marxian economics as a contradiction in terms. For Postone the critique of political economy does not amount to an argument for a better labour economy. Fundamentally it amounts a critique of labour economy.

11   Adorno, *Negative Dialectics*, 251. See also Karl Marx, *Capital*, vol. 1, translated by Ben Fowkes (London: Penguin, 1990), 280.

12 On liberal egalitarianism and contemporary normative social theory, see Tony Smith, *Beyond Liberal Egalitarianism: Marx and Normative Social Theory in the Twenty-First Century* (Chicago: Haymarket Books, 2018).

13 It is, however, the case that not every individual is either a means or a medium of capitalist wealth. Some are neither. Keynes called them the involuntarily unemployed. Dimitra Kotouza, *Surplus Citizens* (London: Pluto, 2019) is less forgiving in her terminology.

14 Although critical theory conceives of capitalist society as a real abstraction, its conceptualization of money as the form of value has developed only since the 1970s. See the pioneering contribution by Hans-Georg Backhaus, 'Materialien zur Rekonstruktion der Marxschen Werttheorie 2', in *Gesellschaft. Beiträge zur Marxschen Theorie 3* (Frankfurt/Main: Suhrkamp, 1975), 122–59. For more recent contributions see Chris Arthur, 'Value and Money', in *Marx's Theory of Money*, edited by Fred Moseley (London: Palgrave, 2005), 111–23; Martha Campbell, 'The Objectivity of Value versus the Idea of Habitual Action', in *The Constitution of Capital: Essays on Volume I of Marx's Capital*, edited by Riccardo Bellofiore and Nicola Taylor (London: Palgrave, 2004), 63–87; Christian Lotz, *The Capitalist Schema* (London: Lexington Books, 2014); Werner Bonefeld, 'Capital *Par Excellence*: On Money as an Obscure Thing', *Estudios de Filosofía* 62 (2020): 33–56.

15 Marx, *Capital*, 255.

16 Joan Robinson, *Economic Philosophy. An Essay on the Progress of Economic Thought* (London: Penguin, 1962), 68.

17 Marx, *Capital*, 494, fn. 4.

18 See Theodor W. Adorno, *Introduction to Sociology*, translated by Edmund Jephcott (Stanford: Stanford University Press, 2000).

19 Karl Marx, 'Letter to Lasalle, 22.2.1858', in *Marx Engels Werke*, vol. 29 (Berlin: Dietz, 1963), 550. 'The economists' connotes a generic term to depict a disciplinary effort at determining the meaning of the economic categories in abstraction from their social foundation. On this, see Werner Bonefeld, *Critical Theory and the Critique of Political Economy* (New York: Bloomsbury, 2014).

20 Marx, cited in Theodor W. Adorno, *History and Freedom: Lectures, 1964–1965*, translated by Rodney Livingstone (Cambridge: Polity, 2006), 118.

21 Marx, *Capital*, 739, 639, 742.

22 Ibid., 639.

23 Ibid.

24 Adorno, *History and Freedom*, 201.

25 Marx, *Capital*, 92.

26 Max Horkheimer and Theodor W. Adorno, *Dialectic of Enlightenment*, translated by John Cumming (London: Verso, 1979), 168–208.

27 This part paraphrases Adorno, *Lectures on History and Freedom*, 100–2.

28 See Werner Bonefeld, 'Antisemitism and the Power of Abstraction', in *Antisemitism and the Constitution of Sociology*, edited by Marcel Stoetzler (Nebraska: University of Nebraska Press, 2014), 314–32, for a development of this point. See also the contributions to the Special Issue on Antisemitism, *Journal of Social Justice*, vol. 9, 2019, edited by Shane Burnley.

29 Theodor W. Adorno, *Einleitung zur Musiksoziologie* (Frankfurt/Main: Suhrkamp, 1962), 30.

30 On this point, see Werner Bonefeld, 'Primitive Accumulation and Capitalist Accumulation', *Science and Society* 75, no. 3 (2011): 379–99.

31 Adorno, *Negative Dialectics*, 375.

32 On the notion of negative totality, see Lars Heitmann, '"Totality": On the Negative-Dialectical Presentation of Capitalist Socialisation', in *The Sage Handbook of Frankfurt School Critical Theory*, edited by Beverley Best, Werner Bonefeld and Chris O'Kane (London: Sage, 2018), 589–606.

33 Adorno, *Negative Dialectics*, 304.

34 Ibid., 320.

35 This view is central to Erik O Wright's account in *Class Counts* (New York: Cambridge University Press, 1997). Professional sociology, argues Horkheimer in 'Traditional and Critical Theory', 221, 'derives its concept of class not from a critique of economy but from its own observations', and determines 'the theoretician's social position… neither by the source of his income nor by the concrete contents of his theory, but by the formal elements of education'. For a critical theory of class, see Tom Houseman, 'Social Constitution and Class', in *The Sage Handbook of Frankfurt School Critical Theory*, edited by Beverley Best, Werner Bonefeld and Chris O'Kane (London: Sage, 2018), 697–713.

36 Marx, *Capital*, 644.

37 Karl Marx and Friedrich Engels, *The German Ideology, Collected Works*, vol. 5 (London: Lawrence & Wishart, 1976), 53.

38 Horkheimer and Adorno, *Dialectic of Enlightenment*, 207.

39 Theodor W. Adorno, *Minima Moralia. Reflections from Damaged Life*, translated by Edmund Jephcott (London: Verso, 2005), 102.

40 Ibid.

41 Adorno, *History and Freedom*, 51.

42 Theodor W. Adorno, *Lectures on Negative Dialectics. Fragments of a Lecture Course 1965/1966*, edited by Rolf Tiedemann, translated by Rodney Livingstone (Cambridge: Polity, 2008), 25.

43 Walter Benjamin, 'Theses on the Philosophy of History', in *idem, Illuminations*, edited by Hannah Arendt, translated by Harry Zorn (London: Pimlico, 1999), 245–55, here 249. Now-time is Benjamin's conception of a time at which the progress of the muck of ages comes to standstill. Now-time rejects the idea of a present

time, which heralds the future as its own being in becoming. On this see Werner Bonefeld, 'Critical Theory, History, and the Question of Revolution', in *Communism in the 21st Century*, vol. 3, edited by Shannon Brincat (Los Angeles, CA: Praeger, 2014), 137–62.

44 Benjamin, 'Theses on the Philosophy of History', 246.

45 Karl Marx and Friedrich Engels, *The Communist Manifesto* (London: Pluto Press, 1996), 18.

46 Adorno, *Minima Moralia,* 102.

47 Benjamin, 'Theses on the Philosophy of History', 254.

48 Adorno, *Negative Dialectics*, 265.

3

Adorno and the critique of political economy

Nico Bobka and Dirk Braunstein
Translated by Lars Fischer

According to Habermas, 'Adorno was not bothered with political economy.'[1] Indeed, on Helmut Reichelt's account, 'in private conversation, Adorno made no secret of his aversion to dealing with the economy'.[2] In short: 'Economics were hardly his thing!'[3] Nor, incidentally, were they Marx's thing. In private, Marx readily confessed his despondency at 'all the economic crap' he was forced to engage.[4] Yet for Adorno, Marx's 'genius' sprang precisely from his determination to grapple with economic issues, his strong aversion to them notwithstanding.[5] 'Proponents of Critical Theory', Adorno told students attending one of his seminars in 1968, 'should not let their aversion to the primacy of the economic deter them from giving the critique of political economy a crack'.[6] Helmut Reichelt recalled that, not long before his death, Adorno had identified the critique of the value and money forms as the 'holy grail' of Critical Theory and its 'encyclopedic analysis' as a crucial desideratum.[7] Building on Marx's contention that the 'anatomy' of bourgeois society needed to be 'sought in political economy', Friedrich Pollock concluded that the latter owned the 'status of an all-encompassing fundamental discipline' and that its critique formed the basis of the revolutionary critique of bourgeois society more generally.[8] This tallies with Iring Fetscher's clarification, in his eulogy for Adorno, that, while Adorno had recently 'admitted to a student just how repulsed he was by the economy, he nevertheless knew that the critique of political economy was the prerequisite of any revolutionary theory or praxis that invokes Marx'.[9]

Adorno did not begin to engage in his own critique of political economy until he was in exile. In fact, as early as September 1937, Adorno informed Benjamin that 'the systematic study of *Capital*' was now among his top priorities.[10] In the first volume of his copy of *Capital,* Adorno noted the date 10 June 1938, suggesting that he indeed began to study it soon after his arrival in New York.[11] Both in New York and in Los Angeles, Adorno familiarized himself with Marx's theory to such an extent that class theory began to feature prominently in his thought. This is indicated not least by the 'Reflections on Class Theory' he wrote in 1942. He began to focus much more intensely on the created nature of society. Adorno came to appreciate that, rather than being a philosophical device that facilitated the conceptualization of modern and premodern social relations alike, the commodity was in fact one category among others required to develop a materialist conception of society and history, and one that applies only to capitalism, at that. Presumably, this also explains why Adorno, his initial enthusiasm in 1936 notwithstanding, largely lost interest in Alfred Sohn-Rethel's analyses of the nexus between the commodity form and the process of cognition.[12] To be sure, the category of the commodity continued to be an important point of reference in his theory, but from a certain point onwards, Adorno was no longer willing to countenance its isolation from the class relations that turn the commodity into a commodity in the first place. Consequently, it could not be an ontological category. He also re-evaluated the significance of class consciousness. Adorno abandoned it as a necessary prerequisite for the existence of classes, instead adopting Marx's understanding of class as determined by the position of the individual in relation to the means of production.

The following passage from *Negative Dialectics* points to the coming together of the critique of political economy and utopian thought in Adorno's philosophy: 'The critique of the principle of exchange in its capacity as the principle that governs how thought assigns identity wants the ideal of free and just exchange, hitherto a mere pretext, to be realized. This alone would transcend exchange.'[13] Adorno's concept of exchange was based on the form of exchange required for consumption to impact on production. This concerns the 'decisive point' at which 'the commodity labour comes into play'. Here, 'everything is both above board and yet not above board'.[14] Since exchange was predicated on 'something being both equal and unequal',[15] the 'illusion in the process of exchange' resided 'in the concept of surplus-value' attached to the very real appropriation of surplus labour by the buyer of the labour under the guise of the exchange of equivalents.[16]

For Adorno, Marx's ability to uncover this nexus demonstrated that, rather than 'merely flirting with its terminology', Marx was genuinely serious about dialectics.[17] The dialectical turn Marx had, on Adorno's account, recognized was that 'the assertion of the equivalence of what is exchanged, as the basis of all exchange, is repudiated by its consequences'. 'As the principle of exchange, by virtue of its immanent dynamics, extends its remit to living human labour it turns into a powerful source of objective inequality.'[18]

Alex Demirović has suggested that this interpretation is only 'partially compatible' with Marx's theory, given the latter's contention 'that the capitalist form of the exchange of equivalents is not fraudulent: labour power is, on average, remunerated at its full value and equality is thus realized.'[19] Yet this is in fact precisely what Adorno himself argued. He merely went one step further in recognizing that the equality in the process of exchange reproduces the inequality of classes and individuals. On Demirović's account, Marx demonstrated 'how the problem of finding a standard for equality is solved by the emergence of an average of socially necessary labour mediated by the market.'[20] Adorno, by contrast, in keeping with Marx, insisted that this measure, precisely by its application in the process of exchange, negated itself. For Adorno, this was 'the decisive turn in Marx':

> Rather than simply say….: none of this is true, he says: in order to change this enormous apparatus at all we want to use its own momentum to set it in motion…. Rather than simply dismiss bourgeois society's claim that it creates harmony, he takes it entirely at its word and asks: does the society you propagate genuinely correspond to its concept? Is there really a free and just society that corresponds to your world of free and just exchange? In this respect too, by saying that it both does and does not, he remains loyal to the principle of dialectics.[21]

When Adorno identified the doctrine of surplus value as the 'centerpiece of Marxian theory',[22] he did so because it offered an account not only of the point of contact between production and consumption, i.e., of an essentially economic phenomenon, but also of 'the social dynamic that holds everything together and produces the conflicts and conditions that govern society. The theory of surplus value was as much about society as it was about the economy and of equal import to both.'[23]

The production of surplus value, which is the result and purpose of the exchange of wage for labour power, marks the very point at which

> Hegel's philosophy of history coincides with classical economic theory and also with Marx – the fact that people pursue their own individual interests makes them at the same time the exponents and executors of that same historical objectivity that is ready to turn against their interests at any moment and thus may assert itself over their heads. There is a contradiction here since it is claimed that what asserts itself despite people's own efforts does so by virtue of them, by virtue of their own interests. But since the society in which we live is antagonistic, and since the course of the world to which we are harnessed

is antagonistic too, what we might term this logical contradiction should not be thought of as merely a contradiction, merely the product of an inadequate formulation. It is a contradiction that arises from the situation.[24]

Consequently, 'the critique of the relationship between scholarly statements and that to which they refer… is inexorably propelled towards the critique of the object itself'.[25] In Adorno, as in Marx, critique therefore has a double meaning. It is social criticism and critique of ideology in one, the critique of reality mediated through the critique of a scholarly praxis predicated on the conceit that reality can be shown to be rational.[26] 'Social critique is a critique of knowledge and vice versa.'[27] Criticism

> must rationally determine whether the shortcomings it encounters are merely the shortcomings of scholarship or the object fails to match the claims scholarship makes about it on the basis of its concepts…. In common parlance, criticism quite rightly implies not merely self-criticism… but also criticism of the object…. Logical criticism and the empathically practical criticism that society must be transformed… are two dimensions of one and the same conceptual process.[28]

On Adorno's account, bourgeois society, as an 'antagonistic totality', was only able to maintain itself *qua* its contradictions.[29] For him, as for Marx, the fundamental antagonism within that totality was one of class. Social totality and social antagonism imply each other. 'Society stays alive, not despite its antagonism, but by means of it.'[30] Since the individual can only reproduce itself within the capital relation, individuals cannot but reproduce the 'coercive character of society', a society by which 'every single one of us is devoured… lock, stock and barrel'.[31] No individual can escape their role in the capitalist process without facing ruin, and, as Adorno wrote in 1942, the 'immeasurable pressure of domination has so fragmented the masses' that 'the oppressed who today, as predicted by theory, constitute the overwhelming majority of mankind are unable to experience themselves as a class', unable to recognize 'that solidarity should be their ultima ratio'. Instead, 'conformity appears more rational to them'.[32] In short, the objective class antagonism persists because society continuously reproduces it. 'Down to the present day life has succeeded in perpetuating itself only because of this division in society, because a number of people in control confront others who have been separated from the means of production.'[33]

Adorno criticized Marx, however, for ultimately affirming this state of affairs. 'You will find', he explained in one of his lectures on *History and Freedom*, that Marx too approves of this affirmation of the coming together of mankind as well as the idea that mankind reproduces itself notwithstanding its sacrifices and sufferings. And if we may look for an element of idealism in Marx, an idealist element in the precise philosophical meaning of the word, this would certainly be the place to find the truly affirmative strand in his thought. It is a strand, moreover, that fits with his predominantly optimistic view of history. The form this Hegelian theme takes in Marx is transformed almost out of all recognition, but retains extraordinary power. It is the highly obscure and difficult theory of the so-called law of value. This is the summation of all the social acts taking place through exchange. It is through this process that society maintains itself and, according to Marx, continues to reproduce itself and expand despite all the catastrophes that may eventuate.[34]

Marx too remained beholden to '"the metaphysics of the forces of production"',[35] ultimately presupposing 'something like the metaphysical substantiality of these productive forces', a metaphysics that amounted to a belief in something that was uncannily 'reminiscent of the Hegelian World Spirit'.[36] 'Ultimately', this led

to the persistence in Marx of a highly dubious theorem of German idealism. We find it explicitly stated, above all by Engels in the *Anti-Dühring*. This is the assertion that freedom really amounts to doing consciously what is necessary, something that is of course meaningful only if what is necessary, the World Spirit, the development of the forces of production is in the right a priori and its victory is guaranteed.[37]

For Adorno, the question of whether it had been unavoidable that humankind perpetuated itself on the basis of this antagonism was moot. 'The strongest argument that can be presented in support of the contention that things could not go any other way,' he noted in his sixth lecture on *History and Freedom*,

hinges on humankind's grappling with physical nature. It found itself in a situation of scarcity and want with which no other form of organization would supposedly have allowed it to cope; only the relations of domination that compelled human beings both to take the scarcity into account and correct it allowed them to do so, and these could not but incubate this antagonism.[38]

Marx and Engels had answered the question in the affirmative, stressing, as Adorno put it, 'that domination, social domination, was a function of the economy, in other words, of the life process, the reproduction of life itself, and not the other way around'.[39] However, if 'economic relations and antagonisms were themselves the product of a fundamental form of domination', Adorno reasoned, 'then their necessity would be extraneous to the historical totality, the life process of society'. It would in fact be 'an accident that could equally well not have occurred'.[40] This suggested that the 'possibility of making a leap forward, of doing things differently, always existed, even in periods when productivity was far less developed', yet the 'opportunity was missed again and again'.[41] This was a motif Adorno borrowed from Walter Benjamin's unorthodox Marxism.[42]

Hitherto, 'the notion that there should be no scarcity, that nobody on earth should suffer hunger, the notion, in other words, of the completion of the abolition of need', presupposed an

> increase in productive forces and, consequently, also the very domination of nature that has become inextricably enmeshed by no means only with the anti-organic principle. It is conceivable only as long as human beings who, after all, are expected to learn how to control not only their external nature but also what is within them, are constantly required to engage in self-denial. The concept of a state of affairs without (self-)denial, the unleashing of the forces of production, the abolition of need, the utopian moment of unlimited fulfilment, in other words, in order to be at all possible, presuppose restraint, asceticism and some element of repression and oppression.[43]

Yet the future of humankind depended precisely on 'whether it is able to extricate itself from this terrible entanglement, the fact that the envisaged alternative state of affairs and the prospective way there, in their quest for realization, develop within themselves the very principle to which they are opposed, and are therefore constantly at risk of relapsing into myth'.[44] The steady increase in the social forces of production invariably perpetuated domination; it merely facilitated the constant change required 'to ensure that everything stays the same'.[45] For all its dynamism, society as a whole always remained the same. It never moved beyond its 'pre-history' yet presented itself 'as constantly different, unforeseen, exceeding all expectation, the faithful shadow of developing productive forces'.[46] In the context of the forces of production, 'the very word "unleashed"', Adorno suggested, 'has undertones of menace'.[47] The constant unfolding of those forces epitomized the 'merciless domination of nature' and was integral to the perpetuation of the ever same that Adorno termed myth.[48]

Nowhere did Adorno come closer to giving a positive outline of sorts of the opposing utopian state of affairs than in his much-cited aphorism 'Sur l'eau' in *Minima Moralia*.[49] At its heart lies a form of human existence beyond the compulsion to produce:

> The naively imputed unambiguous development towards increased production is itself a piece of that bourgeois outlook which permits development in only

one direction because, integrated into a totality, dominated by quantification, it is hostile to qualitative difference. If one conceives of emancipated society as emancipation from precisely that kind of totality, then vanishing-lines come into view that have little in common with increased production and its human reflections. Unrestrained individuals may by no means be the most agreeable or even the freest. Yet a society rid of its fetters would surely be able to (re)discover that the forces of production are not the ultimate substratum of humankind either but in fact reflect a specific historical form of humanity tailored to the production of commodities. Perhaps the true society will grow weary of expansion and take the liberty of passing on possibilities rather than follow its manic compulsion to conquer alien planets. Indeed, it might dawn on a humankind unfamiliar with need, not only how chimerical and futile the efforts previously undertaken to escape need were, but also that, with increasing wealth, they have only reproduced it at an advanced level.[50]

Adorno's point of reference at this point was Marx's treatment of the relations of production as placing limits on the forces of production. At an important juncture in *Capital*, Marx, construing a historical-philosophical argument with no basis in the critique of political economy, referred, not without pathos, to the revolutionary impact of the centralization of capital.

> The monopoly of capital becomes a fetter upon the mode of production, which has sprung up and flourished along with, and under it. Centralisation of the means of production and socialisation of labour reach a point where they become incompatible with, and burst, their capitalist mantle. The bell tolls for capitalist private property. The expropriators are expropriated.[51]

The notion that identified progress with the growth of the forces of production and material wealth ultimately sprang from an idealistic philosophy of history that Adorno was unwilling to countenance. Not that Adorno would have questioned Marx's analysis that 'the wealth of those societies in which the capitalist mode of production prevails, presents itself as "an immense accumulation of commodities"' and the commodity was its basic unit.[52] However, what Marx had overlooked, however, was that, hopelessly embroiled in the commodity form, 'the gifts of fortune themselves become elements of misfortune'.[53] In 'Late Capitalism or Industrial Society?', Adorno noted wryly that there was 'only one respect' in which the relations of production had so far

> failed to shackle the forces of production: that of total annihilation. But the dirigiste methods for controlling the masses presuppose a concentration and centralization that have a technological dimension as well as an economic one,

something that would have to be shown from a study of the mass media. For
this would demonstrate how, from a few points, the consciousness of countless
people can be brought into line simply by the selection and presentation of news
and commentary.[54]

As long as humankind dominated nature, it was itself, in turn, dominated by
nature because its attempts to rise above it entangled not only the forces of
production with the domination of the relations of production but also the
socially conditioned individuals with nature. So far, human beings had only ever
had the choice 'between their subjugation to nature and its subjugation to the
self'.[55]

Regardless of whether, in its desire to combat need and fear, humankind
originally had no choice but to become perpetually entangled with
uncomprehended nature or not, fact was that now, following the disenchantment
of nature, it was no longer compelled to do so. Domination could be abolished,
and that abolition was long overdue. Yet society perpetuated its subjection
to nature, despite its long since having become obsolete, 'as the permanent,
organized compulsion which, reproducing itself in individuals as systematic
self-preservation, rebounds against nature as society's control over it'.[56] As long
as humankind, still unaware of itself and unthinkingly defined as a species, not
least, in terms of its domination over nature, prolonged the compulsion of nature
it could constitute itself only as a 'gigantic public company for the exploitation of
nature' of which society at large and the individuals shaped by it assume that it is
their only option.[57] 'Civilization is the triumph of society over nature – a triumph
which transforms everything into mere nature.'[58] If the domination of nature
ceased, humankind would no longer be beholden to it and could long since have
been reconciled with it. For Adorno, this reconciliation of subject and object,
the 'theological archetype' of his utopian vision,[59] had nothing to do with some
notion of a return to nature.[60] 'Freedom', Adorno noted in *Negative Dialectics*,
'can come to be real only through coercive civilization, not by way of any "Back
to nature"'.[61] Adorno wanted to transcend the dichotomy of nature and society.
Only this, by means of determinate negation, 'would set the nonidentical free
and take even the intellectualized compulsion from it. Only it would facilitate a
multiplicity of difference beyond the grasp of the dialectic. Reconciliation would
be the recollection – anathema to subjective reason – of the manifold which
would then no longer be inimical.'[62]

Building on Marx's critical insight that exchange involved 'things that are
equal and yet unequal', Adorno insisted that the 'goal of the critique of the

inequality within equality is still equality, regardless of our skepticism in the face of the hostility the bourgeois ideal of egalitarianism displays towards all things qualitatively different.[63] This scepticism, he clarified, concerned the way in which the hollow equality of bourgeois society promoted conformism, not against a 'state of affairs which would make it an act of repression to count the beefburgers because everyone could have as many as they liked anyway, while others may, under these circumstances, decide that eating meat is beneath them altogether. Until then, the vulgar-materialist phraseology of sharing remains valid.'[64] In the meantime, 'there is tenderness only in the coarsest demand: that no-one shall go hungry anymore.'[65]

Although Adorno repeatedly emphasized just how much the current state of the forces of production would already facilitate,[66] it would take more to create a truly emancipated society and allow humankind genuinely to come into its own. The coexistence of excess, on the one hand, and existential need, on the other, resulted not from inefficient administration. One resulted from the other. Overcoming capitalism to set free the forces of production alone would not suffice to reconcile society. The conflict between the general and the particular, for example, would remain unresolved. The 'integral bureaucratic domination' that formed an indispensable prerequisite for the high levels of repression and compulsion required to perpetuate society and keep it and those within it on the road guaranteed that 'the horrific too can function in perpetuity.'[67] Today, proletarians most certainly did have 'more to lose than their chains. Measured against conditions in England a century ago as they were evident to the authors of the *Communist Manifesto*, their standard of living has not deteriorated but improved.'[68] Consequently, Marxist immiseration theory, which claimed that the material deprivation endured by proletarians not only united them as a self-confident class but also formed the basis of their revolutionary power, had lost its credibility. Yet Adorno concluded that it is not the thrust of the theory that should be modified but the concept of immiseration that needs to be revisited. 'The theater of a cryptogenic – as it were censored – poverty, however, is that of political and social impotence.'[69] One could only describe the process by which late capitalism turned all human beings into administrative units as a form of 'dehumanization'.[70] The totality had integrated the oppressed, shaped them in its image. Whereas their wretchedness had once set them apart, it now 'lies in the fact that they can never escape'.[71]

Providing for everyone's material needs would neither rule out a new form of domination nor would it be a sufficient guarantee for the 'happiness of humankind which would be the happiness of the individual'.[72] As early as 1944, Adorno had noted:

> [I]n today's objective situation, the notion of a necessary period of transition towards fully fledged socialism contradicts the standard of the material forces of production to such an extent that it sounds rather like an excuse for the consolidation of domination. In their defence, one should note that even the most measured Marxists who had more or less stopped being Marxists altogether assumed the initial phase would be shorter than the period Christians expect to lapse between the birth of Jesus and the Parousia, which is pretty much the entirety of this-worldly time.[73]

For Adorno, happiness is not, as Rolf Tiedemann has suggested, 'a plurale tantum: happiness is the happiness of the species or it does not exist'.[74] For, 'if humanity were a totality that no longer contained any limiting principle, it would be free from the coercion that subjects all its members to such a principle. It would thereby cease to be a totality so that it might finally become a totality'.[75] The 'vision of happiness without shame' points to human beings who are no longer phylogenetically and socially enmeshed and mere specimens of their species, but nor would they be juxtaposed to society as outcasts.[76] 'Utopia', as Adorno saw it, would be a state of affairs in which 'the subject could own its nonidentity without sacrifice'.[77] The 'bad equality' peddled by 'the familiar argument of tolerance', according to which all human beings are the same,[78] would be transcended by a form of association in which human beings 'could be different without fear'.[79] An emancipated society 'would not be standardized' and instead 'achieve the universalizing reconciliation of differences';[80] it would create a 'state of differentiation without domination in which the differentiated elements are mutually accepting of one another'.[81]

Adorno took issue with the 'cult of community as an end in itself'. It indicated 'that one has forgotten about the content of community, the goal of creating a world worthy of humankind. ... A genuine community could only be one comprising free human beings'.[82] This would require exchange to become what it could, given its origin in the identity principle, *also* be: just. 'In society as it ought to be, exchange would be not only abolished but fulfilled.'[83] To be sure,

> Humanity requires that the law of an eye for an eye, the quid pro quo, be brought to an end; that the odious exchange of equivalents, in which age-old myth is recapitulated in rational economics, cease. The process, however, has its dialectical crux in the requirement that what rises above exchange not fall back behind it; that the suspension of exchange not once again deny human

beings, as the objects of order, the full fruit of their labor. The abolition of the exchange of equivalents would be its fulfillment; as long as equality reigns as law, the individual is cheated of equality.[84]

Following the demise of exchange in its current form, all systematic economic categories would disintegrate. Exchange would no longer be an economic phenomenon. Humankind would be 'redeemed from just exchange by its finally unfolding in a just manner'.[85]

According to Adorno, the injustice that springs from the fact that 'the doctrine of like-for-like is a lie' has prevailed from the beginnings of recorded human history to this day.[86] This was borne out, *inter alia*, by Anaximander's 'ur-bourgeois' dictum that 'the Non-Limited is the original material of existing things; further, the source from which existing things derive their existence is also that to which they return at their destruction, according to necessity; for they give justice and make reparations to one another for their injustice, according to the arrangement of Time'.[87] For Adorno, 'Anaximander's curse' provided early evidence of the 'sort of right that makes a mockery of justice'.[88] It was characterized by 'an aspect of archaic legal vindictiveness', legitimized by myth.[89] 'The law that defined itself as punishment for lawlessness comes to resemble it and itself becomes lawlessness, an order for destruction: that, however, is the nature of myth as it is echoed in pre-Socratic thought'.[90] Anaximander had already outlined the ongoing dynamic that 'reproduced the same pattern over and over again'.[91] Subjects were 'not completely in control, either of themselves, or of society'.[92] 'To this day', in other words, 'not matter how one tries to construe it, history lacks a total subject'.[93]

'All the rationalizations notwithstanding', Adorno explained, 'the social process is stuck in an irrational cycle. In a sense, and this is already the case in Hegel, the historical dialectic implies constant transience. What Marx, at one point, with hopeful melancholia, called pre-history epitomizes all recorded history to this day, the realm of bondage'.[94] This negative motif also featured in Adorno's 'Reflections on Class Theory'. The theory that all history to date had been a history of class struggle – a concept that emerged only once the proletariat entered the stage – 'by extending the concept of class to prehistory... denounces not just the bourgeois, whose freedom, together with their possession and education, perpetuates the tradition of the old injustice. It also turns on prehistory itself'.[95] 'By exposing the historical necessity that had brought capitalism into being', the critique of political economy emerged as a 'critique of history in its entirety'.[96] In short, 'all history is the history of class struggles because it was always the same thing, namely, prehistory'. This insight provided 'a pointer as to how we can recognize what history is. From the most recent form of injustice, a steady light reflects back on history as a whole'.[97] This was why 'dialectical theory insisted on perennial categories that merely changed their appearance in the modern, rational, form of society. Consequently, the terms Marx uses, for instance, when calling free wage labour "wage slavery", are no mere metaphors'.[98] History had hitherto encompassed the perpetual repetition of the ever same, of exploitation, domination and oppression, and progress – from overt theft to concealed theft through exchange, from slavery to wage labour,[99] from arbitrary rule to the rule of law – had amounted merely to a 'change in the form of this servitude'.[100] The potential for regression drawing on ever more refined techniques of violent domination and control was constantly present.[101] As long as this was the case, myth had only seemingly been overcome and history continued to impose itself, uncomprehended and fate-like, on the individual with even greater force.

And yet, the injustice inherent in the exchange of equivalents was also 'the condition for possible justice. The fulfillment of the repeatedly broken exchange contract would converge with its abolition; exchange would disappear, if truly equal things were exchanged; true progress would not be merely an Other in relation to exchange, but rather exchange that has been brought to itself'.[102] For Adorno, the fact that an emphatic notion of justice had not previously been realized was no reason to abandon it. The abstract negation of the principle of equality or abolition of the exchange of equivalents offered no solution. After all,

> If we proclaimed, to the greater glory of the irreducibly qualitative, that parity should no longer be the ideal rule – we would be creating excuses to relapse into the old injustice. The main characteristic of the exchange of equivalents has, since time immemorial, been that unequal things would be exchanged in its name, that the surplus value of labor would be appropriated.[103]

Indeterminate negation would 'skip over individual interests in an abstract way' and 'reproduce particularity in the bad sense. Dwelling on – lingering with – the concrete is an inextinguishable aspect of anything that frees itself from particularity. At the same time, that movement of emancipation shows the specificity of particularity to be just as limited as the blind domination of a totality that does not respect particularity'.[104] This, then, was the perpetually unresolved dilemma of all previous history in general and bourgeois society in particular: 'how reason can liberate itself from the particularity of obdurate particular interest, on the one hand, without then falling prey to the no less obdurate particular interests of the totality again, on the other. It is not just philosophy that has hitherto failed in the face of this challenge – so too has the organization of humankind.'[105] For Adorno, the decisive question in need of both a logical and a practical solution was always how a whole could 'exist without doing violence to the individual part'.[106] In the current society, exchange takes the form of value equivalence. Once it had been abolished, unmediated unequal exchange could not be the solution. 'If comparability as a category of measure were simply annulled', Adorno wrote, 'the rationality which is inherent in the exchange principle – as ideology, of course, but also as promise – would give way to direct appropriation, to force, and nowadays to the naked privilege of monopolies and cliques.'[107] The suggestion that, in 'post-capitalist societies... exchange will have ceased to take place', was nonsense.[108] Rather, exchange would become inherently just, the justice of the particular would no longer be quashed by a totality that subordinated the individual.

Adorno's critique of political economy takes issue with a society in which progress, all its inherent dynamism notwithstanding, always remains static insofar as it never points to anything beyond itself. It is entirely an end in itself, progress for the sake of progress. The Marxian critique of political economy, Adorno argued, was flawed insofar as it regressed into 'reified and, in many cases, truly "economistic" thinking' and succumbed to a 'fetishization of the economic sphere'.[109] By contrast, Adorno wanted to

uncover the dialectical core of Marx's economy, which exists *malgré lui-même*, as it were, and demonstrate that the decisive categories – such as the commodity, the forces of production, the rate of profit – really do have their own momentum. This presupposes, however, that, contrary to his aspirations, one does not think of this core as a form of systematic economics or even as a representation of the developmental laws of the capitalist economy but, rather, assumes that each concept, at its heart, is objectively determined by critical intention. He was not trying to outline the dynamics of free and just exchange but plays the tune of 'If you would dance, my pretty Count': you speak of free and just exchange. Well then, here you have your free and just exchange, but it will transpire that, precisely by unfolding in accordance with its concept, it is the opposite of free and just exchange, and the appropriation of surplus value is innate to its purpose. To put it in a less economistic way: exchange relations, raised to the level of a totality, are class relations. Equal is unequal. For us, this core, which, alas, orthodox Marx exegetes would be the last to acknowledge, is dialectical.[110]

Notes

1 Jürgen Habermas, 'Theodor Adorno: The Primal History of Subjectivity – Self-Affirmation Gone Wild (1969)', in *Philosophical-Political Profiles*, translated by Fredrick G. Lawrence (Cambridge, MA: MIT Press, 1983), 99–109, here 109.

2 Helmut Reichelt, 'Marx's Critique of Economic Categories: Reflections on the Problem of Validity in the Dialectical Method of Presentation in Capital', *Historical Materialism* 15, 4 (2007): 3–52, here 4.

3 Jürgen Ritsert, 'Realabstraktion. Ein zu recht abgewertetes Thema der kritischen Theorie?', in *Kein Staat zu machen. Zur Kritik der Sozialwissenschaften*, edited by Christoph Görg and Roland Roth (Münster: Westfälisches Dampfboot, 1998), 324–48, here 331.

4 Karl Marx, letter to Friedrich Engels, 2 April 1851, in Karl Marx and Friedrich Engels, *Collected Works* (New York: International Publishers, 1974–2004), hereafter MECW, vol. 38, 325–26, here 325 (translation amended).

5 Hans-Georg Backhaus, 'Theodor W. Adorno on "Marx and the Basic Concepts of Sociological Theory". From a Seminar Transcript in the Summer Semester of 1962', translated by Verena Erlenbusch-Anderson and Chris O'Kane, in *Historical Materialism* 26, no. 1 (2018): 154–64, here 164. Reprinted in the Appendix of this book.

6 Lecture course *Introduction to Sociology*, seminar minutes, 9 July 1968, quoted in Dirk Braunstein, *Adornos Kritik der politischen Ökonomie* (Bielefeld: transcript, 2016), 10.

7 Helmut Reichelt, *Neue Marx-Lektüre. Zur Kritik sozialwissenschaftlicher Logik* (Freiburg: Ça ira, 2013), 39.

8 Karl Marx, 'A Contribution to the Critique of Political Economy', in MECW, vol. 29, 257–417, here 262; Friedrich Pollock, 'Zur Geldtheorie von Karl Marx', reprint in *idem, Gesammelte Schriften*, vol. 1, edited by Philipp Lenhard (Freiburg: Ça ira, 2018), 25–127, here 32.

9 Iring Fetscher, 'Ein Kämpfer ohne Illusion', in *Theodor W. Adorno zum Gedächtnis. Eine Sammlung*, edited by Hermann Schweppenhäuser (Frankfurt/Main: Suhrkamp, 1971), 90–4, here 93.

10 Theodor W. Adorno, letter to Walter Benjamin, 13 September 1937, in Adorno and Benjamin, *Complete Correspondence, 1928–1940*, translated by Nicholas Walker (Cambridge: Polity, 1999), 207–10, here 210.

11 See Braunstein, *Adornos Kritik*, 101.

12 See Theodor W. Adorno, letter to Alfred Sohn-Rethel, 17 November 1936, in Theodor W. Adorno and Alfred Sohn-Rethel, *Briefwechsel 1936–1969* (Munich: edition text + kritik, 1991), 32–4.

13 Theodor W. Adorno, *Negative Dialectics*, translated by E. B. Ashton (London: Routledge & Kegan Paul, 1973), 147.

14 Theodor W. Adorno, *Philosophische Terminologie I und II* (Berlin: Suhrkamp, 2016), 617.

15 Backhaus, 'Theodor W. Adorno on "Marx"', 158 (translation amended).

16 Ibid., 160.

17 Ibid., 158 (translation amended).

18 Theodor W. Adorno, 'Introduction', in *idem et al., The Positivist Dispute in German Sociology*, translated by Glyn Adey and David Frisby (London: Heinemann, 1976), 1–67, here 25 (translation amended).

19 Alex Demirović, 'Freiheit und Menschheit', in *Vereinigung freier Individuen. Kritik der Tauschgesellschaft und gesellschaftliches Gesamtsubjekt bei Theodor W. Adorno*, edited by Jens Becker and Heinz Brakemeier (Hamburg: VSA, 2004), 22–3.

20 Ibid., 23.

21 Adorno, *Philosophische Terminologie*, 616.

22 Theodor W. Adorno, 'Late Capitalism or Industrial Society?', in *Can One Live after Auschwitz? A Philosophical Reader*, translated by Rodney Livingstone, edited by Rolf Tiedemann (Stanford: Stanford University Press, 2003), 111–25, here 115.

23 Seminar minutes from Adorno's seminar, *Economy and Society I*, 3 December 1957, quoted in Alex Demirović, *Der nonkonformistische Intellektuelle. Die Entwicklung der Kritischen Theorie zur Frankfurter Schule* (Frankfurt/Main: Suhrkamp, 1999), 463.

24 Theodor W. Adorno, *History and Freedom: Lectures, 1964–1965*, translated by Rodney Livingstone (Cambridge: Polity, 2006), 26–7.

25 Adorno, 'Introduction', 24 (translation amended).

26 See Alfred Schmidt, 'On the Concept of Knowledge in the Criticism of Political Economy', in *Karl Marx, 1818/1968*, edited by Golo Mann et al. (Bad Godesberg: Inter Nationes, 1968), 92–102, here 92–3.

27 Theodor W. Adorno, 'Subject and Object' in *Subject and Object. Frankfurt School Writings on Epistemology, Ontology, and Method*, translated by E. B. Ashton, edited by Ruth Groff (New York: Bloomsbury, 2014), 149–64, here 156.

28 Adorno, 'Introduction', 24–5 (translation amended).

29 Theodor W. Adorno, 'Aspects of Hegel's Philosophy', in *Hegel: Three Studies*, translated by Shierry Weber Nicholsen (Cambridge, MA: MIT Press, 1993), 1–51, here 28.

30 Adorno, *Negative Dialectics*, 320. 'I shall say here only that the essence of this model of an antagonistic society is that it is not a society *with* contradictions or *despite* its contradictions, but *by virtue of* its contradictions. In other words, a society based on profit necessarily contains this division in society because of the objective existence of the profit motive. This profit motive which divides society and

potentially tears it apart is also the factor by means of which society reproduces its own existence.' Theodor W. Adorno, *Lectures on Negative Dialectics. Fragments of a Lecture Course, 1965/1966*, translated by Rodney Livingstone (Cambridge: Polity, 2008), 8–9.

31   Theodor W. Adorno, *Philosophical Elements of a Theory of Society, 1964*, translated by Wieland Hoban (Cambridge: Polity, 2019), 68 (translation amended).

32   Theodor W. Adorno, 'Reflections on Class Theory', translated by Rodney Livingstone, in Adorno, *Can One Live after Auschwitz?*, 97.

33   Adorno, *History and Freedom*, 51.

34   Ibid., 49–50.

35   Adorno, *Lectures on Negative Dialectics*, 96. As Adorno explained, this concept drew on ideas articulated by Alfred Seidel, one of the friends of his youth. 'In order to present a consistent concept of history', Seidel had noted, '[Marx], like [Hegel], was compelled to assume that there was *one* driving force inherent in history. As a realist, he rejected Hegel's metaphysics of the spirit and substituted the economy for it. . . . Consequently, the driving force inherent in history could only be economic in nature, more precisely, the factors that facilitate or increase the productivity of labour, i.e., the "forces of production". . . . Given that these were supposedly the driving force inherent in history, they were hypostatized as an absolute and metaphysical – albeit immanent metaphysical – entity, inadvertently creating an historical philosophy analogous to its transcendent-metaphysical predecessors from the Old Testament to Hegel.' Alfred Seidel, *Bewußtsein als Verhängnis*, edited by Hans Prinzhorn (Bonn: Friedrich Cohen, 1927), 209–10.

36   Adorno, *Lectures on Negative Dialectics*, 96.

37   Ibid., 96–7. See also, Adorno, *Philosophische Terminologie*, 314–15 and Friedrich Engels, 'Anti-Dühring', in MECW, vol. 25, 5–309, here 105–6.

38   Adorno, *History and Freedom*, 52 (translation amended).

39   Ibid., 52.

40   Ibid., 53 (translation amended).

41   Ibid., 67.

42   See ibid., 89–90.

43   Adorno, *Philosophische Terminologie*, 525.

44   Ibid., 525–6.

45   Alex Demirović, 'Zur Dialektik von Utopie und bestimmter Negation. Eine Diskussionsbemerkung', in *Kritische Wissenschaften im Neoliberalismus*, edited by Christina Kaindl (Marburg: BdWi-Verlag, 2005), 144.

46   Theodor W. Adorno, *Minima Moralia. Reflections from Damaged Life*, translated by Edmund Jephcott (London: Verso, 2005), 234.

47   Adorno, *Negative Dialectics*, 307.

48 Adorno, *Philosophische Terminologie*, 524. 'Myth', Adorno noted in March 1969, 'is *not* that which is not the case. Rather, it is the cobbled together ever same in the world. Resistance to it is spirit, is the subject. In a reality beyond the existential need in which it originates and whose marks it bears, spirit would be able, and compelled, to change, right down to its very core; it will not simply die away. Each time something is rendered concrete, the phantom of abstract nihilism dissipates.... Myth = the conflated world: that is how it is that is how it will always be that is how it is supposed to be.' Theodor W. Adorno, 'Graeculus (II). Notizen zu Philosophie und Gesellschaft 1943–1969', in *Frankfurter Adorno Blätter* 8 (2003): 9–41, here 35.

49 For a more detailed discussion of this aphorism, see Gerhard Schweppenhauser, *Theodor W. Adorno: An introduction*, translated by James Rolleston (Durham, NC: Duke University Press, 2009), 78–90.

50 Adorno, *Minima Moralia*, 156–7 (translation amended).

51 Karl Marx, *Capital*, vol. 1, in MECW, vol. 35, 750 (translation amended).

52 Ibid., 45.

53 Max Horkheimer and Theodor W. Adorno, *Dialectic of Enlightenment. Philosophical Fragments*, translated by Edmund Jephcott (Stanford: Stanford University Press, 2002), xviii.

54 Adorno, 'Late Capitalism or Industrial Society?', 122.

55 Horkheimer and Adorno, *Dialectic of Enlightenment*, 25.

56 Ibid., 149.

57 Adorno, *History and Freedom*, 45.

58 Horkheimer and Adorno, *Dialectic of Enlightenment*, 153.

59 Rolf Tiedemann, 'Concept, Image, Name. On Adorno's Utopia of Knowledge', in *The Semblance of Subjectivity: Essays in Adorno's Aesthetic Theory*, edited by Tom Huhn and Lambert Zuidervaart (Cambridge, MA: MIT Press, 1997), 123–45, here 126.

60 As Eckart Goebel has noted, 'it is astonishing that the notion that Adorno, in the manner of Rousseau, propagated a return to a pristine, unformed nature as it had supposedly existed before man pounced on, and had his way with, it has become a widespread cliché. The dialectic persists, spirit does not give up on spirit.... Formulated *in abstracto*: the accusation that Adorno was a naïve disciple of nature fails to take into account that Adorno is concerned with the in between, with the point of regression and the utopian vision of spirit, *without* relinquishing either of the two poles'. Eckart Goebel, 'Das Hinzutretende. Ein Kommentar zu den Seiten 226 bis 230 der *Negativen Dialektik*', in *Frankfurter Adorno Blätter* 4 (1995): 109–16, here 112.

61 Adorno, *Negative Dialectics*, 147.

62 Ibid., 6 (translation amended).

63 Ibid., 147 (translation amended).

64 Theodor W. Adorno, 'Contra Paulum', in *Briefwechsel 1927–1969, vol. 2: 1938–1944,* *idem* and Max Horkheimer (Frankfurt/Main: Suhrkamp, 2004), 475–503, here 497–8.

65 Adorno, *Minima Moralia*, 156.

66 See, for example, the following comment: 'The forces of production, the material forces of production, have today advanced to such an extent that a rational organization of society would render need obsolete. In the nineteenth century, the contention that this would hold true for the entire planet, at a global level, would have been dismissed with disdain as grossly utopian.... This much seems clear: given how enormously the objective possibilities have increased, the kind of critique of utopian concepts that hinged on the persistence of scarcity is really obsolete.' Theodor W. Adorno, 'Diskussionsbeitrag zu "Spätkapitalismus oder Industriegesellschaft?"', in Theodor W. Adorno, *Gesammelte Schriften*, vol. 8 (Frankfurt/Main: Suhrkamp, 1997), 578–87, here 585. For similar remarks, see also Adorno, *History and Freedom*, 99.

67 Adorno, 'Introduction', 26.

68 Adorno, 'Reflections on Class Theory', 103 (translation amended).

69 Ibid., 105.

70 Ibid., 109 and *passim*.

71 Ibid., 109–10.

72 Adorno, *Negative Dialectics*, 352 (translation amended).

73 Adorno, 'Contra Paulum', 493.

74 Rolf Tiedemann, '"Gegenwärtige Vorwelt". Zu Adornos Begriff des Mythischen (I)', in *Frankfurter Adorno Blätter* 5 (1998): 9–36, here 10.

75 Adorno, *History and Freedom*, 146. See also, *idem*, 'Progress', in Theodor W. Adorno, *Critical Models: Interventions and Catchwords*, translated by Henry W. Pickford (New York: Columbia University Press, 1998), 143–60, here 145–6.

76 Theodor W. Adorno, 'Graeculus (I). Musikalische Notizen', in *Frankfurter Adorno Blätter* 7 (2001): 9–36, here 16.

77 Adorno, *Negative Dialectics*, 281 (translation amended).

78 As Adorno noted in *Jargon of Authenticity*, 'being human becomes the most general and empty form of privilege. It is strictly suited to a form of consciousness that no longer tolerates privilege and yet is still under its spell. Yet, given that it passes over the unmitigated disparities in social power – between hunger and overabundance, between spirit and docile idiocy – this brand of universal humanness is ideology, the grimace of the innate equality of all beings who bear a human countenance. They respond with chaste sentimentality as they allow themselves to be addressed, at no cost to anyone, as human beings'. Theodor W. Adorno, *Jargon of Authenticity*, translated by Knut Tarnowski and Frederic Will (Evanston: Northwestern University Press, 1973), 66 (translation amended).

79 Adorno, *Minima Moralia*, 103.

80 Ibid. (translation amended).

81 Theodor W. Adorno, 'On Subject and Object', in *Critical Models. Interventions and Catchwords*, translated by Henry W. Pickford (New York: Columbia University Press, 1998), 245–58, here 247 (translation amended).

82 Theodor W. Adorno, 'Thesen gegen die musikpädagogische Musik', in *idem, Gesammelte Schriften*, vol. 14 (Frankfurt/Main: Suhrkamp, 1997), 437–40, here 438.

83 Adorno, *Negative Dialectics*, 295–6.

84 Theodor W. Adorno, 'On the Classicism of Goethe's *Iphigenie*', in *idem, Notes to Literature*, translated by Shierry Weber Nicholsen (New York: Columbia University Press, 2019), 418–28, here 425 (translation amended).

85 Adorno, *Jargon of Authenticity*, 152 (translation amended).

86 Adorno, 'Progress', 159. 'To recognize the catastrophic violence in the latest form of injustice, that is to say, the latent injustice contained in fair exchange', Adorno noted, 'means simply to identify it with the prehistory that it destroyed'. Adorno, 'Reflections on Class Theory', 93–4.

87 Theodor W. Adorno, 'The Experiential Content of Hegel's Philosophy', in Theodor W. Adorno, *Hegel: Three Studies,* Translated by Shierry Weber Nicholsen (Cambridge, MA: The MIT Press, 1993), 53–88, here 86. Kathleen Freeman, *Ancilla to The Pre-Socratic Philosophers. A Complete Translation of the Fragments in Diels*, Fragmente der Vorsokratiker (Cambridge, MA: Harvard University Press, 1948), 19.

88 Theodor W. Adorno, *Against Epistemology. A Metacritique*, translated by Willis Domingo (Cambridge: Polity, 2013), 25; Theodor W. Adorno, letter to Max Horkheimer, 10 January 1945, in *idem* and Max Horkheimer, *Briefwechsel 1927– 1969, vol. 3: 1945–1949* (Frankfurt/Main: Suhrkamp, 2005), 10–15, here 12.

89 Adorno, *Negative Dialectics*, 267.

90 Theodor W. Adorno, *In Search of Wagner*, translated by Rodney Livingstone (London: Verso, 2005), 107.

91 Theodor W. Adorno, '"Static" and "Dynamic" as Sociological Categories', translated by H. Kaal, *Diogenes* 9, no. 33 (1961): 28–49, here 45.

92 Ibid.

93 Adorno, *Negative Dialectics*, 304 (translation amended).

94 Adorno, '"Static" and "Dynamic"', 45 (translation amended).

95 Adorno, 'Reflections on Class Theory', 93.

96 Ibid.

97 Ibid., 94.

98 Adorno, '"Static" and "Dynamic"', 45 (translation amended). In texts that were predominantly polemical rather than scholarly, Marx occasionally contrasted 'Capital and Wage Slavery'. Karl Marx, 'The Civil War in France. Address of the General Council of the International Working Men's Association', in MECW, vol. 22, 307–59, here 335 (translation amended).

99　As Marx noted in the first volume of *Capital*, 'the essential difference between the various economic forms of society, between, for instance, a society based on slave labour, and one based on wage labour, lies only in the mode in which this surplus labour is in each case extracted from the actual producer, the labourer'. MECW, vol. 35, 226–7.

100　See ibid., 706 (translation amended).

101　'The horde, a term that… features in the organizational scheme of the Hitler Youth', Horkheimer and Adorno wrote in *Dialectic of Enlightenment*, 'is no relapse into the old barbarism. It is the triumph of a repressive form of egalitarianism, the degeneration of the equality of rights into the wrong inflicted by equals'. Horkheimer and Adorno, *Dialectic of Enlightenment*, 9 (translation amended).

102　Adorno, 'Progress', 159.

103　Adorno, *Negative Dialectics*, 146.

104　Theodor W. Adorno, 'On the Final Scene of Faust', in *idem, Notes to Literature*, translated by Shierry Weber Nicholsen (New York: Columbia University Press, 2019), 124–30, here 128.

105　Adorno, *History and Freedom*, 45 (translation amended).

106　Theodor W. Adorno, *Beethoven. The Philosophy of Music*, translated by Edmund Jephcott (Cambridge: Polity, 1998), 34.

107　Adorno, *Negative Dialectics*, 146–7 (translation amended). 'Since time immemorial', Adorno noted, 'not just since the capitalist appropriation of surplus value in the commodity exchange of labor power for the cost of its reproduction, the societally more powerful contracting party receives more than the other. By means of this injustice something new occurs in the exchange: the process, which proclaims its own stasis, becomes dynamic. The truth of the expansion feeds on the lie of the equality'. Adorno, 'Progress', 159.

108　Adorno, *Introduction to Sociology*, translated by Edmund Jephcott (Stanford: Stanford University Press, 2000), 31.

109　Theodor W. Adorno, letter to Jürgen von Kempski, 27 January 1950, quoted in Braunstein, *Adornos Kritik*, 391.

110　Ibid. Marx and Engels cited 'If you would dance, my pretty Count', the aria from Mozart's *The Wedding of Figaro*, in an article published in the *Neue Rheinische Zeitung* on 12 August 1848. Karl Marx and Friedrich Engels, 'The German Citizenship and the Prussian Police', in MECW, vol. 7, 383–4, here 384. It seems more likely, however, that Adorno, when making this reference, was thinking of a well-known passage in the introduction to the critique of Hegel's philosophy of right, in which Marx referred to the 'petrified relations' that characterized German society and which 'must be forced to dance by singing their own tune to them!' Karl Marx, 'Contribution to the Critique of Hegel's Philosophy of Law. Introduction', in MECW, vol. 3, 175–87, here 178.

4

Adorno, the New Reading of Marx, and methodologies of critique

Charlotte Baumann

Adorno's conceptual understanding of capitalism and his engagement with Marx was fundamental to the emergence of the 'New Reading of Marx' (NRM) developed by some of Adorno's former students, most notably Hans-Georg Backhaus and Helmut Reichelt. Backhaus and Reichelt often suggest that they sought to realize 'Adorno's programme',[1] since he was 'too old to pursue it further'.[2] The literature about the New Reading also tends to highlight the links and similarities between Adorno and his students.[3] In contrast, this chapter explores the differences between Adorno and the New Reading, and, indeed, between Adorno and what some consider the *new* 'NRM' namely 'Open Marxism' (OM).[4]

The aim of the chapter is not to establish whether these new readings are in any way flawed in their conceptualization of capitalism. Rather, it focuses on the methodological difference between them and Adorno's critical theory. Adorno appreciates an internal, systematic critique that explains the functioning, contradictions and shortcomings of capitalism. However, he believes that such a critique is not sufficient because it remains necessarily within the parameters of the capitalist system. It thereby inadvertently copies some of its basic tenets like, for example, the focus on concepts, rather than the matter they organize, as well as the assumption that the system, its laws and (contradictory) structure is what matters most. What it fails to show is why and how the contradictions and tensions in capitalism are bad (for human beings). After all, many liberal economists agree that there are tensions and cycles in capitalism, but they argue that crises create more wealth in the long run and that despite the fact that workers are exploited, their livelihoods in the Western world did improve considerably under capitalism. The disagreements that the systemic approaches to capitalism bring to the fore are necessarily very abstract, like, for example, whether the systemic laws tend towards the decline or further progress of the system or whether contradictions are bad per se or only if they fail to be socially beneficial in the long run. In this mode of theorizing, the underlying disagreements between Marxists and liberals are rather scholarly and principled, and hard to resolve on the basis of anything besides pre-existing sympathies and expectations.

For Adorno, the focus on the systemic is insufficient. He argued for a different, more fundamental critique of capitalism. I hold that Adorno engages in a form of 'epistemic disobedience', to use Mignolo's expression. His critical theory is more than just an immanent critique of the system, its logic and laws. Fundamentally, it turns towards the human beings, whose suffering is key to understanding not only the way economic laws and concepts function, but also the complexities of social reality, which is never completely identical to any conceptual system. Adorno's critical theory stipulates that human suffering, not the system that causes it, ought to be the ultimate, normative foundation of a critical social theory.

For Adorno, the critique of capitalism involves theorizing the friction between capitalist concepts and human bodies, giving voice to how capitalism hurts. Adorno famously claims that 'reified consciousness has become total',[5] the self-definition of human beings is infused with capitalist logic. But this is only achieved through violence, through repression of non-identity, 'the universal, compressing the particular until it splinters, like a torture instrument'.[6] Although Habermas is right that, according to Adorno, reason and its concepts are complicit in capitalism, he is mistaken to assume that Adorno endorses a self-destructive critique of reason. Rather, Adorno proposes another way of reasoning and perceiving that feeds from and is grounded in the bodily and the particular. The critique of capitalism requires an unusual type of empirical analysis, a new and different way of perceiving – that needs to be theorized in its tension with and linkage to the conceptuality of the system. This empirical analysis does not consist in collecting data or theorizing about 'experience' in a general manner. Rather, it means listening to real people, their personal experiences, feelings and lives. Their lives and feelings are crucial not only to properly understand how capitalism works (i.e. in the real world, rather than in economics textbooks) but also as a critical tool for showing why capitalism is bad and envisaging a better society.

Marx, Adorno, proponents of the NRM and OM are all well aware of the conceptuality and systematicity of capitalism. However, while Marx certainly studied the suffering of those affected by capitalism (when, for example, analysing working conditions, struggles against child labour and the length of the working day), he did not attribute to these insights, as Adorno does, any epistemological and theoretical value. On Adorno's reading, Marx remains concerned primarily with the systematic conceptuality of capitalism and does not turn towards human suffering as the key to comprehending social reality. Adorno tried to remedy this, while proponents of the NRM went in the opposite direction focusing on the conceptuality of capitalism exclusively. In contrast to the so-called 'logicians' of the NRM, proponents of OM are more concerned with the systematicity of capitalism as a lived experience, but this interest has not led to the kind of fundamental change in methodology that Adorno calls for.

The chapter has three main sections. It starts by summarizing a few key propositions that characterize an Adornian take on the conceptuality of capitalism and distinguish it from other approaches. It then turns to the differences between Adorno and the NRM and OM. The section asks whether and to what extent Hegel's *Logic* can be useful in the study of capitalism. Theorists of the NRM argue that this is so, citing similarities between the logical structures Hegel's analyses and the structures that are at work in capitalism, at least as studied by Marx. I assume that Adorno noticed problems of conceptuality (in Hegel and capitalism) that proponents of the NRM did not. The third section expounds Adorno's reservations about a purely conceptual analysis of capitalism.

Capitalism as a totalizing conceptual system

The key distinguishing feature between Adorno-inspired types of Marxism and other studies of capitalism is an enhanced awareness of the conceptuality of the capitalist system. To be sure, liberal economists and orthodox Marxists also treat capitalism as a system that involves concepts. Most analysts of capitalism assume that it displays regularities and laws and, hence, has a system-character to the extent that one can capture important developments by graphs and curves and even make predictions as to how prices, savings or investments are likely to behave. What is lacking in many mainstream and orthodox Marxist approaches, however, is the awareness of the extent, meaning and functioning of concepts in capitalism.

In fact, I would say that proponents of the NRM and OM share with Adorno the following three convictions, the first being the most fundamental: (I) Capitalism is conceptual to a much higher degree than previous societies. In capitalism, concepts have a certain autonomy from human beings whose interactions they shape and determine to a large extent. (II) Capitalism is a totalizing system, its concepts are present as determining factors in all spheres of capitalist societies, and capitalism absorbs and profits from pre- and non-capitalist remnants. (III) One cannot extrapolate concepts or contradictions from the capitalist present to the pre-capitalist or even pre-historical past.

(I) Adorno proposes, in a famous passage that Reichelt cites:[7] There is a 'conceptuality in social reality... not merely the constitutive conceptuality of the knowing subject, but the conceptuality which holds sway in reality itself', i.e. in the social world.[8] Elsewhere, Adorno writes that, in capitalist society, there is 'a certain independence of the concept', with 'singular events' counting only insofar as they are measured by the 'social average'.[9] In capitalism, commodities are exchanged by the market price, which is determined by the social average – of supply and demand, or 'profit, material' and the cost of the 'abstract labor-time',[10] depending on the theory one follows. By the term 'conceptuality' Adorno refers to the fact that concrete entities, events and activities are treated as instances of something else, namely of the higher concept 'value'. This contrasts with other societies. In medieval Europe, for example, there was also a concept for what peasants owed the nobles who owned their land: the 'tithe', a tenth of their harvest. However, the tithe was negotiable and could even be lifted if there had been a crop failure or a fatality. There was a direct relation between the noble and the peasant, and the concept of the tithe guided but did not dictate or predetermine their exact interaction. In capitalism, by contrast, the value of a commodity determines who can buy or sell and what investments are made.

Marx had shown in *Capital* that an exchange is only possible because commodities count as comparable. Sohn-Rethel has coined the term 'real abstraction'[11] to describe this implicit, but real-existing abstraction. Before him, Hegel wrote about an 'abstraction from' or 'idealizing' of 'specific things', in the sense of investing them with a new meaning that has nothing to do with any of their concrete qualities; Hegel describes this as the reduction of all commodities to 'signs' of value, which turns all qualitative differences into quantitative ones.[12] The market works because specific things count as indicators of something else, instances or quanta of the higher concept of value – and some entities as pure crystallizations of this value without any additional baggage, namely coins and bills. (This is why Backhaus and Reichelt call money the 'real-existing universal', a 'real-existing abstract' concept or 'universal in the thing', referencing Hegel and Simmel.[13])

Real abstraction is not a subjective mistake, but an objective reality that engenders and presupposes economic laws like Adam Smith's price mechanism.

Smith proposes that, through millions of unconnected acts of buying and selling of the same commodity, one (average) price for this commodity is established on the market, a price that in turn determines who can sell or buy. Of course, Marxists tend to disagree with Smith's notion that supply and demand determine prices, and argue that values and, hence, prices are determined by the average time workers are assumed to require to produce a type of commodity. On both accounts, however, value determines the interactions of individuals, what is produced, how it is done, who manages to sell what and where new investments are made. Value is 'the objective category as such, the category of exchange, by means of which something like a material necessity realizes itself over the heads of the particular subjects and which is in itself something conceptual, spiritual'.[14]

(II) Value thus does not only mediate the sphere of exchange. Rather, more importantly, it also shapes what is produced, how this is done (namely in a profitable way) and how human beings relate to their own productive activity, since what matters is receiving a wage.[15] The objective value and price of a product can even cause subjective pleasure, for example where expensive commodities serve as status symbols. But capitalism is systemic and totalizing even in a broader sense for Adorno: It shapes every aspect of human lives,[16] absorbs, defines and profits from (seemingly) external elements or 'non-capitalist enclaves'.[17] Adorno includes the family among such enclaves. He refers to 'quasi-colonial conflicts',[18] which capitalism profits from and exacerbates; it may be assumed that racism, sexism, and older class or cast distinctions also count among the traditional structures capitalism absorbs and integrates into its totality.

(III) Understanding capitalism as conceptual in this way shows that capitalist concepts only have the power that they do because human beings act upon them within this system. It is true that Marx sometimes speaks of capitalists as personified capital. He does so in order to highlight that managers, investors and entrepreneurs are compelled to follow the logic of capital accumulation, on pain of ruin. While this necessity is real, it is nevertheless only a logical and conceptual necessity that arises from capitalism and to which capitalists respond. There is no super-subject called Capital that literally forces the hands of capitalists. As Adorno puts it, 'Blindly attributing a dialectical movement to subjectless matter amounts to the wildest belief in spirits.'[19]

Furthermore, one cannot treat capitalist concepts as ahistorical constants. Capitalist concepts have their meaning and function within and because of the capitalist system. One cannot appeal to ahistorical contradictions between 'forces' and 'relations of production' propelling history, as if these factors were always the same and as if those concepts had some power and reality of their own independently of human practice.[20] Similarly, one cannot study labour 'in abstraction from society',[21] as something ahistorical and eternal, a human interaction with nature now just as it was at the birth of humanity. While Adorno is sympathetic to Marx's view that production normally requires something other than human beings and concepts, namely nature,[22] he is not as confident as Alfred Schmidt that this is always and necessarily the case.[23] Adorno highlights the point of the late Marx who argues that, in capitalism, anything can have value depending on the circumstances.[24] Marx proposes in his *Theories on Surplus Value* that a writer, who writes on demand and under the guidance of a bookseller, is a productive worker, because 'his product is subsumed under capital from the start'; a singer, who tries to sell her compositions, is an unproductive worker up until the point she gets contracted by a music entrepreneur.[25] For Adorno, this 'reveals the irony' of capitalism and that value is purely 'immanent to the system'[26] – and, hence, unconnected to any pre-capitalist notion of a productive interaction with nature.

Hegel – a boon and a burden

Both Hans-Georg Backhaus[27] and Helmut Reichelt[28] sum up the key methodological commitment of the NRM, by pointing out Marx's indebtedness to Hegel's *Logic* and dialectics, claiming that one cannot truly understand Marx's *Capital* without the more overtly Hegelian *Rohentwurf*, also known as *Grundrisse*. Backhaus and Reichelt interpret Marx by relying on Hegelian figures like illusion/illusory being, appearance, substance, essence and doubling.[29] Not all of these expressions actually appear in Hegel's text, but they certainly refer to definable structures that Hegel discusses in his *Logic*.

It is worth quickly sketching which Hegelian structures fit Backhaus's description. Hegel's entire *Logic* can be read as discussing different structures or constellations, different ways elements can be united into a whole. At the beginning of the Logic of Essence, Hegel discusses the following constellation: a unitary, absolute whole he calls 'essence' posits entities as unposited. Essence brings something about which appears not to have been brought about or made. Hegel calls these things that are posited as unposited 'illusory being'. Being basically means something that has independent existence; things as illusory beings certainly exist but not independently so, since they stem from Essence. The doubling Backhaus refers to is present here insofar as essence occurs twice in this equation: once as posited and once as unposited or rather as the origin or root of illusory beings. That this is a sort of 'doubling' becomes explicit later, when Hegel defines the essence as 'ground', with the ground and grounded being the same content in a different form.[30] Hegel's point is that things (illusory beings or appearances) seem to exist independently, to just be there and the way they are simply by themselves; however, their 'being' or independent existence is an illusion, in the sense that they certainly do exist but not independently so. Essence, for its part, appears to be an absolute, independent, primary force, but is actually dependent on appearing (to be the essence of anything at all) and, indeed, is nothing but what is taken to have its appearance in those seemingly independent things. Hegel discusses similar structures in other places, most notably in Logic of the Concept, where he discusses objective, mechanical laws: Mechanical natural laws are nothing but regular connections between the physical properties of objects, and yet these properties and their links apply to objects as external law – like impositions. The laws are the objects' own properties, which rule them externally and 'violently',[31] because, as Hegel writes, the objects do not control 'out of their own impetus',[32] thereby failing to be 'self-determining' and free.[33]

The similarity of these structures to capitalism is clearly no coincidence, since Hegel concerned himself with the market economy of his time. In many places he deplores that market laws function like 'blind destiny' (WL2 421/720) or 'external' or 'blind necessity' (E3 §532; WL2 440/736). In *Jenaer Systementwürfe I*, Hegel writes that the 'manifold of productive activities have to realize… their abstraction… Money is the real existing concept'.[34] In his *Science of Logic*, when discussing laws of objectivity that externally govern things by using their properties, Hegel does not explicitly mention Adam Smith. However, he calls this mechanism a 'cunning of reason', adding in a note: 'God lets men, who have their particular passions and interests, do as they please and what results is the accomplishment of his intentions.'[35] The links between Smith's 'invisible hand' and Hegel's 'cunning of reason' have been explored in detail by others,[36] but the similarities are clear: Smith's price mechanism refers to how, by accumulating preferences/choices of purchase, the market imposes a specific price for each product that is externally given to market participants and changes against their wills. Hegel says Smith detects the 'principles' governing a multitude of details and thereby reveals the 'appearance of rationality' in the market.[37]

Leaving aside Hegel's own intentional references to the market logic, Reichelt and Backhaus argue that money and, indeed, value is 'both illusion and reality'.[38] Value is illusory insofar as rather than being a natural property of commodities, as it appears to be, value is actually 'posited', a function of and foundation for the capitalist system; however, value is real insofar as it shapes production, employment relations and even consumption/usefulness. In fact, value is both the necessary condition for and expression of a social relation of private and isolated producers.[39] Value, on their reading, has been linked to Hegel's logical essence;[40] value is self-multiplying, self-positing in the form of capital, which appears to be the independent source of things, but only consists in them counting as and producing more value. Other more creative uses of Hegelian structures are present throughout the NRM. The most important 'doublings'[41] they identify include: the doubling of products into value-objects and actual, physical objects, commodities and money;[42] the doubling of productive activities as they also appear as instances of abstract labour or 'work'[43] and the appearance of relations between persons (producer–consumer, employee–employer) as relations between things (commodity–money, labour–money).

Taking a step back, Hegel is clearly useful for those interested in analysing the objective functioning and structures of capitalism. This is so because and insofar as Hegel assumes that concepts are linked according to a structure or logic that is not mental but real and, indeed, because he assumes that concepts can be posited or have a physical form just as much as the form of a law. The specific structures Hegel analyses as well as his general outlook regarding the power and functioning of concepts are attractive, because they are (intentionally) akin to market dynamics. Furthermore, Hegel's *Logic* comes with certain critical tools or angles. Hegel develops critical notions such as illusory being and inversion. These terms help critics to formulate a critique in terms of the problematic (violent, incoherent, discordant, twisted) functioning of a structure, rather than searching for mistakes in terms of subjective misrepresentation of said structure. Hegel's *Logic* comes with a certain moral or social compass, as he considers external, violent, fate-like impositions as bad (i.e. unlikely to endure and unsuitable for human freedom). Hegel favours structures that function by means of a collective and mutually beneficial, harmonious coordination of all elements or, indeed, social groups. After all, Hegel is the same scholar who said the market was a 'monstrous system' that needed to be 'tamed like a wild beast'.[44] (A key difference between Marx and Hegel lies in the fact that Hegel believes that such a 'taming of the beast' is possible and the market can play an integrated, limited, and controlled part within a system of freedoms, that includes a strong element of collective government.)

I do not doubt that Adorno agrees with the general usefulness of Hegel for reading Marx and studying capitalism. Adorno opposes nominalism, according to which universal concepts are nothing but abstractions that human beings have in their minds. 'The concept is the sufficient reason of the thing insofar as the exploration of social objects, at least, becomes flawed, where... you ignore the determination by the totality.'[45] For Adorno, society is 'a real-existing system,[46] an 'objective structure', and 'interconnection of functions' [*Funktionszusammenhang*][47] that has an independence from the individuals who constitute it.

Nevertheless, using Hegel also comes with some major problems. And it is an acute awareness of these problems that, I believe, marks a key difference between Adorno and the NRM. You have to ask yourself: Why does Hegel describe and analyse these structures? What hidden commitments does Hegel have? One commitment, which Backhaus and Reichelt explicitly reject, is Hegel's belief in 'sublation', i.e. that wrong, faulty, problematic structures will or are likely to self-destruct, giving way to a determinate better structure or, indeed, society. But Hegel comes with some additional baggage that Backhaus and Reichelt seem to overlook: Hegel studies these conceptual structures because he thinks that the conceptual, in whatever form, is what truly matters. Metaphysical Hegelians are of course right in that Hegel should not be misunderstood as saying that everything is in the mind or consists in shared conceptions, norms and definitions. The concept or conceptual in Hegel's metaphysics clearly does not merely refer to abstract classifiers or elements in judgements. Nevertheless, Hegel clearly assumes the priority of the 'conceptual' as he proposes that physical, mind-independent nature contains and is characterized not by its physical composition or material existence, but by its structure and regularities, the law-like way elements are organized. Chemical reactions, natural laws, the structured interconnection of organs, etc., this is what the world truly consists in; it is not the blood, but the way it circulates that characterizes the sanguinary system. Hegel thus champions the conceptual (meaning the form or structure of things). This not only entails Hegel's belief that the world can be grasped by human thought (since the structures of things can easily be picked up on by structured human thinking). His assumption that everything is characterized by its structure also comes with the normative implications that all that truly matters are structures and that the consistency or composition of a thing's structure shows whether something is good or bad, harmonically or forcefully organized, stable or likely to self-destruct. This view clearly reverberates in Marx and, indeed, in the NRM, and it is here where Adorno vehemently disagrees.

The non-conceptual and the fallacies of conceptual system analysis

Backhaus and Reichelt have been described as logicians,[48] which is fitting insofar as they take capitalism at its word and study it as a conceptual system even more seriously than classical liberal economists do. They propose to analyse 'the deduction of value as a dialectical movement',[49] developing its 'internal logic'[50] in a series of 'immanent logical contradictions'.[51]

Adorno takes the opposite route from the same starting point. After acknowledging the conceptuality and systematicity of capitalism, Adorno concludes that we need to focus less on the conceptual and the system, and more on the physical, bodily and personal. In order to formulate a critique of capitalism it does not suffice to outline its problematic systematic functioning; one has to reflect on the oppressive character of systems in general and on the fact that any conceptual system is necessarily partly non-identical to the matter it organizes. And the matter is comprised not only of machines, streets, buildings and artefacts like cars, but also human bodies and nature. For Adorno, one must attend to this friction between system and matter, and do so even at the expense of seeming 'amateurish' and 'unstructured' in contrast to strict, clean and coherent economic theorists.[52]

I have argued elsewhere that Adorno criticizes Marx's immanent critique of capitalism, since, for him, Marx buys into capitalism's basic presuppositions, particularly the need to focus on the large scale, the tendencies, laws and concepts.[53] The problems Adorno highlights are three-fold: The first concerns the empirical grip or truth-value of concepts. Adorno writes: 'The task of empirical research is to protect the concept of essential laws from mythologization.'[54] This mythologization consists in forgetting that economic laws are nothing but concrete and accumulated actions of human beings (there is no actual 'invisible hand' of God or, indeed, of revolutionary logic that takes part in human history). Adorno also proposes that it is irrational to 'rant about concepts like imperialism or monopoly – innocent of all reflection upon the real state of affairs which these terms denote and the extent to which they are valid'.[55] If one focuses on the conceptual capitalist system alone, one can end up lacking awareness that capitalist and Marxist concepts need to be constantly checked or corroborated against the empirical world to see whether and how far they still capture empirical reality. Otherwise, those concepts could end up 'spinning in the void', as McDowell puts it. In other words, concepts can end up misrepresenting the current social reality.

In fact, to some extent, capitalist concepts have always partly misrepresented reality. As noted above, capitalism co-opts, absorbs and profits from seemingly external elements. This implies that capitalist concepts structure the present social world, but not exclusively so. Therefore, the following point by Petrucciani is correct with regard to Adorno's overall oeuvre: For Adorno, 'class domination cannot simply be explained with reference to the exchange between capital and labor ... the relations of property, and thus, of domination pre-exist capitalism and perpetuate themselves thanks to its mechanisms'.[56] Colonial and patriarchal structures are certainly among the most relevant ones Adorno has in mind. While capitalism certainly has an impressive structuring power and reach, it is also part of capitalism to trick us into focusing solely on its concepts, overlooking what does not quite fit its pattern, theorizing its problems by copying capitalism and believing that the capitalist system has a uniformity that it only exhibits in textbooks.

The second and related issue is that Marxist concepts need to mean something in people's lives to be relevant – for them. Adorno writes: 'It must be verified with reference to the individual subjects ... If the central differences do not affect people's lives, the theory loses its meaning'.[57] This is of practical concern, insofar as it is hard to convince someone of the problems with capitalism by using notions that bear no relation to their experiences. But it is also a theoretical point, since Marxism is not meant to be a metaphysical system of beliefs, a mere 'declamation of true or alleged insights in the essence of things'.[58] Rather, Marxism is meant to be a critique of an actual social reality that applies and matters to the human beings living within it. As such, the critique of capitalism has to manage to capture how the system operates, and why this reality is bad or undesirable in terms of people's lives and experiences. This is why, while being perfectly aware that the term 'worker' denotes an objective function in the capitalist system, Adorno insists that it would be 'delusional dogma' not to ask whether 'something essential has changed in social objectivity' if 'workers no longer consider themselves to be workers'.[59] The point is that, even if people are workers, objectively speaking, it becomes vacuous and even patronizing to insist that they are so without trying to link this claim to their experience and self-understanding.

The third issue Adorno has with analysing capitalism purely conceptually is that one valorizes the universal over individuals – just as capitalism does. Critics tend to focus on self-destructive laws of capitalism, major contradictions and their conceptual function. As a consequence, critics not only uncritically replicate capitalism's focus on concepts and laws, but also stand in the way of envisioning a world that would care about particular human beings and their lives. The 'obsession with the grand scale' makes it is hard to 'catch sight of the essential'[60] – or, at least, of what ought to be the essential, namely human beings. Adorno rejects the 'idealist proposition' that a focus on the 'higher', conceptual aspects and the larger, systemic tendencies constitutes a moral achievement. Instead, Adorno adopts a materialism that cares about the 'many, dispersed, untamed, nature-like', 'sensations' as they bear traces of 'pain and organic pleasure'.[61] Ultimately, what ought to matter to a critic of capitalism (and, indeed, to any moral being) are real humans in flesh and blood, their needs and well-being – not the system, its concepts and their supposed (in)coherence or the 'functions' that human beings occupy within it.

Adorno's concept of the non-identical, his view that concepts necessarily miss out on materiality including the human body, implies that bodies can never be completely formed by or turn into instances of concepts. This is so even in capitalism with its totalizing tendencies. For Adorno, one ought to 'neither dispense with logical unity... nor dogmatically present the order of thought as the order of things themselves'.[62] While keeping Marxist concepts in mind, one must also be aware that this is only a conceptual system and as such it is never identical to the actual world. Capitalism is, indeed, a totalizing system of concepts that structures social interactions, the physical world, human bodies and minds. Yet, nevertheless, there is some matter to which this system is applied that partly resists this application – for example, human bodies that feel pain and/or anger when being forced to fit into the system. The system defines its members, positions and functions, but human beings are 'more' than that, not in the sense of some hidden, true human essence, but in the sense of someone registering and suffering from the pressures of the system. For Adorno, capitalism hurts. 'Society becomes directly perceptible where it hurts', when you need money or a job and cannot find any,[63] or when you dare to imagine organizing your life without the future sale of your labour power in mind.[64] He speaks of 'the universal, compressing the particular until it splinters, like a torture instrument'.[65] Human beings cannot turn themselves into cogs in a machine; they cannot simply and unconsciously enact their functions within the system. Adorno proposes to trace this incapacity and the suffering it causes and use this as the basis of a critique of capitalism.

The goal of and the best method for a critique of capitalism

In the end, what distinguishes Adorno most clearly from proponents of the NRM – and, indeed, in part OM – is the question of 'what for?' and the appropriate means for critique. For Adorno, the overarching reason to study capitalism is that one wants to contribute to the end of suffering. While NRM and OM share this goal, there is some significant disagreement over the best intellectual approach to achieve it.

Backhaus and Reichelt intend for their work to have an emancipatory effect, insofar as understanding the workings of capitalism reveals the contradictions, inconsistencies and illusory nature of the system. Proponents of the NRM and OM frequently describe their own projects as 'deciphering'. Backhaus intends to 'decipher the doubling of the commodity into commodity and money as an antagonistic relation of things that expresses an antagonistic relations of human beings;'[66] Bonefeld sets out to 'decipher the definite social relations' behind 'mysterious' economic forces.[67] Osborne describes this type of analysis as the 'social-ontological version of ideology-critique'.[68] Without endorsing Osborne's view, it points in the right direction to the extent that these authors want to help us grasp capitalism, understand how it functions, see through and explain its 'objective illusions'.[69] This is emancipatory not only because understanding something better enables one to act accordingly, but also because the illusions create the false assumption that things cannot substantially change and only piecemeal adjustments can happen. Authors of the NRM show us that economic laws are not natural laws arising from the reproductive relation between human beings and nature; rather they only have a logic within the system of capitalism, which is a specific historical social arrangement and can be changed. Bonefeld has criticized this approach as not going far enough, insisting that studying capital as the 'essence' or subject of capitalism as NRM does, mystifies the functioning of capitalism, as the OM fails to specify that and how the logic of capital exists in and through human practice and class relations.[70] This is why Bonefeld and Holloway want to see class antagonism, and not exchange, as the core of capitalism. This is also the reason why Holloway insists on the hypothetical potential to 'stop making capitalism',[71] and why Bonefeld proposes, more cautiously, that we can formulate an immanent, complicated 'no' to the system.[72]

Despite their differences, NRM and OM see the emancipatory or critical element of their work in the uncovering of necessary illusions, revealing a hidden social reality – which human beings can act on and change. What OM offers beyond NRM is an emphasis on the exact points where we can change the system, the class antagonism and daily work practice, thereby highlighting the need to overcome class antagonism and separation via an emancipatory self-abolition of class. Nevertheless, from an Adornian perspective, proponents of the NRM in particular, but also the OM, have been sucked into capitalist logic, its conceptual systematicity overriding the small, personal, particular and bodily, which has led them to assume that laying bare conceptual contradictions is an effective critique and a route to improvement. To believe that conceptual clarification leads to real-life improvements is a leap that a Hegel-inspired thinker may underestimate. The typical link orthodox Marxists draw between contradictions and a better world has been a Hegelian conception of 'sublation' and Marxist crisis theory. Proponents of the NRM and OM reject this link and deny the existence of necessary, self-destructive laws in capitalism and beyond. Nevertheless, they do not consider sufficiently what this entails for their critique; in fact, one may wonder whether they simply substitute the conception of sublation or necessary self-destruction with the demand or expectation that people (ought to) change their world when they become aware of its contradictions and their roles in it.

What OM and the NRM do not ask, unlike Adorno, is whether the system, its foundation and the practices that constitute it, ought to be what we most care about. Adorno answers in the negative. Capitalism exists and shapes our lives as a matter of fact, but what matters or ought to matter are human beings in flesh and blood, their needs, bodies and well-being. Reichelt[73] follows Marx in speaking of human beings as 'bearers' of functions of capitalism; Holloway has introduced the notion of the 'scream',[74] the visceral, non-rationalized first urge to resist capitalism that exists in all of us. Human beings thus appear in their theories as instances of or functions for something else (e.g. capitalism or its end). Bonefeld's notion of 'concrete man'[75] is curious not only because it is a *contradiction in adjecto*, but because he tries to overcome this take on humans as instances, claiming that concrete circumstances and needs matter. Nevertheless, Bonefeld does not seem to fundamentally adapt his methodology to this insight. Ultimately, despite the notion of 'concrete man', Bonefeld retains his focus on the system and its functioning, with human beings featuring only in terms of their roles in (maintaining or confronting) it.

The rule of the universal or system over individuals is indeed how capitalism functions, but does a critic of capitalism really need to copy this reality in his critical approach? Adorno thinks not. While one cannot deny the power of capitalist concepts and their systemic connection, one ought to engage in an act of 'epistemic disobedience' and focus on the matter the system makes invisible and orders about, particularly on human beings, their personal lives and experiences. The term 'epistemic disobedience' does not imply that Adorno presupposes an alternate reality, which one can discover (reducing capitalism to a narrative one can choose not to share). Nor does he assume his decision to study the unimportant is purely subjective and wilful, with no link to objective reality. Rather, for Adorno, capitalism is certainly a system and a reality structuring all aspects of our lives. There is no hidden essence or wholesome life-world to fall back on to ground one's critique. Nevertheless, it is never a purely conceptual, logical or mathematical system, but a system that structures bodies and lives that suffer from and partly resist this structuring: 'Experience of objects like society, which are themselves essentially subjectively mediated, becomes the more concise the more subjective it is.'[76] In another famous passage, Adorno says: 'suffering is objectivity that weighs upon the subject'.[77]

Thinking against capitalism, looking at the small, unimportant, personal, bodily, partially non-conceptual and undertheorized has an objective truth-value, as well as an ethical and practical import. For Adorno, suffering is best suited to reveal what capitalist concepts really mean (in the lives of human beings living under capitalism) and to ground a critique of the capitalist system by simple argumentative resources and relevant normative grounds. Pain is bad simply because it hurts, and we instinctively want it to stop. As Adorno says, citing Nietzsche: 'Woe speaks: Go'.[78] If capitalism systematically generates pain, anxiety, stress, eating disorders, workplace accidents, racialized violence, domestic violence then it is to be overcome in a direction that is likely to generate less pain. 'The telos of such an organization of society would be to negate the physical suffering of even the least of its members, and to negate the internal reflexive forms of that suffering.'[79]

Human stories, lives and bodies should feature in a critique of capitalism, and they should do so not merely as an element or datum for explaining the workings of the system. Rather, human lives ought to be the 'explanandum', the object of analysis, as well as the reason and ethical ground of critique. Human lives, bodies and well-being matter – both in the sense that they ought to matter in reality and in one's theorizing, and in the sense that only by consulting those lives can one truly understand and define what capitalism actually means.

This is so not only because Adorno famously assumes that capitalist conflicts have become less acute and perceivable in the core capitalist countries, as they are externalized as 'quasi-colonial conflicts',[80] and only appear on the micro level as 'marginal phenomena' and 'the most internal, psychological conflicts'.[81] Already, Adorno's fundamental concept of the non-identical implies a call for humility on the theorist's part: The concepts of any theorist only ever partially capture reality. Hence, theorists need to listen, search for empirical input, discover what capitalist concepts really mean in people's lives and study the traffic jam skirmishes and domestic disputes over TV programmes that Adorno reflects on in *Minima Moralia*. In these seemingly banal phenomena, one can detect the stress and suffering that human beings have to endure when trying to make themselves fit into the system, the suffering they experience because they can never be solely bearers of functions, but always remain partly non-identical to this role. This is how Adorno tries to keep Marxism fact-sensitive and to 'use the critical notions that were once valid without erecting them as invariants' with the aim of 'exhausting them' and 'thereby possibly developing them further'.[82]

Admittedly, some of the everyday examples of suffering under capitalism that Adorno gives in *Minima Moralia* seem comical and silly. Adorno was influenced by Husserl and Freud when developing 'micrological' accounts of experiences, describing them in detail without treating them as 'mere examples' or a 'specimen' of general concepts.[83] Thus, it is unsurprising that Adorno spent much time micro-analysing his own experiences and the suffering and sublimations therein. However, I believe Adorno would have helped his programme immensely if he had been more aware of the racist and sexist elements of capitalism – or, indeed, if he had been familiar with Mari Matsuda's method of 'looking to the bottom'[84] or 'seeing the world from the standpoint of the oppressed'.[85] As Audre Lorde proposes: A white woman may manage to ignore the pains of the system, until 'a man needs her job' or she 'dares to verbalize resistance'. By contrast, speaking for Black women, Lorde says, 'violence weaves through the daily tissue of our lives'.[86] This says a lot about how capitalist society works. Listening attentively to those who suffer most is a way of putting into practice Adorno's reasoning about the non-identical: With the word 'non-identical' Adorno is trying to capture the difference that he hopes still exists between (capitalist or other) concepts and actual human beings. Adorno is interested in the difference and, hence, friction between system and bodies; it therefore makes sense to look for the people who experience this friction most strongly, people who are trying to express how the system and its concepts hurts them. Adorno's notion of the non-identical denotes a demand for humility that is meant to counteract the belief in and dominance of big concepts. It is a call to keep an open, unforced attention to how actual human beings live, what they feel and experience, without assuming that phrases like 'class antagonism', or, indeed, the 'non-identical' express all that needs to be said. Listening in this way, rather than lecturing people about the system or their supposed duty to change it, is not only more humane; it also contributes to a richer, more nuanced and relevant comprehension of the capitalist system.

Conclusion

I have argued that, while sharing the basic account of capitalism as a conceptual and totalizing system, Adorno parts ways with NRM and OM primarily when it comes to the right methodology for critique. By finding conceptual contradictions and highlighting tensions in the capitalist system, proponents of the NRM certainly analyse and criticize capitalism. But unless one is a dogmatic Hegelian, one cannot simply assume that conceptual contradictions necessarily entail real-life improvements. Having rejected a Hegelian notion of 'sublation', and therewith self-destructive laws that necessarily lead to the creation of something new, these thinkers are left with a gap between their conceptual and critical study of capitalism and the real world this study is meant to positively impact. The NRM and OM do not fundamentally break with the method of conceptual analysis; they do not ask themselves whether this conceptuality, while real and man-made, is or ought to be the main matter of critical concern.

In contrast to NRM and OM, Adorno distinguishes between giving a critical account of the internal logic of the capitalist system and questioning the validity of systematicity per se. The latter reveals the shortcoming and oppressive nature of system thinking in general and takes the form of a partly external critique, that analyses how the system affects human lives and how it is met by a certain resistance in the very least in the form of feelings of inconformity and suffering. The du Boisian notion of 'second sight'[87] would have been a great addition to Adorno's reasoning, since the term denotes the cultural work of collectively understanding and thinking against oppression. On this Adornian approach, the conceptual analysis of capitalism certainly remains important. NRM-style critiques remain vital in gaining a better understanding of the functioning of capitalism, which conditions all our lives. However, while he is certainly interested in the market laws, Adorno believes that the focal point of all analysis and practice ought to be concrete, personal situations of suffering. Rather than intending to formulate a grand theory, give a complete and coherent account of all the types of 'doubling' in the system, the aim is to understand concrete experiences and their law-like, systemic, but complex interconnectedness.

Adorno's method helps us understand what capitalist concepts truly mean (in the lives of human beings) and reminds us that while Marxist categories like class and exploitation certainly have an objective reality, they also need to exist and be perceivable somehow for the human beings to whom Marxists apply such notions. Otherwise, Marxists are in danger of being not just dogmatic, but paternalistic, imposing a view, demanding actions that neither resonate with nor connect to the experiences, dreams and self-perceptions of the individuals they are trying to appeal to. The ethical assumption behind Adorno's method is that any critique of capitalism ought to be grounded on the notion of human suffering, hence showing how the stress, working conditions, inequality and arbitrariness of capitalism harm human beings in their everyday lives and experiences. This care for people's personal lives, the particular over the universal, is also a precondition for envisioning a better and more humane society.

Acknowledgements

I want to thank Werner Bonefeld and Chris O'Kane for their extremely helpful feedback and comments.

Notes

1   Helmut Reichelt, 'Die Marxsche Kritik der ökonomischen Kategorien', in
    Emanzipation als Versöhnung, edited by Irving Fetscher and Alfred Schmidt
    (Ljubljana: Verlag Neue Kritik, 2002), 148.
2   Helmut Reichelt, 'From the Frankfurt School to Value-Form Analysis', *Thesis Eleven*
    4, no. 1 (1982): 166.
3   See, for example, Mario Schäbel, 'Die Bedeutung der Frankfurter Schule für die
    neue Marx-Lektüre', in *Karl Marx*, edited by Dominik Novkovic and Alexander
    Akel (Kassel: Kassel University Press, 2018), 93–112.
4   For this take on Open Marxism, see: Frederick Harry Pitts, 'Value-Form Theory,
    Open Marxism and the New Reading of Marx', *Open Marxism*, vol. 4, edited by
    Ana Cecilia Dinerstein et al. (London: Pluto Press, 2020), 63–75.
5   Theodor W. Adorno, *Negative Dialectics*, translated by E.B. Ashton (London:
    Routledge, 1973), 346.
6   Ibid., 346.
7   Reichelt, 'Die Marxsche Kritik der ökonomischen Kategorien', 142–3.
8   Theodor Adorno, *The Positivist Dispute in German Sociology*, translated by Glyn
    Adey and David Frisby (London: Heinemann, 1977), 80.

9   Theodor W. Adorno, *Philosophische Terminologie. I und II (1962–1963)* (Berlin: Suhrkamp, 2016), 617. Translations from German sources are the author's own.

10 Theodor W. Adorno, 'Theodor W. Adorno on Marx and the Basic Concepts of Sociological Theory. From a Seminar Transcript in the Summer Semester of 1962', translated by Verena Erlenbusch-Anderson and Chris O'Kane, *Historical Materialism* 26, no. 1 (2018): 159. Reprinted in the Appendix of this volume.

11 Alfred Sohn-Rethel, *Geistige und körperliche Arbeit* (Weinheim: VCH 1989), 11; see also Alfred Sohn-Rethel, *Materialistische Erkenntniskritik und Vergesellschaftung der Arbeit* (Berlin: Merve, 1971), 16ff. Reprinted in the Appendix of the book.

12 G.W.F. Hegel, *Elements of the Philosophy of Right*, translated by Hugh Barr Nisbet (Cambridge: Cambridge University Press, 1991), §63 including addition and note. For the notion of idealizing specific qualities, see Charlotte Baumann, 'Irrationality and Egoism in Hegel's Account of Right', *British Journal of the History of Philosophy* 26, no. 6 (2018): 1132–52. See also Adorno's definition of abstraction as 'disregarding the determinate use – values, that is, the sensible immediacy of objects or things that are being exchanged. Exchange only exists insofar as there are concepts' (Adorno, *Philosophische Terminologie. I und II*, 315).

13 Backhaus, 'Adorno und die metaökonomische Kritik', 48, 57, 33.

14 Adorno, *Philosophische Terminologie. I und II*, 315.

15 See Werner Bonefeld, 'Abstract Labour: Against Its Nature and on Its Time', *Capital & Class* 34, no. 2: 257–76.

16 Theodor W. Adorno, *Gesammelte Schriften*, vol. 4 (Frankfurt: Suhrkamp, 1997), 262.

17 Adorno, *The Positivist Dispute*, 107.

18 Adorno, *Gesammelte Schriften*, vol. 8, 189.

19 Adorno, *Philosophische Terminologie. I und II*, 316.

20 Werner Bonefeld, 'Negative Dialectics and the Critique of Economic Objectivity', *History of the Human Sciences* 29, no. 2 (2016): 70.

21 See Werner Bonefeld, *Critical Theory and the Critique of Political Economy* (New York: Bloomsbury, 2014), 3.

22 Adorno, *Philosophische Terminologie. I und II*, 625, 627.

23 Alfred Schmidt, *Der Begriff der Natur in der Lehre von Marx* (Hamburg: Europäische Verlagsanstalt, 1993), 83.

24 Adorno, *Philosophische Terminologie. I und II*, 634.

25 Karl Marx, *Marx Engels Werke*, vol. 26.1 (Berlin: Dietz Verlag, 1965), 376f.

26 Adorno, *Philosophische Terminologie. I und II*, 783.

27 Hans-Georg Backhaus, *Dialektik der Wertform* (Freiburg: ça ira, 1997), 14ff.

28 Helmut Reichelt, *Zur logischen Struktur der Kapitalbegriffs bei Marx* (Freiburg: ça ira, 2001), 13.

29 Reichelt, *Zur logischen Struktur der Kapitalbegriffs bei Marx*, 168ff.

30   See G.W.F. Hegel, *Science of Logic* (Amherst, NY: Humanity, 1969), 456.

31   Ibid., 567.

32   Ibid., 746.

33   Ibid., 740.

34   G.W.F. Hegel, *Jenaer Systementwürfe*, vol. 1 (Hamburg: Meiner, 1986), 230. For
     the official English translation, see: H.S. Harris and T.M. Knox (eds. and trans.),
     Jenenser Realphilosophie (Albany, NY: SUNY Press, 1979), 249. See also Lisa
     Herzog, *Inventing the Market* (Oxford: Oxford University Press, 2013), 51–8. See
     also: James Henderson and John B. Davis, 'Adam Smith's Influence on Hegel's
     Philosophical Writings', *Journal of the History of Economic Thought* 13 (1991):
     184–204.

35   G.W.F. Hegel, *The Encyclopaedia Logic*, translated by T.F. Geraets, W.A. Suchting
     and H.S. Harris (Indianapolis, IN: Hackett Publishing Company, 1991), §209 and
     §209 addition.

36   See, for example, Edna Ullmann-Margalit, 'The Invisible Hand and the Cunning of
     Reason', *Social Research* 64, no. 2 (1997): 181–98; John B. Davis, 'Smith's Invisible
     Hand and Hegel's Cunning of Reason', *International Journal of Social Economics* 16,
     no. 6 (1989): 50–66.

37   G.W.F. Hegel, *Elements of the Philosophy of Right* (Cambridge: Cambridge
     University Press, 2008), §189 addition.

38   Backhaus, *Dialektik der Wertform*, 58.

39   See Hans-Georg Backhaus, 'Zur Dialektik der Wertform', in *Beiträge zur
     Marxistischen Erkenntnistheorie*, edited by Alfred Schmidt (Frankfurt:
     Suhrkamp, 1969), 147.

40   See Bonefeld, *Critical Theory*, 9.

41   Helmut Reichelt, *Zur logischen Struktur der Kapitalbegriffs bei Marx* (Freiburg: ça
     ira, 2001), 168ff.

42   Backhaus, 'Zur Dialektik der Wertform', 146.

43   Helmut Reichelt, 'Kapital als Handlung und System', interview by Hanno Pahl and
     Lars Heitmann, 2009, http://www.rote-ruhr-uni.com/cms/IMG/pdf/Kapital_als_
     Handlung_und_System.pdf

44   Hegel, *Jenenser Realphilosophie*, 249.

45   Adorno, *Negative Dialectics*, 164.

46   Helmut Reichelt, *Neue Marx-Lektüre* (Hamburg: VSA-Verlag), 22.

47   Reichelt, *Neue Marx-Lektüre*, 23; see Adorno, *Gesammelte Schriften*, vol. 5, 266.

48   Werner Seppmann, *Subjekt und System* (Hamburg: Laika, 2011), 60.

49   Backhaus, 'Zur Dialektik der Wertform', 130.

50   Hans-Georg Backhaus, 'Der widersprüchliche und monströse Kern der
     nationalökonomischen Begriffsbildung', in *Emanzipation als Versöhnung*, edited by
     Irving Fetscher and Alfred Schmidt (Ljubljana: Verlag Neue Kritik, 2002), 113.

51 Reichelt, 'Die Marxsche Kritik der ökonomischen Kategorien', 144.

52 Theodor W. Adorno, *Introduction to Sociology*, translated by Edmund Jephcott, edited by Christoph Gödde (Cambridge: Polity Press, 2000), 144.

53 For a more detailed account, see: Charlotte Baumann, 'Marx and Adorno: The System and the Non-Identical', in *The Oxford Handbook on Adorno*, edited by Martin Shuster and Henry Pickford (Oxford: Oxford University Press, forthcoming).

54 Adorno, *The Positivist Dispute*, 84.

55 Adorno, *Gesammelte Schriften*, vol. 8, 357.

56 Stefano Petrucciani, 'Adorno's Criticism of Marx's Social Theory', in *Critical Theory and the Challenge of Praxis*, edited by Stefano Giacchetti Ludovisi (London: Ashgate, 2015), 21. See also Theodor W. Adorno, 'Reflections on Class Theory', in *Can One Live After Auschwitz? A Philosophical Reader*, translated by Rodney Livingstone, edited by Rolf Tiedemann (Palo Alto, CA: Stanford University Press, 2003), 100.

57 Theodor W. Adorno, *Philosophical Elements of a Theory of Society*, edited by Tobias ten Brink and Marc Phillip Nogueira, translated by Wieland Hoban (London: Polity Press, 2019), 127.

58 Adorno, *Introduction to Sociology*, 21–2.

59 Adorno, *The Positivist Dispute*, 84; see also Adorno, *Gesammelte Schriften*, vol. 8, 355.

60 Adorno, *Introduction to Sociology*, 19.

61 Alfred Schmidt, 'Adornos Spätwerk: Übergang zum Materialismus als Rettung des Nicht-Identischen', in *Emanzipation als Versöhnung*, edited by Irving Fetscher and Alfred Schmidt (Ljubljana: Verlag Neue Kritik, 2002), 91 and 95 respectively.

62 Adorno, *Philosophical Elements*, 102.

63 Adorno, *Introduction to Sociology*, 36.

64 Theodor W. Adorno, *Philosophie und Soziologie (1960)* (Frankfurt: Suhrkamp, 2011), 55.

65 Adorno, *Negative Dialectics*, 346.

66 Backhaus, *Dialektik der Wertform*, 57.

67 Bonefeld, *Critical Theory*, 6.

68 Peter Osborne, 'Adorno and Marx', in *A Companion to Adorno*, edited by Peter Gordon (London: Blackwell, 2020), 309.

69 Backhaus, *Dialektik der Wertform*, 273.

70 Bonefeld, *Critical Theory*, 7.

71 John Holloway, *Crack Capitalism* (New York: Pluto Press, 2010), 254.

72 Bonefeld, *Critical Theory*, 224–5.

73 Reichelt, *Zur logischen Struktur des Kapitalbegriffs*, 86, 231.

74 John Holloway, *Change the World without Taking Power* (New York: Pluto Press, 2005).

75   Bonefeld, *Critical Theory*, 8, 128.

76   Adorno, *The Positivist Dispute*, 82.

77   Adorno, *Negative Dialectics*, 17–18.

78   Ibid., 203.

79   Ibid., 203–4.

80   Adorno, *Gesammelte Schriften*, vol. 8, 189.

81   Ibid.

82   Theodor W. Adorno, 'Aus einem Entwurf zur Neuausgabe der Dialektik der Aufklärung. Frankfurt Februar 1969', in *Frankfurter Adorno Blätter*, vol. 8, edited by Rolf Tiedemann (München: text+kritik, 2003), 7.

83   Adorno, *Negative Dialectics*, 408.

84   Mari Matsuda, 'Looking to the Bottom', *Harvard Civil-Right Civil Liberties Law Review* 22, no. 2 (1987): 323–99.

85   Mari Matsuda, *Where Is Your Body?* (Boston, MA: Beacon Press, 1996), 8.

86   Audre Lorde, *Zami, Sister Outsider, Undersong* (New York: Quality Paperback, 1993), 119.

87   W.E.B Du Bois, *Souls of Black Folk*, edited by Brent Hayes Edwards (Oxford: Oxford University Press, 2007), 8.

5

Marxian economics and the critique of political economy

Chris O'Kane and Kirstin Munro

Moishe Postone's critique of Marxian economics[1] and his negative critique of labour are essential to the development of the critique of political economy as a critical social theory. In *Time, Labour and Social Domination,*[2] Postone demonstrated that mid-twentieth-century Marxian economics consisted in a foreshortened 'positive' critique of capitalism as a mode of unequal distribution premised on an ontological understanding of labour as the source of wealth. In distinction to Marxian economics, Postone conceived of the critique of political economy as a negative critique of the historically specific capitalist form of labour. Yet the rise of interest in democratic socialism and expanded interpretations of Marx premised on reproductive labour and the state call into question the applicability of Postone's critique of Marxian economics. These prevalent interpretations of Marx also indicate that Postone's negative critique of the historically specific form of labour as a critical social theory was incomplete as it did not critique the state, the household and the reproductive labour of state employees and household members.

This chapter critically expounds on Postone's critiques of Marxian economics and labour. Part One provides an overview of Postone's critique of Marxian economics and of his interpretation of the critique of political economy as a critique of labour. Part Two builds on Postone's critique of Marxian economics to establish that democratic socialism, Social Reproduction Theory (SRT), and the synthetic theories of Jason E. Moore and Nancy Fraser expand on the presuppositions of traditional Marxism and the categories of Marxian economics to offer a positive critique of capitalist society as a mode of distribution from an expanded standpoint of labour. We show that these approaches conceive of socialism as the realization of labour, and as a result these approaches unwittingly promote the perpetuation of capitalist society. Part Three disentangles Postone's negative critique of labour from Postone's positive emancipatory dynamic, and then extends Postone's critique of labour to the state and household to develop a negative critique of capitalist society as a historically specific form of labour. The conclusion recaps the argument to demonstrate the vitality of Postone's critique of labour for the development of critical theory.

Postone's critiques

In *Time, Labour and Social Domination,* Postone develops a distinction 'between two fundamentally different modes of critical analysis: a critique of capitalism *from the standpoint of labour,* on the one hand, and a *critique of labour* in capitalism, on the other'.[3] The *critique of labour* in capitalism, in turn, also serves as the grounds for Postone's critique of the analysis of capitalism that proceeds *from the standpoint of labour.*

Postone's analysis of the critique of capitalism from the standpoint of labour is premised on his interpretation of the work of mid-twentieth-century Marxian economics, primarily that of its leading exponents: Maurice Dobb, Paul Sweezy and Ernest Mandel. Postone argues that according to this approach to Marxian economics, 'Labour is the ontological ground of society', 'the only source of wealth' and hence the standpoint of a 'positive' critique of 'the mode of distribution'.[4] In Marxian economics, capitalism is characterized by the contradictory creation of wealth by social labour, which is appropriated by the capitalist class due to their private ownership of the means of production. Yet, according to Marxian economics, this process of production and appropriation is veiled by the market where it appears that workers are fairly compensated for their labour. Consequently, according to Marxian economics:

> The essential thrust of Marx's critique [of political economy] is, accordingly, to reveal beneath the appearance of the exchange of equivalents the existence of class exploitation. The market and private ownership of the means of production are considered to be the essential capitalist relations of production, which are expressed by the categories of value and surplus value. Social domination is treated as a function of class domination which, in turn, is rooted in 'private property in land and capital'.[5]

For Marxian economists, Marx's labour theory of value is tantamount to a 'positive' critique of political economy from the standpoint of labour.

In distinction to Marxian economics' critique of capitalism as a mode of distribution from the standpoint of labour, Postone conceives of the critique of political economy as a 'negative critique' of the historically specific form of labour. According to Postone, the historically specific form of capitalist labour consists in a unique type of social interdependence of 'impersonal' 'quasi-objective' social domination that is 'effected by historically unique forms of social relations that are constituted by determinate forms of social practice'.[6]

Value and wealth are not synonymous, labour is not transhistorical, and capitalism is not a mode of exploitation and appropriation premised on private ownership. Rather, capitalist labour is historically specific and possesses twofold dimensions: private and social, abstract and concrete. Marx's categories do not capture the unequal distribution of goods in a system of market exchange premised on private property. Rather, they are categories that critically grasp the historically specific capitalistic organization of production and distribution on the basis of the reciprocal social mediation of abstract and concrete labour. The categories of the commodity, value, surplus value, et cetera, 'necessarily express the forms of being [*Daseinsformen*], the determinations of existence [*Existenzbestimmungen*]' of the historically specific capitalist form of labour as a quasi-objective and abstract type of social domination. Consequently, contra traditional Marxism, 'The abstract domination and the exploitation of labour characteristic of capitalism are grounded, ultimately, not in the appropriation of the surplus by the non-labouring classes, but in the form of labour in capitalism.'[7]

Following from this interpretation of the critique of political economy as a critique of capitalist labour, Postone argues that traditional interpretations of Marx, exemplified by mid-twentieth-century Marxian economics, fail to grasp the dual character of labour and its historical specificity – ultimately, Marxian economics fails to grasp capitalism. This leads to traditional Marxism's foreshortened understanding of how capitalism might be overcome. Socialism is conceived as the 'realization of labour'. Capitalism's 'unconscious' mode of distribution – private property and the market – is replaced with the 'conscious' public ownership of the means of production and the public planning of distribution.[8] According to Postone, such a conception of socialism unwittingly reproduces capitalism. The realization of labour in socialism may do away with private property and the market. Yet it perpetuates the capitalist organization of labour and Marx's critical categories, and as a result perpetuates the capitalist form of labour. In Postone's negative critique, the historically specific form of the dual character of labour – and with it capitalist production and distribution – must be abolished in order to overcome capitalism.

In this overview of Postone's critique of Marxian economics and his critique of the historically specific form of labour, we have shown that there is a stark difference between traditional Marxism's critique of capitalism *from the standpoint of labour* and Postone's critical theory of the historically specific form of labour. The critique of capitalism *from the standpoint of labour* offers a 'positive critique' of capitalism as a mode of private distribution from the standpoint of social labour and conceives of socialism as the realization of social labour via public ownership and distribution. Postone's critical theory of the historically specific form of labour, on the other hand, provides a negative critique of capitalism as a historically specific form of labour that possesses a dual character inclusive of its private and social, abstract and concrete dimensions that amounts to impersonal social domination. So socialism consists in the abolition of labour.

In what follows, we will argue that Postone's critique of traditional Marxism and his critique of the historically specific form of capitalist labour are essential to the development of critical theory today. We will also show that the current broad applicability of Postone's notion of traditional Marxism is missed if it is simply applied to contemporary Marxian economics. Moreover, Postone's critique of labour ultimately does not amount to a negative critical theory of capitalist society. The purpose of our critique of Postone's critique of labour is to further develop these critical aspects.

II

As the work of Richard Wolff and Stephen Resnick,[9] Fred Moseley[10] and David Brennen and colleagues[11] demonstrates, Postone's critique of Marxian economics is undoubtedly still relevant. Yet this critique of Marxian economics in itself is incapable of critiquing an array of prevalent criticisms of capitalism – from social democratic notions of political economy, to the new Marxist-feminist offshoot SRT, to synthetic theories of capitalism – that expand the standpoint of labour to include the domains of reproductive labour and treat the relationship between the state and the economy as central to their criticisms of capitalism as a mode of distribution.

Postone himself did not predict these developments, let alone provide a broader conception of traditional Marxism that would enable critiquing them. One of the foundational justifications for Postone's interpretation of Marx was that traditional Marxism did not respond to the demands of the new social movements.[12] It is true that Postone points to the wider significance of his critique of traditional Marxism. In particular, Postone points to the parallels between the standpoint of labour and normative social and political philosophy. In this vein, he discusses how the standpoint of labour parallels the normative critique of the state from the standpoint of civil society, while asserting that his interpretation of the critique of political economy holds that 'the changing relationship of state to civil society, as well as the character and development of institutions in each sphere... can be understood only in terms of the intrinsic dynamic of capitalist society'.[13] Postone indicates that, '[i]n this sense (and only in this non-sociologically reductive sense), the difference between the two forms of social critique' – that is, the positive critique of the standpoint of labour and the negative critique of labour – 'is that between a "bourgeois" critique of society, and a critique of bourgeois society'.[14] Yet Postone did not develop these points. In this section we expand on Postone's critique of Marxian economics to show how social democratic political economy, SRT and synthetic theories of capitalism offer positive critiques of capitalism as a mode of distribution from an expansive standpoint of labour – inclusive of reproductive labour that takes place in state institutions and households – that unwittingly promote the reproduction of capitalism.

Democratic Socialist Political Economy

What we call 'democratic socialist political economy' is prominent in heterodox economics and the new interdisciplinary project of law and political economy.[15] This notion of democratic socialist political economy undergirds the ideas of democratic socialism that are now prevalent in the Anglophone world. Democratic socialist political economy includes the Ricardian interpretations of Marxian economics discussed by Postone. However, these contemporary interpretations also amalgamate Marx's work alongside classical political economy, John Maynard Keynes, and Karl Polanyi. Elements identified in Postone's critique of traditional Marxism are essential to democratic socialist political economy's critique of capitalism as a mode of distribution. However, democratic socialist political economy has a broader worldview that is premised on the standpoint of labour but also includes the relationship between the economy and the state in its distinction between capitalism and socialism.

Social democratic political economy has a transhistorical notion of labour as the source of all wealth. However, it differs from Marxian economics in viewing the fundamental social contradiction that typifies capitalist society as not just between social production and private appropriation premised on private property, but between the public and the private, the state and the economy, encompassing different types of norms, reason and governance. As a consequence, democratic socialist political economy opposes itself to capitalist political economy by distinguishing between the capitalist and democratic socialist ordering of modern society. In democratic socialist political economy, capitalism is viewed in terms of the public realm of the state serving the private interests of capitalists by enforcing laws and policies that lead to the unequal distribution of wealth created by labour.[16]

The social democratic critique of capitalism proceeds from the standpoint of labour to criticise capitalism as a mode of distribution. This positive social democratic critique demonstrates that the state facilitates the private distribution of social labour, demystifying the supposed separation between the state and the economy. Marxian, Polanyian and Keynesian categories are seen as the hidden creation of the state; these categories capture capitalist processes of unequal distribution. Socialism, in contrast, is conceived of as democratic state policy that serves the general interest of the public, fairly distributing the wealth created by labour.

Social Reproduction Theory

Social Reproduction Theory is a self-designated interdisciplinary current in contemporary Marxist feminist theory. The notable theorists in SRT – Susan Ferguson, Tithi Bhattacharya, Alan Sears and Cinzia Arruzza – have developed what they have dubbed the 'Marxian approach to SRT' by drawing on selective interpretations of accounts of the reproduction of labour power by Lise Vogel[17] and Italian autonomism[18] and integrating them into a 'classical Marxist' framework.[19]

As Ferguson puts it, 'The Marxian School of social reproduction feminism observes that Marx did not extend his political-economic critique of capitalism to unpaid social reproductive labour.'[20] Yet as the self-designation 'classical Marxist' suggests, SRT develops such a 'political-economic critique' by extending the presuppositions of the standpoint of labour to reproductive labour.[21] SRT draws on and expands the traditional Marxist interpretation of the critique of political economy by including the reproductive labour of 'life-making' in the standpoint of labour. While SRT contends that productive labour is the transhistorical source of wealth, reproductive labour is conceived of as the transhistorical type of labour that constitutes and sustains the life that is necessary for labour to create wealth.

For SRT, the 'life-making' of reproductive labour – in tandem with productive labour – provides the standpoint of SRT's 'positive' critique of capitalism as a mode of distribution. SRT argues that the reproductive labour of life-making makes exploitation and unequal distribution possible. According to SRT, the relationship between reproductive labour and profit is veiled by capitalist society. According to SRT, reproductive labour is either unpaid or underpaid and yet is essential to the production and reproduction of labour power, to the exploitative level of wages, and as a result to exploitation and unequal distribution. Moreover, reproductive 'life-making' creates and reproduces the 'desired human qualities and capacities'[22] that capital exploits, by meeting the needs that are necessary to create and sustain life. Following traditional Marxist presuppositions, SRT offers an expanded critique of capitalism as an exploitative and dominating process of distribution which is extrinsic to the form of capitalist production and reproduction itself.

SRT also expands the traditional Marxist conception of communism. Reproductive labourers are members of the proletariat because they sustain the proletariat; reproductive workers are also dominated and indirectly exploited by the capitalist class. For SRT, the contradiction between the development of the forces and relations of production immiserate reproductive labour. So, according to this perspective, the seizing of totality and communism entails seizing and unleashing the productive forces and the reproductive forces of life-making under common ownership and public planning.

Fraser and Moore's synthetic theories

Nancy Fraser[23] and Jason E. Moore's[24] synthetic theories of capitalism draw together the social democratic and social reproductive criticisms of capitalism to criticize capitalism as a mode of distribution from an expanded standpoint of labour while advocating for an expanded idea of socialism.

Fraser conceives of capitalism as an 'institutionalized social order' that is premised on the exploitation of labour and the unpaid expropriation of the 'background spheres' of reproductive labour and nature. Fraser further contends that such an institutionalized social order is facilitated by the state and is realized in profit. Yet it is 'disavowed.' Fraser's 'positive' critique of the capitalistic institutionalized order of modern society unveils this process of exploitation and appropriation from the standpoint of productive and reproductive labour. Her 'expanded idea of socialism'[25] consists in the democratic state management of the distribution of the surplus created by productive and reproductive labour premised on the norms of each of these spheres of modern society.[26]

Moore in his own work and in his work with Raj Patel[27] argues that capitalist profit is made possible through the 'cheapening' of productive and reproductive labour, money, lives and nature. Socialism consists in 'reparation ecology', a process premised on 'recognition, reparation, redistribution, reimagination, and recreation',[28] in which people, activities and the environment are valued at their worth and society is democratically ruled on this basis.

Consequences of this expanded standpoint of labour

As this overview of democratic socialist political economy, SRT and Fraser and Moore's synthetic theories of capitalism demonstrates, Postone's critique of Marxian economics is both fundamental and inadequate to these theories. These three contemporary approaches certainly conceive of capitalism as an unconscious mode of distribution that is criticized from the standpoint of labour. Yet the conception of labour is expanded. The object of criticism for these approaches is capitalist distribution; however, while this criticism is ostensibly directed at the market, it is ultimately directed at the state's central role implementing capitalist distribution. Rather than simply seeing Marx's categories as economic categories of exploitative distribution, these categories are said to be made possible by the state and reproductive labour – and even nature. For these approaches, Marx's categories are concealed not only by the market but are also veiled by society. Following Postone, socialism is certainly conceived in these theories as the 'conscious' social regulation of distribution by public planning, yet socialism is grounded on this expanded conception of labour and expressed through the democratic state management of distribution.

Postone's critique of Marxian economics focuses on the mid-twentieth-century work of Dobb, Sweezy and Mandel, but his critique of the standpoint of labour is all too relevant today. At the same time, Postone's critique of Marxian economics is too limited. For democratic socialist political economy, SRT, and Fraser and Moore's synthetic theories of capitalism expand on these presuppositions to develop positive theories of the mode of distribution of entirety of bourgeois society. These notions of socialism unwittingly promote the perpetuation of capitalism, transforming labour into a broad ontological principle that envisions socialism as 'the realization' of productive and reproductive labour by overcoming 'its mode of distribution' (private property and the market) and replacing it with the public ownership of the means of production and the public planning of distribution at the behest of a democratic state that distributes the proceeds of labour on the basis of extant norms.

While these contemporary approaches leave much to be desired, they still point to the shortcomings of Postone's negative critique with respect to a negative critical theory of society. In the next section, we show the vitality of Postone's negative critique of capitalism as a historically specific form of labour by extending Postone's critique to the state, the household and the reproductive labour of state employees and household members.

III

The tension between Postone's negative critique of the historically specific form of capitalist labour and Postone's emancipatory dynamic need to be addressed. In Postone's negative critique of labour, capitalism consists in a historically specific form of labour that needs to be abolished to achieve human emancipation. Yet this negative critique sits uneasily with Postone's larger effort to revitalize critical theory. Postone's attempts to revitalize critical theory mirror Habermas's justification for formulating his own approach to critical theory: they share the contention that Adorno and Horkheimer's critical theory is one-dimensional and lacks an emancipatory basis.[29] While the emancipatory grounds Habermas and Postone developed were certainly distinct from one another, their ensuing social theories nonetheless possess striking similarities. Postone's approach to rejuvenating critical theory consists in grasping the emancipatory potential of a pre-existing social dynamic whose further development he believed points to the emancipatory overcoming of capitalism – an approach he shares with Habermas and even the traditional Marxism that Postone criticizes.[30]

For traditional Marxism, the forces of production will, in the course of their development, come into contradiction with the relations of production. This contradiction will lead to the revolutionary seizure of the forces of production by the proletariat, and the realization of labour as the unfettering of the productive forces. Habermas argued that the evolution of contemporary society led to complexity and the systematic differentiation of the spheres of the economy, state and life world. The unmooring of the neutral spheres of the state and the economy had come into contradiction with the private sphere. For

Habermas, the public sphere should use the state as a 'conveyor belt', unleashing the democratic rule of the public sphere over the state and the economy. For Postone, the development of the forces of production would lead to the displacement of labour and the diminishment of value. The development of the forces of production, the displacement of labour and the diminishment of value would serve as the emancipatory grounds for:

> a growing contradiction between the sort of labour people perform under capitalism and the sort of labour they could perform if value were abolished and the productive potential developed under capitalism were reflexively used to liberate people from the sway of the alienated structures constituted by their own labour.[31]

Since Postone's interpretation of this dynamic of development, displacement and diminishment does not consider relative surplus value, or countervailing state measures his interpretation of the dynamic of accumulation is called into question. The emancipatory basis of Postone's attempt to rejuvenate critical theory is akin to a sociological model of progressive technological future-oriented social development that mirrors both the classical Marxist notion of an emancipatory crisis and Habermas's notion of social development. It is also fetishistic and distinct from a negative critique of the historically specific form of labour. Postone's emancipatory dynamic of development, displacement and diminishment relies on the continuing domination of the reified subject of capital and the exploitation of labour to realize emancipation, but negative critique implies an emancipatory notion of the contemporary necessity of the collective negation of the organization of the historically specific social form of capitalism in response to social domination. In what follows, we separate Postone's negative critique of capitalist society as a historically specific critique of labour from Postone's emancipatory dynamic.

We also extend Postone's negative critique of capitalist society as a historically specific form of labour to a critique of the state, the household and the reproductive labour of state employees and household members. Postone's negative critique of labour does not critique these dimensions of capitalist society. However, the state, the household, and the reproductive labour of state employees and household members are implicit in Postone's general statements that '[i]n constituting a self-grounding social mediation, labour constitutes a determinate sort of social whole – a totality'[32] and that

> the historically specific character of this labour is intrinsically related to the form of social interdependence characteristic of capitalist society. It constitutes

a historically specific, quasi-objective form of social mediation that, within the framework of Marx's analysis, serves as the ultimate social ground of modernity's basic features.[33]

As Postone demonstrates in his analysis of Marx's categories, 'value' refers to the capitalist organization of production, while Marx's categories describe objective–subjective modes of being.

Hence:

> within the framework of Marx's analysis, value is a form of wealth that is not extrinsic to production or to other social "institutions" in capitalism but, rather, is intrinsic to them and shapes them; as a form of mediation, it generates a process of ongoing transformation and reconstitution.[34]

Postone states that civil society and the state are not separate but are 'embedded' and 'transformed' by this value-mediated 'process of transformation and reconstitution'.[35] Although Postone does not specifically apply this insight to reproductive labour, the non-separability of reproductive labour, civil society, and the state can be inferred given that much of reproductive labour is carried out by employees of the state, while other aspects of reproductive labour are carried out in households. Proletarian households do not represent a separate 'domestic sphere', but rather are linked to the state and economy via the value dynamic of 'transformation and reconstitution'.

In order to sketch how the historically specific form of labour constitutes a 'determinant' 'social whole' inclusive of the state, household and reproductive labour it is necessary to begin by supplementing Postone's account of the historically specific form of labour with an account of its genesis. While Postone points to 'determinate social relations that constitute' the historically specific form of labour, he does not elaborate on their genesis, nor the genesis of the other institutions in this 'social whole'.[36]

Following Bonefeld,[37] the historically specific social form of capitalist society was created by the violent process of primitive accumulation. The state separated people from their means of reproduction and expropriated land and wealth for the ruling class. This created the capital relation and the historically specific forms of labour and wealth. The state was transformed into the capitalist state and the private household emerged.

Now that we have outlined the 'social ground' of this whole, we turn to indicate how it is 'shaped' by a 'historically specific, quasi-objective form of social mediation'.[38] We follow Postone in holding that capitalist production does not consist in the transhistorical production of wealth that is unequally distributed due to the institutions of private property and the market. Furthermore, Marx's categories do not capture this market-veiled unequal allocation of social wealth. Instead labour is characterized by its historically specific dual character. Value is the historically specific form of wealth. Capital shapes production and produces goods with the sole intent of valorizing value. Marx's categories capture the necessary appearance of this historically specific form of labour in the form of value (money) and its ensuing dynamic of accumulation and reproduction as 'determinate modes of being' that mediate and compel concrete activity 'generat[ing] a process of ongoing transformation and reconstitution', in the separate yet interrelated spheres of the economy, state and household.

Since capitalists are 'personifications of economic categories', they are compelled to compete with other capitalists by this 'quasi-objective' form of social mediation (the historically specific natural laws of accumulation) to acquire profit in the form of money. Since workers are free from the means to sustain themselves and free to sell their labour power, they are compelled to compete with other proletarians to sell their labour power for money in order to sustain themselves. Since profit is incumbent upon selling commodities while maximizing surplus value, capitalists compete to increase working hours, lower wages and increase productivity. This competition between capitalists to increase productivity leads to the revolutionizing of production via supervision, a strict division of labour and an increasing reliance on machinery. This dynamic is replicated across the social division of labour as whole. The result is a blind, crisis-ridden process that produces reoccurring crises, the accumulation of wealth at one pole and misery at the other, and the 'multiplication' of the proletariat and the reproduction of separation on an 'extended scale'.

The capitalist state is 'the organized force of society'.[39] Since this society is capitalist society, and not merely the capitalist organization of the distribution of the proceeds of modern society, it is a force for 'social enslavement'[40] and the object of the critique of political economy. Following Clarke[41] and Bonefeld,[42] the capitalist state protects property and perpetuates the propertyless, reinforcing and perpetuating the historically specific form of labour. Constitutions codify the historically specific form of labour and displace class antagonism to the representative politics of the political sphere. In the political sphere, elected officials ostensibly vie to represent the general will of the public on the basis of different social and economic policies.

While these policies can undoubtedly be progressive or regressive, they are nevertheless realized in bureaucracies by reproductive workers employed by the state who administer the population, reproducing individuals as bearers of the commodity labour power, thus perpetuating the capitalist social form. As Munro[43] shows, state employees in state bureaucracies – ranging from education, to welfare, to health care – are not virtuous life-makers. They do not instil children with the skills and norms that are needed to produce goods that would meet human needs barring the capitalist mode of distribution. Nor do they sustain adults who already possess these skills and norms. Rather education consists in what Adorno calls 'house training', eradicating autonomy and critical thinking, and instilling the discipline, authority and competitiveness necessary for bearers of the commodity labour power to beat out their competitors and excel at jobs that entail a range of activities preformed by the capitalist division of labour. Welfare subjects the unemployed to a punitive bureaucracy that pays them a bare minimum to tide them over until they find new work. This reinforces the wage and ultimately capital accumulation. Health care subjects people to an administration tasked with sustaining people's ability to sell the commodity of labour power in order to valorize value. Finally, the police promote the reproduction of the commodity of labour-power via enforcing laws that protect property and administer social individuals to act as virtuous sellers of labour power by incarcerating troublesome law breakers. Consequently, these state bureaucracies and their functionaries enact 'reproductive life-making' by administering the population, depoliticizing class struggle, raising and preserving individuals as bearers of the commodity of labour power. These state institutions and these activities impose market dependency, maim individuals and contribute to the reproduction of the historically specific form of labour. Expanding on Clarke,[44] the general interest of society and the general will of the public is the general interest of capital.

Like the state and reproductive labourers employed by state bureaucracies, reproductive domestic labour in households is not a virtuous activity of 'life-making' 'thwarted' by the capitalist mode of distribution. Rather, '[p]rivate life, the zone of individuality, is absorbed by so-called social activities and thus likewise moulded by… the schemata of society'.[45] As Munro[46] shows, the household and household production are mediated by and mediate the crisis-ridden dynamic of capital accumulation and reproduction. The very existence of the household is incumbent on primitive accumulation, private property, law enforcement, wages and state provision of goods and services. Sustaining a household necessitates selling labour power for a wage and performing domestic labour that – along with commodities purchased with wages and state inputs – sustains household members' ability to perform productive and reproductive labour. Households combine commodities purchased with wages, state goods and services, and domestic labour in shifting proportions to produce day-to-day life, contributing to the crisis-ridden process of accumulation both directly and indirectly. Households create a new generation of workers to be exploited, sustain those who are underemployed or between jobs, and sustain those unable to work, keeping down wages. By responding to the crisis-ridden process of accumulation via these activities of reproduction, households are a part of it – contributing to the reproduction of labour power and thus capitalist society as a historically specific form of labour.

Productive and reproductive labour in the state and the household are integral to reproducing the negative totality of capitalist society as a historically specific form of labour. In contrast to democratic socialist political economy, SRT, and synthetic theories of capitalism, such a society is not characterized by the capturing of the proceeds of productive and reproductive labour by capital on the basis of state policies that serve these private interests. Rather productive labour and reproductive labour of the state and the household are integral to the historically specific form of labour as a form of social mediation of the social whole that shapes and reproduces its institutions. Productive labour is realized in a crisis-ridden dynamic of abstract and concrete labour that maims and displaces a labour force that overproduces junk for the sake of profit. The reproductive bureaucracies of the state as well as the household dominate and sustain social individuals as bearers of the commodity labour power, reproducing the historically specific form of labour. In critiquing this negative form of social unity, we have expanded on Postone's critique of labour to provide a negative critique of capitalist society, indicating how a historically specific form of labour is constitutive of a 'quasi-objective' form of social mediation that shapes the social whole. We have also pointed how the state, the household and the reproductive labour of state employees and household members reproduce the historically specific form of labour. Taken together these moments perpetuate the social whole. In this perspective, socialism does not consist in the realization of productive and reproductive labour and the fair distribution of its proceeds via a social democratic state, but rather their abolition.

Conclusion

Moishe Postone's critique of Marxian economics and his negative critique of labour are essential to the development of the critique of political economy as a critical social theory. However, Postone's critique of Marxian economics is not sufficient to critique the now-prevalent approaches of democratic socialist political economy, SRT, and the synthetic theories of capitalism that draw these approaches together. Moreover, Postone's negative critique of labour is supplanted by an emancipatory account of progressive technological development that mirrors traditional Marxism and Habermasian critical theory. Finally, Postone's critique of the historically specific form of labour does not critique the state, household or reproductive labour. This chapter has sought to demonstrate the vitality of Postone's critique of Marxian economics and his negative critique of the historically specific form of labour by expanding on them in this regard.

We first demonstrated that democratic socialist political economy, SRT, and Fraser and Moore's synthetic theories of capitalism extend Marxian economics' critique of capitalism as a mode of distribution by conceiving of productive and reproductive labour as the transhistorical source of life and wealth that is unequally distributed because the state acts in the private interests of capitalists. These approaches expand upon Marxian economics' interpretations of Marx's economic categories as categories of distribution that are veiled by the market, arguing that unpaid reproductive labour (and even nature) are ultimately represented in profit. For these approaches, this process is veiled by what Fraser calls the disavowal of institutionalized order of capitalist society. The expanded idea of socialism envisioned in these approaches is conceived as the 'realization' of this extended notion of labour via the democratic social state's public management of distribution.

We then turned to illustrate the importance of Postone's negative critique of capitalism as a historically specific form of labour for the critique of political economy as a critical social theory. Expanding on Postone's definition of labour as a structuring form of social mediation, we showed that the critique of labour can be extended to encompass the negative dynamic unity of the economy, state and household, and thus how capitalist society is constituted and reproduced by the historically specific unity of productive and reproductive labour.

This chapter indicates the centrality of Postone's critique of Marxian economics and his critique of labour to the further development of the critique of political economy as a critical social theory. In the first place, we have demonstrated how democratic socialist political economy, SRT, and Fraser and Moore's synthetic theories of capitalism extend Marxian economics, offering a critique of capitalism as a mode of distribution from an expanded standpoint of labour that unwittingly promotes the perpetuation of capitalism rather than its abolition. In the second place, we have demonstrated that the negative critique of labour also entails the negation of the historically specific institutions and types of reproductive labour that reinforce and reproduce it. Postone's insights can be used to further develop the critique of political economy as a critical social theory by showing that it is necessary to negate not only productive labour but also the state, the household and the reproductive labour of state employees and household members.

Acknowledgements

The authors would like to thank Edward Henry for invaluable research assistance.

Notes

1   Following Postone, 'Marxian economics' is used here as a general term, rather than as a name for the specific interpretation of Marx by Richard Wolff, Stephen Resnick, and their followers.

2   Moishe Postone, *Time, Labour, and Social Domination* (Cambridge: Cambridge University Press, 1994).

3   Postone, *Time, Labour*, 5.

4   Ibid., 60.

5   Ibid., 52–3.

6   Ibid., 3.

7   Ibid., 161.

8   'The difference between socialism and capitalism, then, aside from whether private ownership of the means of production exists, is understood essentially as a matter of whether labour is recognized as that which constitutes and regulates society – and is consciously dealt with as such – or whether social regulation occurs nonconsciously. In socialism, then, the ontological principle of society appears openly, whereas in capitalism it is hidden.' Postone, *Time, Labour*, 60–1.

9   Richard D. Wolff and Stephen A. Resnick, *Contending Economic Theories* (Cambridge MA: MIT Press, 2012).

10   Fred Moseley, *Money and Totality: A Macro-Monetary Interpretation of Marx's Logic in Capital and the End of the 'Transformation Problem'* (Leiden: Brill, 2017).

11   David Brennan, David Kirstjanson-Gural, Catherine P. Mulder and Erik K. Olson (eds.), *Routledge Handbook of Marxian Economics* (London: Routledge, 2017).

12   See Postone, *Time, Labour*, 14.

13   Ibid., 278.

14   Ibid., 64.

15   The contours of this discourse is established in a number of recent textbooks (Sam Bowles, Frank Roosevelt, Richard Edwards and Mehrene Larudee, *Understanding*

Capitalism, 4th ed. (Oxford: Oxford University Press, 2017), Ira Katznelson, Mark Kesselman and Alan Draper, *The Politics of Power*, 7th ed. (New York: W. W. Norton, 2013); theoretical works (Robert Skidelsky, *Money and Government* (New Haven: Yale University Press, 2018), James Crotty, *Keynes Against Capitalism* (London: Routledge, 2019), Bhaskar Sunkara, *The Socialist Manifesto* (New York: Basic Books, 2020); journals and periodicals such as *Jacobin, Tribune, Catalyst, Law and Political Economy*; and policy proposals such as the Green New Deal and Jobs Guarantee.

16   Feminist economics emerged in the late 1980s and early 1990s as a branch of progressive/democratic socialist economics that aims to overturn male bias in the discipline of economics and argues that women's contributions to the capitalist economy through gendered labour – unpaid or underpaid – are not sufficiently recognized by economists, governments, and society. Feminist economics argues for the recognition of this gendered labour via proposals such as alternative measures of national output that include household production and on the basis of categories such as 'care work'. Lately, in light of the success of SRT, feminist economics has moved to assimilate and co-opt Marxian categories such as 'social reproduction'. Feminist economics broadens the domain of democratic socialist political economy's standpoint of labour, but the precise boundaries between feminist economics and SRT have recently become blurred. For that reason, we have refrained from discussing it in detail here.

17   Lise Vogel, *Marxism and the Oppression of Women: Toward a Unitary Theory* (Leiden: Koninklijke Brill, [1983] 2013).

18   Mariarosa Dalla Costa and Selma James, *The Power of Women and the Subversion of the Community* (Bristol: Falling Wall Press, 1975); Silvia Federici, *Revolution at Point Zero: Housework, Reproduction, and Feminist Struggle* (Oakland: PM Press, 2012).

19   Cinzia Aruzza, 'Functionalist, Determinist, Reductionist: Social Reproduction Feminism and Its Critics', *Science & Society* 80, no. 1 (2016): 9–30; Tithi Bhattacharya, 'How Not to Skip Class: Social Reproduction of Labour and the Global Working Class', in *Social Reproduction Theory: Remapping Class, Recentering Oppression*, edited by Tithi Bhattacharya (London: Pluto Press), 68–93; Susan Ferguson, 'Building on the Strengths of the Socialist Feminist Tradition', *Critical Sociology* 25, no. 1 (1999): 1–15; Alan Sears, 'Body Politics: The Social Reproduction of Sexualities', in *Social Reproduction Theory: Remapping Class, Recentering Oppression*, edited by Tithi Bhattacharya (London: Pluto Press), 171–91.

20   Susan Ferguson, *Women and Work: Feminism, Labour, and Social Reproduction* (London: Pluto Press, 2019), 126.

21   Kirstin Munro, '"Social Reproduction Theory," Social Reproduction, and Household Production', *Science & Society* 83, no. 4 (2019): 451–68.

22 Silvia Federici, *Revolution at Point Zero: Housework, Reproduction, and Feminist Struggle* (Oakland: PM Press, 2012), 99; cited in Ferguson, *Women and Work*, 130.

23 Nancy Fraser and Rahel Jaeggi, *Capitalism: A Conversation in Critical Theory* (Cambridge: Polity, 2018).

24 Jason E Moore, *Capitalism in the Web of Life: Ecology and the Accumulation of Capital* (London: Verso, 2015).

25 Nancy Fraser, 'What Should Socialism Mean in the Twenty-First Century?' *Socialist Register* (2020): 1–13.

26 Chris O'Kane, 'Critical Theory and the Critique of Capitalism: An Immanent Critique of Nancy Fraser's "Systematic" "Crisis-Critique" of Capitalism as an "Institutionalized Social Order"', *Science & Society* 85, no. 2 (2021): 207–35.

27 Jason E Moore and Raj Patel, *A History of the World in Seven Cheap Things* (Berkeley: University of California Press, 2017).

28 Ibid., 207.

29 See Jürgen Habermas, *Theory of Communicative Action*, vol. 1 (Boston: Beacon Press, 1985), particularly chapter 4 339–403; Jürgen Habermas, *Theory of Communicative Action*, vol. 2 (Oxford and Cambridge: Polity, 1992), particularly chapter VI, pp. 113–99 and chapter VIII, 301–405; and Jürgen Habermas, 'Excursus on the Obsolescence of the Production Paradigm and the Entwinement of Myth and Enlightenment: Max Horkheimer and Theodor Adorno', in *Philosophical Discourse of Modernity: Twelve Lectures*, edited by Jürgen Habermas (Cambridge MA: MIT Press, 1985).

30 As Werner Bonefeld has pointed out, Postone's reconstruction of the critique of political economy does not discuss primitive accumulation as the process that constitutes the historically specific form of labour. See Werner Bonefeld, *Critical Theory and the Critique of Political Economy: On Subversion and Negative Reason* (London: Bloomsbury, 2014). In a 2016 interview, Postone himself acknowledges his reconstruction of the critique of political economy did not reach chapter 25 of *Capital* vol. 1. Indeed, Postone does not reconstruct Part Seven of *Capital* vol. 1, where Marx discusses accumulation and reproduction. This means not only does Postone fail to account for the creation of social form and social categories in capital, but also does not link his emancipatory dynamic to accumulation and reproduction. Martin Thomas, 'Moishe Postone Interview: "Work, Time, and the Working Class"', *Worker's Liberty* (29 June 2016). Retrieved 29 July 2021, from https://www.workersliberty.org/story/2017-07-26/work-time-and-working-class.

31 Given the focus of the chapter, we leave aside a discussion of the veracity of Postone's account of this emancipatory dynamic, but feel inclined to point out that relative surplus value calls the anachronism of value into question. Recent studies that show how automation has led to deskilling and the erosion of conditions of work rather than redundancy call Postone's labour displacement into question. See

for example: Aaron Benanav, *Automation and the Future of Work* (London: Verso, 2020); Jason E. Smith, *Smart Machines and Service Work* (London: Reaktion Books, 2020).

32 Postone, *Time, Labour*, 151.

33 Ibid., 5.

34 Ibid., 397.

35 Ibid., 58.

36 Ibid., 397.

37 Bonefeld, *Critical Theory*.

38 Postone, *Time, Labour*, 5.

39 Karl Marx, 1976. *Capital: Volume I*, translated by Ben Fowkes (London: Penguin Books, [1867]1976), 915.

40 Karl Marx, *The Civil War in France*. https://www.marxists.org/archive/marx/works/download/pdf/civil_war_france.pdf, ([1871] 2010), 23.

41 Simon Clarke, *Keynesianism, Monetarism, and the Crisis of the State* (Cheltenham: Edward Elgar, 1988).

42 Bonefeld, *Critical Theory*.

43 Kirstin Munro, 'Unproductive Workers and State Repression', *Review of Radical Political Economics* 53, no. 4 (2021).

44 See Clarke, *Keynesianism*.

45 Theodor W. Adorno, *Philosophical Elements of a Theory of Society* (Cambridge: Polity, [1964] 2019), 64.

46 Munro, 'Social Reproduction Theory'.

Part Two

Critique of Political Economy as a Negative Dialectic of Society

6

Economic objectivity and negative dialectics: On class and struggle

Werner Bonefeld

The chapter presents negative dialectics as a dialectics of society in the form of the economic object. Negative dialectics refuses to accept the economic categories as categories of economic nature. Instead, it sets out to expose them as categories of historically specific social relations. Its conception of economic nature as a socially constituted nature entails the class antagonism in the concept of economic objectivity. Negative dialectics is the presentation of capitalist social praxis in the form of seemingly independent economic categories.

The assertion that Adorno's negative dialectics amounts to a critique of the constituted relations of economic objectivity, is not a common view. Martin Jay and Jürgen Habermas no less have argued that Adorno's critical theory did not concern itself with political economy or economics, be it bourgeois economics or Marxian economics.[1] However, what would a critical theory of society amount to if it were not to concern itself with the manner in which society maintains itself? Why, really, does this content, human social reproduction, take the form of seemingly self-moving economic forces and what therefore is the content of these economic forces?[2] Adorno's characterization of negative dialectics as critique of 'the ontology of the wrong state of things', which is to establish that 'all concepts, even the philosophical ones, refer to non-conceptualities', does not exclude the economic concepts.[3] Even the philosophical concepts are not excluded![4] According to Adorno 'illusion dominates reality' and it does so because '[e]xchange value, merely a mental configuration when compared with use value, dominates human needs and replaces them.'[5]

This chapter emerged from various earlier drafts that appeared in English in *History of the Human Science* 29, no. 2 (2016): 60–76; in Spanish in *Constelaciones* 8, no. 8–9 (2016): 3–27; and in Korean in *Jinbo-Pyŏnglon*, 71 (2017): 269–305.

The subtitle, 'on class and struggle', comprises a second uncommon view. Critical theory is normally discussed as an immanent critique of philosophical concepts, social phenomena and cultural experiences, not as a negative dialectics of political economy and its class theory.[6] The chapter holds that the negative dialectics of the relations of economic objectivity recognizes human suffering and social struggle as the non-conceptual premise of the economic categories.[7] The non-conceptual is not only the vanished premise of the economic concept of, say, price. It also appears in it – with a price tag. It is, however, the case that Jürgen Habermas introduced a theory of social practice as communicative action.[8] For him communicative action is the means of reason, which announces itself in public speeches and pronouncements, and parliamentary deliberations. Communicative action is about the achievement of a civilized society.[9] In distinction, the class struggle, which is about 'crude and basic material things', belongs to an uncivilized society, in which the class tied to work struggles to make a living.[10] Indeed, one could argue that communicative action is the means of overcoming the conflicts and hardships of a class-ridden society through the application of reason. It is to civilize bourgeois society for the sake of humanity, peace and tranquillity according to the norms of justice, equality and liberty.

Honneth's theory of recognition expands on Habermas. According to Axel Honneth bourgeois society contains within itself the 'promise of freedom'.[11] This would suggest that bourgeois society also contains within itself the 'promise' of a freedom from want and therewith from the class struggle to make ends meet. For the sake of this freedom, Honneth's argument implies that the existing form of society has to develop its potential to the full in order to make good on its promises. In this view, the struggle for access to crude material things, the satisfaction of human needs, is not innate to capitalist society. Rather, it manifests a social pathology of unfreedom that can be overcome through a politics of social justice or recognition.[12] Bourgeois society ought to be civil, just and fair in the treatment of its workers. Who would object to that view? Yet, what really does this mean?[13]

In contrast to the contemporary critical theory represented by Honneth and Habermas, Adorno understood that in capitalist society 'the needs of human beings, the satisfaction of human beings, is never more than a sideshow'.[14] For Adorno the 'total movement of society' is 'antagonistic form the outset'[15] and 'society remains class struggle'.[16] For him, what existing society promises is not freedom from want. Rather, it promises that those without property, free traders in labour power, will have to struggle to make a living.

The presentation of Adorno's negative dialectics as a critique of society in the form of the economic object takes its cue from Max Horkheimer's remarks that 'human beings produce, through their own labour, a reality that increasingly enslaves them' and that therefore Marx's critique of political economy amounts to a 'judgment on existence'.[17] The account starts with a section on economic objectivity as the subject matter of negative dialectics. It argues that 'materialism is not the dogma indicted by clever opponents, but a dissolution of things understood as dogmatic'.[18] Then follows a section on Adorno's dictum that 'society remains class struggle'. It argues that class is a negative category and it develops this point with reference to Adorno's critique of the capitalist exchange relations. The final section – Looking on the Bright Side of the Wronged World – is the conclusion. It sums up the negative dialectics of economic objectivity and argues that, like Marx's critique of political economy, it too is a manifestation of philosophy's search for the good and reasonable organisation of life.[19] It holds that 'there is a tenderness only in the coarsest demand: that no-one should go hungry anymore'.[20]

Economic objectivity and negative dialectics

In the disciplinary division of academic labour, Adorno's negative dialectics as a critique of bourgeois society in the form of the economic object is found wanting. Sociology is the dedicated science of the society. According to the established view, it deals with the relationships between people. It analyses interpersonal relationships 'without paying too much attention to their objectified economic forms'.[21] It observes the social relations, analyses the social facts and attributes meaning to them, and then classifies their social attributions into ideal-typical models of social inter-action, without ever once asking itself why society organizes its reproduction in the form of independent economic categories, of profit, cash and rent. It considers the comprehension of the forms of social wealth, conceived by Marx as the independent, ghost-like movement of value, as a matter of economics. However, like sociology, economics, as the dedicated science of economic matter, does not pay attention to the objectified economic forms either. Economics recognizes economic quantities, represents their movements with mathematical accuracy, rationalizes the economic aspects of society with the help of algebraic formulae, predicts on the basis of available economic data what markets will do next, describes the manner in which the human agents (have to) adjust to market demands for the sake of achieving greater economic efficacy, and explores the means of state as the public authority of economic regulation to achieve optimum factor efficiency – for the sake of economic progress measured by the rate of growth.

For economic thought the essence of economics is not Man (*Mensch*), her needs and desires. Rather, the essence of economics is economic nature, which it presumes to be valid because of itself. Yet, it does not tell us what it is. Economics ascribes subjective power to economic things and argues that the movements of economic quantities express value preferences, which reveal a rationality of economic action that expresses itself in the form of price movements, which manifest a dynamic of competition that 'is supposed to keep the whole process alive and even cause it to progress, as if it were moved by an "invisible hand"'.[22] As the designated science of economic matter, economics translates quantities of 'capital' into algebra and, on the condition of undistorted competition in undivided markets, assigns the power of economic regulation to some omnipotent invisible hand that tells the social individuals what to buy, where to invest, and how to achieve optimum factor efficiency of themselves as embodiments of human capital.[23]

There really is, as Dirk Braunstein remarks drily, no economist by the name of Adorno.[24] Nor is there a sociologist by the name of Adorno. According to Adorno negative dialectics 'flouts tradition'[25] and he argues that the division between economics and sociology 'sets aside the really central interests of both disciplines'.[26] Neither focuses on the manner in which society organizes the satisfaction of its needs and neither concerns itself with the specific form of capitalist wealth – money that yields more money – its production, circulation, law of movement, and its financial forms and crisis-ridden character.[27] In the hands of the economists economic laws are 'metamorphosed...into a pretended law of nature'[28] and for the sociologists 'society is nothing but the average of individual reactive moves'.[29] Both disciplines recognize that the social conflicts have to do with the competitive struggle over the distribution of wealth – who gets what and how much – yet, neither scrutinizes the social relations of production.

> What is entirely overlooked is that this conflict of interests, as manifested in competition, is itself a dilute derivative of much deeper conflicts, those between classes. The former conflicts are really the ones which take place after the central conflict over control of the means of production, has already been decided, so that the competition is carried on within the sphere of an already appropriated surplus value.[30]

A few notable exceptions apart, there is hardly a book or journal article that raises the issue of economic objectivity as a topic of negative dialectics and this despite Adorno's insistence that 'a critical theory of society [is] represented prototypically by that of Marx.'[31] Marx, argues Adorno, directed his critique of political economy 'at the substance' of society, that is, the 'social production and reproduction of the life of society as a whole.'[32] For Marx, the focus of critique is the social relations of production, that is, 'the actual, given relations of life… which… have become apotheosized'[33] in the form of seemingly self-moving economic forces that economic science sets out to quantify with mathematical precision and that sociology fails to recognize when it investigates interpersonal relations based on income, labour market position, educational status, gender, ethnicity, health, etc.[34] Adorno captures this process of the inversion of social relations into seemingly self-moving mysterious economic forces when he argues that 'the objective rationality of society, namely that of exchange, continues to distance itself through its own dynamic, from the model of logical reason. Consequently, society – what has been made independent – is, in turn, no longer intelligible; only the law of becoming independent is intelligible.'[35] The recognition of society as an autonomic economic subject entails its critique.[36] What appears in the appearance of society as a movement of real economic abstractions, how is it that 'the life of all men hangs by' it,[37] and what gives it a consciousness and a will?

Social reproduction governed by 'real economic abstractions' entails both chance and necessity, which are experienced as 'fate'. The mythological idea of fate becomes no less mythical when it is demythologized 'into a secular "logic of things"' that on the pain of ruin judges the actions of the actual individuals in cold, exacting ways.[38] Such fate is a category of a ghostlike society.[39] Its secret is, however, not some invisible hand that regulates the economic development. Rather, and as argued since Marx, what manifests itself 'behind the backs of the acting subjects… is their own work,'[40] and it is their own work that endows the cold society of economic reason with a will and that condemns them as economic 'character masks' (Adorno) or 'personifications of economic categories' (Marx).[41] That is, 'the social relations… do not appear as direct social relations between persons in their work, but rather as material (*dinglich*) relations between persons and social relations between things.'[42] Adorno's conception of dialectics has to be understood against this background. It is to find out what is active in things and holds sway in them, and what holds sway in them asserts itself not only over the social individuals but also through and by means of them.

Negative dialectics refuses 'to lend itself to sanctioning things as they are'.[43] Intended as a theory without 'affirmative traits', it purports to demystify rigidified, thing-like, congealed relationships, rendering their immediacy transparent – as socially constituted things that are imbued and endowed with an independent will and consciousness through the social practices of the individuals that act in and through them as personfications of their own social world. For example, Marx writes that in the money fetish, 'a social relation, a definite relation between individuals... appears as a metal, a stone, as a purely physical external thing which can be found, as such, in nature, and which is indistinguishable in form from its natural existence'.[44] There is only one world, and that is the world of appearances. What counts is money and money counts only as more money. However, what is appearance an appearance of, and what therefore appears in appearance? The social objectivity of a 'purely physical thing' (Marx) that appears in the form of money as incarnation of social wealth, 'does not lead a life of its own'.[45] That is to say, the social relations assume the form of a relationship between things and make themselves manifest as a relationship between money and more money. Society in the form of self-moving economic objects remains social, however perverted in its economic forms of appearance. That is, the social relations vanish in their economic appearance as a relationship between coined metals, and this appearance of the social relations is real. What appears in the appearance of society as a 'stone', or a 'coin', is thus a definite social relationship between individuals subsisting as a relationship between 'coins'. In this 'coined' relationship the social individuals vanish, only to reappear as personifications of economic reason, some, 'the owners of money',[46] calculating the movement of economic quantities, winnings and losses, others, the sellers of labour power, labouring for the sake of money as more money, which is the condition of maintaining themselves through sustained wage income.

As argued previously, for Adorno 'all concepts, even the philosophical ones, refer to non-conceptualities'.[47] Say, the economic concept of profit entails what it is not; that is, it entails the definite social relations between individuals as the vanished premise of its economic force. What has vanished cannot be conceptualized. That is, 'the definite social relations between men themselves... assume here, for them, the fantastic form of a relation between things' and in this form Man in her social relations appears as a mere character mask of her own social world – a mere price-taking agent, 'human material' for 'money which is worth more money, value which is greater than itself', capital which begets more capital and which has thus succeeded in avoiding competitive erosion and the threat of bankruptcy 'through the conquest of social wealth' by means of the progressive accumulation of the extracted surplus value and therewith the 'extension of the area of the exploited human material' that is under its sway.[48]

The social individuals are not visible in the movement of the economic quantities that govern them – instead of personal relations of domination, capitalist society is ruled by abstractions. Their freedom is a freedom of economic compulsion. What counts is money as more money, on the point of ruin. Their needs and desires are a metaphysical distraction to the calculation of all things economic. Nevertheless, as argued by Marx, this distraction is all-important. Capital is not 'a very mystic being' of (economic) nature. It is a very mystic being of a definite form of social relations.[49] Critically conceived, then, historical materialism opens 'up the non-conceptual with the aid of the concept, without reducing it to the concept'.[50] That is, it explores the economic concept from within by thinking in and through it, and in this manner it 'extinguishes the autarky of the concept, strips the blindfold from our eyes. That the concept is a concept even when dealing with things in being does not change the fact that on its part it is entwined with a non-conceptual whole', that is, the non-conceptuality of Man in her social relations as the vanished premise of the economic object.[51]

For Adorno, therefore, the traditional notion of historical materialism as a materialism of the historically unfolding forces of production is in its entirety tied to the natural appearance of the existing social relations. Critically conceived, historical materialism is not a metaphysis of an unfolding economic nature that transitions the social relations from mode of production to mode of production, akin to Adam Smith's fable of the stages of history. Rather, it is critique of the existing relations of economic nature, one that dissolves the dogma of natural economic forces on a social basis. Economic nature is a social nature; it is a nature of the actual relations of life.[52] Thus, historical materialism is critique of society in the form of the economic object. It comprehends the forces of production as the forces of historically specific social relations.[53] Man vanishes in her economic appearance and her own sensuous practice manifests itself as the practice of sensuous supersensible things that make the world go around not in spite of the social individuals but, rather, in and through, and by means of them.[54] What prevails over society exists through society.

Adorno's dialectics is negative on the condition that it 'thinks' against the dazzling spell of the supersensible world of economic objectivity.[55] It thinks 'in contradictions, for the sake of the contradiction once experienced in the thing, and against that contradiction'. It is 'suspicious of all identity' and it therefore resists the temptation to identify reified (economic) things.[56] What appears in reification? What appears is the social relations in the form of a relationship between economic things. This appearance is as real as the fact that the producers of surplus value depend on the effectiveness of their exploitation, the profitability of their labour, to make a living. Capitalist 'society stays alive, not despite its antagonism, but by means of it'.[57] Truth exists as an existing untruth. The fetishism of commodities does not disguise the 'real' social relations. Rather, the fetishism of commodities expresses the 'real' social relations. The social individual is governed by the price mechanism, belongs to the price mechanism, acts through the price mechanism as the existing calculus of their social reproduction, and, as the living material of valorization, struggles to make ends meet – as a price taker.

Society in the form of the economic object is bewitched. It is governed by a ghostlike movement of incomprehensible economic quantities. However, their movement does not create the coldness of capitalist society. It represents it and, as such, it presents it to the social individuals. The identity of the bewitched world of the economic categories is entirely abstract. It is governed by the spectre of value, a ghostlike thing that appears in glimpses in the form of money as more money. Just as the critique of religion does not criticize God on the basis of God, the critique of political economy does not criticize real economic abstractions on the basis of real economic abstractions. Rather, the critique of religion deciphers the social relations that assume the form of God and vanish in the idea of God only to reappear as cowed believers in God, mere human derivatives of divine rule. Similarly, the critique of economic objectivity is not a critique from the standpoint of economic nature. Like the critique of religion, it too deciphers the definite social relations that manifest themselves in mysterious, seemingly extra-mundane economic forms and forces that prevail in and through the social individuals as living personifications of their own world that manifests itself in the form of an independent movement of real economic abstractions, which compels them as living means of a process beyond their control. It thus explores the economic concept from within to comprehend the 'actual relations of life' that assume the form of value as a thing of 'nature'.[58]

The independent movement of the economic forces, of cash, rent and profit, manifests the 'objective necessity' of the existing relations of social reproduction, 'to which we owe everything and that yet [threaten] to bury us all'.[59] Adorno's dialectical theory – like Marx's – sets out to comprehend the social subject in the form of the reified object. That is, the demystification of society in the form of the economic object is, therefore, more than just a matter of an a*d hominem* critique of the economic categories.[60] It is also a '*reductio hominis*, an insight into the delusion of the subject that will style itself an absolute'.[61] What is reified? Appearance [*Schein*] 'is the enchantment of the subject in its own world'.[62] The essence [*Wesen*] of society manifests itself in the form of a 'fatal mischief [*Unwesen*] of a world that degrades men to means'[63] and sets them loose as subjects to struggle to make ends meet, to compete and make profits, and, if need be, to maim and kill. Madness characterizes the mode of reified men, mere personifications of their own social world set loose.

In conclusion, *negative dialectics* is the presentation of the wrong state of things. It argues that the idea of society as 'subject to natural laws is ideology if it is hypostasized as immutably given by nature'.[64] Instead, it holds that the economic forces find their rational explanation in human social practice and in the comprehension of this practice, however perverted this practice might be in the form of the economic object. It thus argues that the relations of economic objectivity manifest the social nature of an inverted [*verkehrte*] and perverted [*verrückte*] world of definite social relations. That is, it amounts 'to a conceptualised praxis (*begriffene Praxis*)' of the capitalist social relations.[65] Negative dialectics is the cunning of reason in a bewitched world.

Economic abstraction and class

I have argued that Adorno's critical theory holds that society in the form of self-moving economic categories is not intelligible. What remains intelligible is the 'law' of economic autonomization in the form of objectively valid exchange relations between one economic quantity and another.[66] The social relationship disappears in the commodity form, which manifests the vanished social subject as a personification of a spectre of ghost walking economic categories. Exchange value dominates use-value, and exchange value manifests itself in money as the form of value. On the pain of ruin, use-value production has to appear as production for money. Money needs to be made. Everything else is a waste of time, effort, intelligence, productive application and wealth itself. What cannot be transformed into money has no value in exchange and might as well be left to rot. Use-values that have no value in exchange count for nothing and the labour that went into their production is socially speaking invalid and was thus worthlessly expended. What matters is not the satisfaction of needs. What matters is the avoidance of devaluation and bankruptcy through the valorization of capital. The value validity of the expended labour time is of the essence. For the dependent seller of labour power, the consequences are formidable, from increased pressure to make her expenditure of labour count as a socially valid expenditure that assumes the form of money, cutting down on meal-times, speeding up, etc., to wages pressure and loss of employment, weakening the strength of her link to the means of subsistence. The world of value is an inhospitable world. Empathy, human warms and fellow feelings do not make money. Nothing is personal. Everything is just business. On the pain of ruin, money needs to be made. How long a time, then, did this concrete labour take and how much quicker could it have been expended – what is its productivity relative to all other appropriated social labour and what needs to be done to enhance it – to sustain its social validity as a labour of money making? Time is money.

This section argues that the capitalist subject is a value subject of profitable equivalent exchange relations. It expounds the meaning of this last sentence. Exchange is either an exchange between equivalent values or it is profitable; in bourgeois society it is both – a contradiction in terms, which is 'immanent to [its] reality'.[67] What is exchanged and what is the critical category of a profitable equivalence exchange relationship? The section explores the value subject as a class subject and expounds surplus value as the critical category of an equivalent exchange between unequal values.

In Adorno's argument, the 'law which determines how the fatality of mankind unfolds itself is the law of exchange'.[68] The exchange relations are equivalent exchange relations. Between two equal value-things there is no difference or distinction. That is, '[o]ne hundred pounds worth of lead or iron is of as great a value as one hundred pounds worth of silver or gold'.[69] The act of an equivalent exchange therefore 'implies the reduction of the products to be exchanged to their equivalents, to something abstract, but by no means – as traditional discussion would maintain – to something material'.[70] The substance of value equivalence cannot be found in 'the geometrical, physical, chemical or other natural property of commodities. Such properties come into considerations only to the extent that they make the commodities useful, i.e., turn them into use-values'.[71] Value equivalence expresses something invisible that is, however, neither divine nor natural in character. Rather, it is an entirely social substance, which becomes visible in the money form.

The traditional idea that money expresses the value of a commodity is uncritical. It supposes value as a substance that is innate to individual commodities. However, the value of a commodity is its social value. Its value is thus a property of exchangeability and money is the independent social form of that property. In clarification, money is not the measure of value. This conception presupposes a pre-monetary existence of value. One hundred pounds of this is the same as one hundred pounds of that. Concrete labour produces this and that. But what labour produces one hundred pounds? Contrary to the traditional theory of value, this or that expenditure of labour does not count. What counts is the social validity of this or that expenditure of labour. Marx conceives of the socially valid labour as abstract labour.[72] Whether this or that expenditure of concrete labour represents a socially necessary and therewith valid expenditure of social labour, of abstract labour, becomes clear only in exchange for money. Money is the socially valid form of measurability.[73] What cannot be exchanged for money has no value-validity and is thus worthless. It is a failed commodity, which weights like a noose around the necks of those who committed an expenditure of a concrete labour that turned out to be socially unnecessary and is therefore not 'measurable' in the form of a certain quantity of money. The logic of abstract labour, of the socially necessary expenditure of labour by the dissociated producers, 'holds sway in reality (*Sache*) itself'.[74] It is independent from the specific temporalities of the individual expenditures of concrete labour; and yet, results 'from the actions of the producers'.[75] Socially necessary labour time is not fixed and given. It is a fluid category. Its establishment is 'no greater an abstraction, and is no less real than the resolution of all organic bodies into air'.[76] The dynamic of capitalist wealth comprises a 'social process that goes on behind the backs of the producers' and yet, it is their work.[77]

Adorno's negative dialectics presents the law of value with reference to Marx's concept of socially necessary labour time. In Adorno's words, 'society… determined… by exchange' entails an 'abstract element' that does not manifest something material in the traditional sense of the word.[78] In fact, what is exchanged are 'average necessary amounts of labour time'.[79] This reduction of the product to 'social labour time [necessarily disregards] the specific forms of the object to be exchanged… ; instead they are reduced to a universal unit'.[80] Marx's familiar definition of the social constitution of value – 'socially necessary labour time is the labour-time required to produce any use-value under the conditions of production normal for a given society and with the average degree of skill and intensity of labour prevalent in that society' – expresses its social character in the form of a universal commensurability of a time made abstract.[81] This time appears as a force of nature – everybody labours to make the cut in time, and then the value validity of the expended labour is effected or denied in exchange. Whether something has value is a matter of exchangeability and measurability, and what is exchanged are equal amounts of socially necessary labour time. In capitalism 'time is ontologised'.[82] This ontologized time is the time of value, and the time of value is the socially necessary labour time – the value-validity of expended labour is like a ghost that either becomes visible in the form of money or it does not, in which case, it becomes visible in the form of a hard-hitting invisible hand.

The holy trinity of social labour, socially necessary labour time and value-validity in exchange is invisible. Its objectivity is spectral. I have argued that the ghostlike objectivity of value becomes visible in the money form. Back in production the ghost of value appears as a Vampire that feeds on living labour as the human material of valorization. Socially necessary labour time is not fixed and given. The labour time that 'was yesterday undoubtedly socially necessary for the production of a yard of linen, ceases to be so to-day'.[83] Whether the concrete expenditure of labour time is a valid, socially necessary expenditure of labour time can only be established *post-festum* in exchange. On the pain of ruin, the expenditure of living labour is thus done in the hope that it will turn out to be socially necessary and that it will thus achieve value-validity in exchange with money. 'Time is money', said Benjamin Franklin, and one might add that therefore money is time. If then, capitalism reduces everything to time, an abstract time that is dissociated from concrete human circumstances and purposes, then, time really is everything. If *'time is everything, [then] man is nothing; he is, at the most, a time's carcase'*[84] – a carcass of 'personified labour-time'.[85] Expenditure of socially valid labour does not occur in in its own good time. It occurs within time, that is the time of value as expenditure of socially necessary labour time. The abstraction of the exchange process 'lies therefore not in the abstracting mode of though by the sociologist, but in society itself' (Adorno 2000: 32). Something abstract, intangible and invisible, holds sway in reality and compels its conduct.

Finally turning to the point that the capitalist exchange relations posit the exchange of money for more money as an equivalent exchange between unequal values (M... M'), how does money '[bring] forth living off springs'?[86] What appears in the appearance of an equivalent exchange of money as more money is the 'difference between the labour-time expended by the worker and that needed for the reproduction of his life'.[87] The fundamental relationship is thus between the value of labour power and the value produced by the consumption of labour power during the social working day. The mysterious character of an equivalent exchange of money for more money has thus to do with the transformation of the commodity labour power into a surplus value producing resource (M... P... M').[88] For the sake of more money, the curtailment of the labour-time spent by the worker to reproduce the value of labour power is of the essence. It is the condition for extending the surplus labour time beyond the time necessary for the (simple) reproduction of society. This extended labour time is the source of the expansion of social wealth, creating a surplus in value, the foundation of profit. The understanding, then, of the mysterious character of an equivalence exchange between unequal values, of money for more money, lies 'in the concept of surplus value'.[89] Adorno thus argues that the equivalence exchange relations are founded 'on the class relationship' between the owners of the means of production and the producers of surplus value, and he argues that this social relationship vanishes in its economic appearance as an exchange between one quantity of money for another.[90]

Economic thought identifies the properties of the economic categories as the revealed truth of society. It recognizes the profitable accumulation of some abstract form of wealth for its own sake as a social necessity. Its identification of profit as a social necessity is not untrue. Failure to make a profit entails great danger. To the vanishing point of death, the life of the sellers of labour power hangs by the success of turning her living labour into a profitable means for its buyer. The profitability of her labour is the fundamental condition of achieving sustained wage-based employment. Yesterday's profitable appropriation of surplus labour buys the labour power of another Man today, the buyer for the sake of making a profit, so that he avoids bankruptcy by enriching himself, the sellers in order to make a living through wage income.

In *Capital*, Marx develops the capitalist class relations from the sale of the commodity labour power. In truth, however, 'the sale of labour power presupposes coercion as the foundation of its sale'.[91] The labour market is the institution that regulates the economic compulsion to make ends meet in the form of an equal exchange relationship between the traders in labour power. Behind the freedom of trade stands the free labourer who divorced from the means of subsistence is at liberty to enter into contracts of employment. On the other side of freedom is the daily struggle to secure the means of subsistence through wage income and to curtail the buyer's acquired right to consume the seller's labour power no matter what during the contracted hours of work. Freedom appears in the form of the economic compulsion to trade labour power for a wage, and not only that, it appears also in the necessity to produce surplus value for its buyer as the condition of future employment.

The struggle for employment and conditions takes the form of a competition between the sellers of labour power on a global scale.[92] For the seller of labour power, competition is not some abstract economic law. Rather, its conceptuality is experienced in the form of precarious labour markets, wage pressure, risk to redundancy, and loss of income. 'Proletarian language is dictated by hunger'.[93]

Class society exists in the form of individualized commodity owners, each seeking to maintain themselves in competitive, gendered, racialized, and territorialized labour markets where the term 'cutthroat competition' is experienced in various forms, from arson attack to class solidarity, and from destitution to collective bargaining, from gangland thuggery to communal forms of organizing subsistence-support, from strike-breaking to collective action, nationalist flag-waiving to international solidarity strikes.

For the science of economic matter, the unemployed represent an economic zero since they lack both in productive contribution and effective demand. This economic calculation of the unemployed is not untrue. It makes clear that the life of the traders of labour power really 'hangs by' the profitability extraction of surplus value.[94] Labouring for the sake of a surplus in value is innate to the concept of the worker. She belongs to a system of wealth in which her labouring existence has a utility only as a means of surplus value extraction. Her subsistence depends on the profitability of her living labour.

Contrary to a whole tradition of Marxist theory, and critical theory too, from Habermas to Honneth and from Fraser to Jaeggi,[95] the social relations of production do not harbour within themselves a 'progressivist' resolution through schemes of communicative action, recognition or application of Marxian economics. They harbour within themselves the requirement of surplus value extraction from the living labour of dispossessed workers. Surplus value extraction is the condition of social reproduction in capitalist society. Unprofitable buyers of labour power go out of business; profitable ones maintain demand for labour power. The profitable accumulation of yesterday's yield of surplus value is the condition of today's wage-based access to the means of subsistence. The dispossessed surplus value producers do not struggle for abstract ideas. They struggle to make a living and they work for profit.

Looking on the bright side of the wronged world

I have argued that economic reproduction is social reproduction. It takes place 'in and through' the perverted 'totality' of the social relations of economic objectivity that feed on the surplus value producing labour of a class of dispossessed workers.[96] For Adorno, 'the organic nature of capitalist society is both an actuality *and* at the same time a socially necessary illusion. The illusion signifies that within this society laws can only be implemented as natural processes over people's heads, while their validity arises from the form of the relations of production within which production takes place.'[97]

Adorno's critical theory holds that the forces of production do not manifest some economic nature. Rather, they manifest 'congealed relationships, which have become autonomous, objectified vis-à-vis human beings'.[98] He thus rejects the orthodox conception of a dialectics between the forces of production as some trans-historically active economic nature and the historically specific relations of production as a 'perverter of Marxian motives'. He criticizes it as a 'metaphysics' which conceives of history as a 'basic ontological structure of things in being',[99] in which, as Patrick Murray puts it, the '"forces of production" are not social-form-determined but, on the contrary, are the ultimate determinant of the "relations of production"'.[100] The traditional view not only naturalizes the economic categories. It also, Adorno argues, denies the 'spontaneity of the subject, a *movens* of the objective dialectics of the forces and relations of production'.[101] In his understanding the forces of production manifest '"relationships between human beings and not, as they appear to us, the properties of things"'.[102] What therefore appears in the appearance of society as an object of the economic forces is not some general economic nature that imposes itself behind the backs of the individuals. Rather, what appears are the actual social relations in the form of independent economic forces. Economic abstractions as such do not exist, except as a negative ontology of 'perverted' (*verrückte*) social relations.

The reality in which the social individuals move day in and day out has no invariant character, that is, something which exists independently from them. As a critical theory of society, and as argued here with reference to Alfred Schmidt,[103] the critique of political economy amounts to a conceptualized social praxis in the form of the economic object, that is, the entire meaning of the 'relations of production resides precisely in the fact that we are here concerned not with direct action but, if you like, congealed action, or with some form of congealed labour' or with society in the form of independent economic forces.[104] Economic nature is a social nature. Its reality is immanent to its own social context.

The crucial category of economic objectivity is the concept of surplus value as 'the invisible and unknown essence' of profit.[105] It is produced by a class of dispossessed sellers of labour power whose access to the means of subsistence depends on the profitability of their living labour. Surplus value is the difference between the value of the commodity labour power and the total value extracted from its consumption during the social working day. To be an unexploitable worker is a fate much worse than being an exploited worker. How to make a living without wage-income? What can be traded if labour-power can't – how many for organ sales? The producers of surplus value belong to a world that is 'hostile to the subject' and the equivalent exchange relations between the buyers of labour power and its sellers presuppose coercion in the conceptuality of social freedom and equality.[106] Bourgeois society does not contain within itself the promise of freedom from want. Rather, it contains within itself dispossessed producers of surplus value who struggle to dodge the 'freedom to starve' as personifications of surplus labour time.[107]

Adorno's dictum that 'society remains class struggle' does not express something positive or desirable.[108] His negative dialectics of the false society resists the bright side view. It holds that 'the abolition of hunger [requires] a change in the relations of production.'[109]

Notes

1   According to Martin Jay, *The Dialectical Imagination* (London: University of California Press, 1973), 152, 'Horkheimer and Adorno, however broad the scope of their interests and knowledge, were never really serious students of economics, Marxist or otherwise'. According to Jürgen Habermas, *Philosophical-Political Profiles*, translated by Fredrick G. Lawrence (London: Heinemann), 1983, 109, 'Adorno was not bothered with political economy.'

2   The question is Marx's, see his 'The Fetishism of Commodities and the Secret Thereof', in Karl Marx, *Capital*, vol. 1, translated by Ben Fowkes (London, Penguin, 1990), 163–77.

3   Theodor W. Adorno, *Negative Dialectics*, translated by E. B. Ashton (London: Routledge, 1990), 11.

4   Theodor W. Adorno, *Metaphysics: Concepts and Problems*, translated by Edmund Jephcott, edited by Rolf Tiedemann (Cambridge: Polity, 2001).

5   Theodor W. Adorno, 'Sociology and Empirical Research', in *The Positivist Dispute in German Sociology*, edited by Theodor W. Adorno, Hans Albert, Ralf Dahrendorf, Jürgen Habermas, Harald Pilot and Karl Popper, translated by Glyn Adey and David Frisby (London: Heinemann, 1976), 68–86, here 80.

6   Following Simon Clarke, *Marx, Marginalism and Modern Sociology* (London: Palgrave, 1992), traditional Marxist conceptions of class are fundamentally Smithean in origin. See also the contributions to Ana Cecelia Dinerstein and Mike Neary, *The Labour Debate* (Aldershot: Ashgate, 2002).

7   See also Charlotte Baumann's contribution to this volume; and Matthias Benzer, 'Social Critique in the Totally Socialized Society', *Philosophy & Social Criticism* 37, no. 5 (2011): 575–603.

8   Jürgen Habermas, *Theory of Communicative Action*, translated by Thomas McCarthy (Cambridge: Polity, 1986).

9   On Habermas' critical theory, see Christopher Henning, 'Jürgen Habermas: Against Obstacles in Public Debates', in *The Sage Handbook of Frankfurt School Critical Theory*, edited by Beverley Best, Werner Bonefeld and Chris O'Kane (London: Sage, 2018), 402–16, and Helmut Reichelt, 'Jürgen Habermas' Reconstruction of Historical Materialism', in *The Politics of Change*, translated by William Martin and Joseph Fracchia, edited by Werner Bonefeld and Kosmas Psychopedis (London: Palgrave, 2000), 105–45.

10   Walter Benjamin, 'Theses on the Philosophy of History', in *idem, Illuminations*, translated by Harry Zorn, edited by Hannah Arendt (London: Pimlico, 1999) 245–55, here 246.

11   Axel Honneth, *The Pathologies of Individual Freedom*, translated by Ladislaus Löb (Cambridge MA: Princeton University Press, 2010), 10.

12   As discussed by Nancy Fraser and Axel Honneth in their *Redistribution or Recognition* (London: Verso, 2013).

13   It might of course be the case that Honneth's idea of 'freedom' does not include the freedom from want. If that were to be the case, his freedom does not promise very much, if anything at all. On Honneth's theory of recognition, see Richard Gunn and Adrian Wilding, *Revolutionary Recognition* (London: Bloomsbury, 2021) and Michael J. Thompson 'Axel Honneth and Critical Theory', in *The Sage Handbook of Frankfurt School Critical Theory* (London: Sage, 2018), 564–584.

14   Theodor W. Adorno, *History and Freedom: Lectures, 1964–1965*, translated by Rodney Livingstone (Cambridge: Polity, 2006), 51.

15   Adorno, *Negative Dialectics*, 304.

16   Theodor W. Adorno, 'Society', in *Critical Theory and Society*, edited by Stephen Eric Bronner and Douglas Kellner (London: Routledge, 1990), 267–275, here 272.

17   Max Horkheimer, 'Kritische und Traditionelle Theorie', in Max Horkheimer, *Kritische und Traditionelle Theorie* (Frankfurt: Fischer, 1992), 205–59, here 229. Translations from German original sources are by the author.

18   Adorno, *Negative Dialectics*, 196.

19   Max Horkheimer, 'Nachtrag', in *idem, Kritische und Traditionelle Theorie*, 261–70.

20   Theodor W. Adorno, *Minima Moralia. Reflections from Damaged Life*, translated by Edmund Jephcott (London: Verso, 2005), 156.

21   Theodor W. Adorno, *Introduction to Sociology*, translated by Edmund Jephcott (Cambridge: Polity, 2000), 141. Even Weber's concern about the relationship of economy to society has vanished from contemporary sociology. For Weber, this

relationship is a central sociological problem. His sociology does however not conceptualize the economic categories as historically specific forms of social reproduction. He rather keeps them separate, views them as distinct spheres of action, and analyses their interrelationships. These points paraphrase Adorno's argument in *Introduction to Sociology*. On Adorno's sociology, see Matthias Benzer, *The Sociology of Theodor Adorno* (Cambridge: Cambridge University Press, 2014).

22 Ibid., 67.

23 On economics as a science of 'incomprehensible concepts', see Joan Robinson, *Economic Philosophy. An Essay on the Progress of Economic Thought* (London: Watts, 1962). 88. Hans-Georg Backhaus, 'Some Aspects of Marx's Concept of Critique in the Context of his Economic-Philosophical Theory', in *Human Dignity: Social Autonomy and the Critique of Capitalism*, edited by Werner Bonefeld and Kosmas Psychopedis (London: Routledge, 2017), 13–29, and Werner Bonefeld, *Critical Theory and the Critique of Political Economy* (London: Bloomsbury, 2014), 21–51.

24 Dirk Braunstein, *Adornos Kritik der politischen Ökonomie* (Bielefeld: Transcript, 2011), 10. See also the contribution by Nico Bobka and Dirk Braunstein to this volume.

25 Adorno, *Negative Dialectics*, xix.

26 Adorno, *Introduction to Sociology*, 144.

27 See Marx, *Capital*, chaps 4 and 5. For a critical theory of capitalist wealth see, for example, Beverley Best, *Marx and the Dynamic of Capital Formation* (London: Palgrave, 2010); Simon Clarke, *Marx's Theory of Crisis* (London: Macmillan, 1994); Michael Heinrich, *Die Wissenschaft vom Wert* (Münster: Westfälisches Dampfboot, 2017); Patrick Murray, *The Mismeasure of Wealth* (Chicago: Haymarket, 2018); and Maximiliano Tomba, *Marx's Temporalities* (Chicago: Haymarket, 2014).

28 Adorno, *History and Freedom*, 118.

29 Adorno, *Negative Dialectics* 198.

30 Adorno, *Introduction to Sociology*, 67.

31 Ibid., 145.

32 Adorno, *Introduction to Sociology*, 84, 141.

33 Marx, *Capital*, 494, fn. 4.

34 The mistake, says Adorno, *Negative Dialectics*, 149, 'in traditional thinking is that identity is taken for the goal'. What is identified and what does the identity of an economic quantity identify? It identifies quantitative differences. Identity thinking affirms what negative dialectics dissolves – the autarky of the socio-economic object as a thing in itself.

35 Theodor W. Adorno, 'Introduction', *The Positivist Dispute in German Sociology*, 1–67, here 15.

36 Contrary to the argument attempted here, Christian Lotz, *The Capitalist Schemata* (London: Lexington), 2014, 22, holds that Adorno 'identifies capitalism with the exchange principle' and that he therefore did not conceptualise the class-divided character of the capitalist social relations. The focus on the exchange principle was key to the New Reading of Marx in (West-)Germany. Helmut Reichelt, *Die Neue Marx Lektüre* (Hamburg: VSA, 2008). On the new reading, see Ingo Elbe, 'Helmut Reichelt and the New Reading of Marx', translated by Jacob Blumenfeld, *The Sage Handbook of Frankfurt School Critical Theory*, 367–85; Ricardo Bellofiore and Tommaso R. Riva, 'Hans-Georg Backhaus: The Critique of Premonetary Theories of Value and the Perverted Form of Economic Reality', ibid., 386–401; and Elena Lange, 'Moishe Postone: Marx's Critique of Political Economy as Immanent Social Critique', ibid., 514–32. In the case of Adorno, the exchange principle was understood as a real social abstraction. However, and surprisingly so, the form of the abstraction, that is the money form, was not discussed at all. On real abstraction and the money form of wealth, see Frank Engster, *Das Geld als Maß, Mittel und Methode* (Berlin: Neofelis, 2014) for a comprehensive, though convoluted, account. On Postone's critique of the economic object, see also Chris O'Kane and Kirstin Munro, in this volume. On Adorno's critique of the capitalist exchange relations, see also Charles Prusik, *Adorno and Neoliberalism* (London: Bloomsbury, 2020) and his contribution to this volume.

37 Adorno, *Negative Dialectics*, 320.

38 Ibid., 319.

39 On the invisible character of 'economic' value, its appearance in the money form, and on the labour that produces it see Riccardo Bellofiore, 'A Ghost Turning into a Vampire', in *Re-reading Marx: New Perspectives after the Critical Edition*, edited by Riccardo Bellofiore and Renato Fineschi (London: Palgrave, 2009), 178–94; Werner Bonefeld, 'Abstract Labour: Against Its Nature and on Its Time', *Capital & Class*, 34, no. 2 (2010), 257–76.

40 Herbert Marcuse, *Negations* (London: Free Association Press, 1988), 151.

41 Adorno, 'Sociology and Empirical Research', 78; Marx, *Capital*, 92.

42 Marx, *Capital*, 166.

43 Adorno, *Negative Dialectics*, 159.

44 Karl Marx, *Grundrisse* (London: Penguin, 1973), 239.

45 Theodor W. Adorno, 'On the Logic of the Social Sciences', in *The Positivist Dispute in German Sociology*, edited by Theodor W. Adorno, Hans Albert, Ralf Dahrendorf, Jürgen Habermas, Harald Pilot and Karl Popper, translated by Glyn Adey and David Frisby (London: Heinemann, 1976), 105–22, here 107.

46 Marx, *Capital*, 270.

47 Adorno, *Negative Dialectics*, 11.

48 Marx, *Capital*, 165, 740, 257, 739–40.

49 Karl Marx, *Capital*, vol. 3 (London: Lawrence & Wishart, 1966), 837.

50 Adorno, *Negative Dialectics*, 65.

51 Ibid., 12.

52 The actual relations of life are the non-conceptual premise of the economic categories. On this, see Marx, *Capital*, vol. 1, 493–4, fn. 4.

53 According to Adorno, *Negative Dialectics*, 197, 'Horkheimer's phrasing "critical theory"… seeks not to make materialism acceptable but to use it to make men theoretically conscious of what it is that distinguishes materialism – distinguishes it from amateurish explications of the world as much as from the "traditional theory" of science'.

54 See Marx, *Capital*, 165. For an exposition of Marx's notion of sensuous supersensible practice, see Helmut Reichelt, 'Social Reality as Appearance: Some Notes on Marx's Conception of Reality', in *Human Dignity*, edited by Bonefeld and Psychopedis (London: Routledge, 2017), 31–67.

55 Of course, 'it', critical theory, does not think. We do. On real abstraction and forms of thought, see Alfred Sohn-Rethel, *Warenform und Denkform* (Frankfurt: Suhrkamp, 1978). For a critical theory of real abstraction, see the contributions by Ingo Elbe, Chris O'Kane and Patrick Murray to Antonio Oliva, Angel Oliva and Ivan Novara (eds.), *Marx and Contemporary Critical Theory* (Palgrave: London, 2020).

56 Adorno, *Negative Dialectics*, 145.

57 Ibid., 320.

58 Marx, *Capital*, 494, fn. 4. Adorno, *Negative Dialectics*, 355.

59 Ibid., 55.

60 Adorno, 'On the Logic of the Social Sciences', 121.

61 Adorno, *Negative Dialectics*, 186.

62 Theodor Adorno, *Stichworte, Kritische Modelle 2* (Frankfurt/Main: Suhrkamp, 1969), 159.

63 Adorno, *Negative Dialectics*, 167.

64 Ibid., 355.

65 Alfred Schmidt, 'Praxis', in *Gesellschaft: Beiträge zur Marxschen Theorie 2* (Frankfurt/Main: Suhrkamp, 1974), 264–308, here 207. On critical theory as a critique of capitalist socialization (*Vergesellschaftung*) see Lars Heitmann, '"Totality": On the Negative-Dialectical Presentation of Capitalist Socialisation', in *The Sage Handbook of Frankfurt School Critical Theory*, translated by Jacob Blumenfeld, 589–606; and Patrick Murray, 'Critical Theory and the Critique of Political Economy', ibid., 764–82.

66 See Adorno, 'Introduction', 15.

67 Adorno, 'Sociology and Empirical Research', 80.

68 Ibid.

69 Marx, *Capital*, 127–8.

70 Adorno, 'Social and Empirical Research', 80.

71 Marx, *Capital*, 139.

72 For an exposition, see Werner Bonefeld, 'Wealth and Suffering', *Dialogue and Universalism*, 28, no. 3 (2018), 123–40.

73 See Chris Arthur, 'Value and Money', in *Marx's Theory of Money*, edited by, Fred Moseley (London: Palgrave, 2005), 111–23.Werner Bonefeld, 'Capital Par Excellence: On Money as an Obscure Thing', *Estudios de Filosofía*, 62 (2020), 33–56.

74 Adorno, 'Sociology and Empirical Research', 80.

75 Moishe Postone, *Time, Labour and Social Domination* (Cambridge: Cambridge University Press, 1993), 191, also 215.

76 Karl Marx, *Contribution toward a Critique of Political Economy*, MECW 29 (London: Lawrence & Wishart, 1987), 272.

77 Marx, *Capital*, 135.

78 Adorno, *Introduction to Sociology*, 31, 80.

79 Ibid., 31.

80 Ibid., 32.

81 Marx, *Capital*, 129.

82 Adorno, *Negative Dialectics*, 331.

83 Marx, *Capital*, 202.

84 Karl Marx, *The Poverty of Philosophy*, MECW 6 (London: Lawrence & Wishart, 1975), 127.

85 Marx, *Capital*, 525–53.

86 Ibid., 255.

87 Adorno, *Minima Moralia*, 73.

88 M … P … M' and M … M' are classical expressions for first, the transformation of Money into the Production of essentially surplus value that is realised in exchange in the form of a greater amount of Money that expresses the extracted surplus value in the form of profit. Second, M … M', which is the general formula of capital, money making, expresses the exchange relationship between Money and more Money, say, £100 [M] = £120 [M'].

89 Theodor W. Adorno, 'Seminar Mitschrift von 1962', Appendix to Hans-Georg Backhaus, *Die Dialektik der Wertform* (Freiburg: Ça Ira, 1997), 501–13, here 508. See also Chris O'Kane's important introduction to this text by Adorno, both published here in the Appendix.

90 Ibid., 506.

91 Adorno, cited in Braunstein, *Adornos Kritik der politischen Ökonomie*, 217.

92 See, for example, Werner Bonefeld, 'The Spectre of Globalisation', in *The Politics of Change*, edited by Werner Bonefeld and Kosmas Psychopedis (London: Palgrave, 2000), 31–68. Tony Smith, *Globalisation: A Systematic Account* (Leiden: Brill, 2005).

93   Adorno, *Minima Moralia*, 102.

94   Adorno, *Negative Dialectics*, 320.

95   Nancy Fraser and Rahel Jaeggi, *Capitalism: A Conversation in Critical Theory* (Cambridge: Polity, 2018).

96   Adorno, *History and Freedom*, 47.

97   Ibid., 118.

98   Adorno, *Introduction to Sociology*, 82.

99   Adorno, *Negative Dialectics*, 358.

100 Patrick Murray, 'Marx's "Truly Social" Labour Theory of Value', *Historical Materialism*, 6, no. 1 (2000), 27–65, here 64, fn. 21.

101 Adorno, *Negative* Dialectics, 205. Translation amended.

102 Adorno quoting Marx, *Introduction to Sociology*, 82.

103 Schmidt, 'Praxis'.

104 Adorno, *Introduction to Sociology*, 105.

105 Marx, *Capital*, vol. 3, 43.

106 Adorno, *Negative Dialectics*, 167.

107 Adorno, *Introduction to Sociology*, 201.

108 Adorno, 'Society', 272.

109 Adorno, 'Introduction', 62.

The liquidation of the individual as a critique of political economy

Fabian Arzuaga

For Theodor W. Adorno, the historical emergence of the waged-worker and the capitalist marks not just the economic roles of the principal classes of modern society but also heralds 'the individual' as a new anthropological type. Hardly older than the Italian Renaissance, the individual coalesces new qualities of 'self-responsibility, foresight, self-sufficiency, as well as a rigid compulsion of conscience and an internalized bond to authority'.[1] If, as Adorno argues, the 'individual owes its crystallization to forms of political economy, especially the urban marketplace [Marktwesen]', it seems that the dissolution of these forms would auger the same for the individual.[2] With the reorganization of capitalism at the turn of the twentieth century, 'competition and the market economy [Marktwirtschaft]' began to cede their coordinating functions to conglomerates of monopoly capital and to state forms oriented to managing economic crises and integrating the proletariat. These economic changes brought forth what Adorno calls 'the anthropological transformations under late industrial mass culture' wherein human beings become 'mere receptive apparatuses' and 'nodal points of conditioned reflexes'.[3] With these changes, however, it seems that even the faint promise buoyed by the ideology of the bourgeois individual drifts beyond all hope of rescue. 'The concept of the individual, historically originated, reaches its historical limit.' [4]

For the second- and third-generation Frankfurt School, the meaning and implications of Adorno's assessment are unambiguous: the individual exists in name only, leaving Adorno to elegize the bourgeois individual as one of

I would like to thank the editors of this volume and Jeta Mulaj for their generous critical feedback on drafts of this chapter.

its last representatives. While other commentators rightly point out that this liquidation does not amount to a deformation but to an anthropological transformation,[5] interpretations following Jürgen Habermas have emphasized decline. The dead-end of such a 'relentless pessimism' has been understood as the inevitable outcome of the abiding influence of the 'state capitalism thesis' on Adorno's thought.[6] According to this reading, if monopoly capital and the interventionist state effectively abolish the market, the structural contradictions of the capitalist economy would no longer be central for a theory of society. With the market made obsolete, so too the bourgeois norm of individualism and the possibility of its immanent critique. The upshot of Adorno's thesis, according to Axel Honneth, leaves 'the individual a helpless victim' at the mercy of 'the calculated interests of the major corporations and the planning capacity of the state organs'.[7]

Despite the influence of the subsequent generations of the Frankfurt school on the reception of Adorno's work, such interpretations remain one-sided. No matter how withering or even pessimistic Adorno's remarks may appear at first glance, the movement of his analysis never halts at an abstract negation. In Adorno's own words: 'to think that the individual is being liquidated without a trace is over-optimistic'. Liquidation 'does not take the form of a radical elimination of what existed previously'. Instead, individuality persists by being 'dragged along dead, neutralized and impotent as ignominious ballast'.[8] While Adorno leaves no doubt that 'the socialization of society has enfeebled and undermined' the individual, he also claims that within this same process 'the individual has gained as much in richness, differentiation, and vigor'.[9] This contradictory status of the individual does not foreclose immanent critique but demands it. Indeed, as Adorno puts it, '[i]n the age of the individual's liquidation, the question of individuality must be raised anew'.[10] The related claim that Adorno's theory reflects the one-dimensionality of the state capitalism thesis – an effective revocation of the critique of political economy – is equally dubious.[11] According to Adorno, the individual persists in the process of its liquidation because the form of its self-preservation continues to require the human being to function as an 'agent of value'.[12]

It is through the critique of political economy that we can better track how Adorno's critical analysis of the contradictory status of the individual seeks not to eulogize but to redeem or rescue its promise. In this chapter, I argue that Adorno's thesis of the 'liquidation of the individual' develops the critique of political economy as a critical social theory. A cluster of meanings present themselves in the liquidation thesis, which can be hewn into three closely related moments within a larger contradictory whole: i) individuality as a means of self-preservation, ii) individuation as a mode of social conformity, and iii) the fungibility of every individual. The first two moments elucidate the transformation of bourgeois individuality as an anthropological type. Under existing conditions, the preservation of the self withers and fragments the individual subject, who increasingly conforms to pre-established patterns in an effort to adapt to the exigencies of capital. The third moment – the fungibility of the individual – entails the liquidation of actually living individuals, or what Marx calls the production of a 'surplus population'. While each moment appears within seemingly different spheres of social life, the expositional separation presented below is strictly heuristic. As will be evident, these moments of the individual's liquidation are unified by a shared basis in the capitalist form and organization of labour and the subordination of the human being to the 'regulative law' of socially necessary labour-time.

After introducing the three moments of the liquidation of the individual below, we turn to Marx's critique of political economy to show the continuity between the liquidation of the individual as anthropological type and what I call the liquidation of 'actually-living individuals'. While it will be shown that Adorno sets up this transition by linking fungibility to its social basis in the universal commensurability of abstract labour-time, he does not explicitly connect this insight to capital's tendency to render labour superfluous in the form of human beings. Instead, Adorno somewhat vaguely detects this inversion in the pervasive suspicion that '[e]veryone knows that he could become superfluous [*überflüssig*] as technology develops as long as production is only carried out for production's sake'.[13] To better substantiate Adorno's insights, part II of this chapter turns to Marx's concept of 'socially necessary labor-time' as the 'law of value' which reveals how capital distinguishes between social 'necessity' and social 'superfluity', or waste. This distinction extends to human beings in the production of a 'surplus population', an outcome of what Marx calls the 'changing organic composition of capital'. After assessing the contributions and shortcomings of Adorno and Marx on the related immiseration thesis in part III, the final section considers how the developmental tendencies in the productivity of labour-time suggest possibilities for the emancipation of the individual, which can occur only in an emancipated society, i.e. a society not controlled by labour-time but 'in control of itself'. The chapter closes by considering how Adorno's critique of 'objectively untrue' yet 'real conceptualities' discloses not just what is promised by the concept of the individual but also what can be redeemed from the 'real untruth' of the superfluity and fungibility theorized as the liquidation of the individual.

I. Liquidation of the individual

As described at the outset of this chapter, Adorno's thesis of the 'liquidation of the individual' first presents itself as an anthropological transformation emerging from the historical dissolution of the bourgeois individual. As capital continues to reorganize the labour process according to the demands of ceaseless self-valorization (what Marx calls the 'real subsumption of labor under capital'), the individual proves to be increasingly incompatible with self-preservation. Under the conditions of advanced capitalism, the preservation of the self turns out to wither the individual subject as it effaces its own individuality by conforming to pre-established patterns in reflex-like adaptation. Echoing Marx's insight that life as simply a means to life becomes a lifeless thing, Adorno underscores the stark contrast between the potential of individuality and its disfigurement when yoked to self-preservation.[14] As merely a means, and therefore a by-product of self-preservation, the prevailing form of individuality experiences 'the possibility of sustaining one's life' as its freedom.[15] Such 'freedom' to pursue one's own needs amounts to the 'cover-image of the total social necessity, which compels the individual towards ruggedness, so that it survives'.[16] Under prevailing social conditions, individuality has been made inessential for the survival of a living-individual: 'self-preservation annuls life in subjectivity'.[17]

The subordination of individuality to the preservation of the self entails a second moment of its liquidation as individuation by means of social conformity. To be sure, the critique of conformism comprises some of the better-known features of Adorno's analysis of the culture industry and mass consumption. For instance, Adorno describes the 'pseudo-individuality' of consumer choice, wherein individuals mistake as their own acts of choosing what really is chosen for them on the basis of the increasing standardized differentiation of cultural products for consumption.[18] Yet, it would be a mistake to consider conformism as 'merely' subjective, psychological, or cultural. The compulsion to conform emanates from the form and organization of labour in capitalism. This objective basis comes into focus if we keep in mind that the ultimate criterion of self-preservation in a capitalist society is the individual's 'successful or unsuccessful adaptation to the objectivity of their function and the schema assigned to it'.[19] The necessity to seek out and fulfil a function in the social division of labour cuts across the class dimensions of capitalist society in that individuals must preserve themselves either through the successful sale of their labour power or by acting as 'capital personified' by carrying out the logic of endless accumulation. The reproduction of capitalist society as a whole depends on the fulfilment of these functions, in which the form of social organization reduces human-beings to 'bearers' [*Träger*] of objectified social relations. Whether proletarian or bourgeois, individuals 'must mold themselves to the technical apparatus body and soul'.[20]

Just as self-preservation remains tethered to the labour process as it becomes all the more subsumed under capital, Adorno consistently explains the hallmarks of conformity as adapting, adjusting, submitting, and ultimately identifying with one's function within the capitalist social division of labour. Marx articulates this objective compulsion to conform most strikingly in his analysis of large-scale industry, wherein the worker must 'learn to adapt his own movements to the uniform and unceasing motion of an automaton'.[21] Adorno extends this analysis by tracing this compulsion from the detailed division of labour in the factory to the social division of labour in capitalist society:

> People are still what they were in Marx's analysis in the middle of the nineteenth century: appendages of the machine, not just literally workers who have to adapt themselves to the nature of the machines they use, but far beyond that, figuratively, workers who are compelled right down to their most intimate impulses to subordinate themselves to the mechanisms of society and to adopt specific social roles without reservation. Today, as in the past, production is for the sake of profit.[22]

Here, Adorno indicates that not only can the social roles of individuals be deduced from their 'individuated function in the modern economy as mere agents of value', but also their 'inner constitution'.[23] The individual must mould themselves according to their social function within the division of labour while also expressing gratitude so far as this function lasts – social conformity aims to create an 'atmosphere of social contentment'.[24]

Just as capital must concern itself with the particular qualitative dimensions of production only insofar as they are relevant for producing surplus-value, so too is the worker 'required to be capable of the same flexibility or *versatility* in the way he applies his labor'.[25] Marx arrives at this insight by tracing how proletarian labour becomes increasingly less specialized, which means that workers must in principle conform to any specific concrete tasks assigned to their functions within the whole. So central is this objective compulsion to conform to one's function, that it renders all feats of 'adaptation, all acts of conformity described by social psychology and cultural anthropology' as 'mere epiphenomena'.[26] In this light we can understand why Adorno chides the conservative complaints about the 'mechanization of man'. Such an idea assumes a dualistic opposition of individual and society in which the individual is conceived either as a residuum of pure subjectivity or as deformed by social objectivity that remains external to it.[27] Neither side of this dualism grasps the 'individual' as itself an historical product of capitalist society. In other words, society 'realizes itself through the interaction of the individuals' who produce it, while the 'substance' of those producers is itself 'essentially' already society.[28] By bemoaning the individual's 'inauthenticity, hypocrisy, and narrow egoism', conservative individualism 'blames the hypostatized individual for his fungibility and his existence as a "character-mask" of society rather than as a real self'.[29] Conformity is not a function of an individual's incapacity or indolent unwillingness to develop an independent or autonomous individuality. Rather, '[i]t is the concrete conditions of labor in society which enforce conformism – not the conscious influences which additionally render the oppressed stupid and deflect them from the truth'.[30] In short, individuals tend to conform by virtue of the objective threat of being impoverished, ostracized or even annihilated via forced economic exclusion.[31]

If this 'fear of unemployment'[32] helps explain why individuals willingly participate in the dissolution of their own individuality through self-effacing self-preservation and relentless conformity, the objective basis of that fear brings us to the third moment of liquidation: the fungibility of every individual.[33] As the mutual interchangeability of things identical in kind, fungibility inheres within the exchange of commodities. Given the centrality and ubiquity of exchange in capitalist society, fungibility not only encompasses the products of labour taking the commodity-form but swallows potentially all objects, and, to the extent we can call ourselves 'subjects', individual human beings. The fungible individual contradicts the historically emergent idea of the 'individual' as a human being with a unique character and special potentialities.[34] Despite the failure of liberalism to make such an idea a reality, this concept of 'individual' still held the unfulfilled promise that every human being could also determine themselves *as* individuals up through the mid-nineteenth century. However, the fungibility of every individual, which follows from the ongoing real subsumption of labour under capital, threatens to dissolve what the concept 'individual' promises by making every individual identical (and therefore interchangeable and replaceable) with every other individual. In their *Dialectic of Enlightenment*, Adorno and Horkheimer explain: 'Through the mediation of total society, which encompasses all relationships and impulses, human beings are being turned back into precisely what the developmental law of society, the principle of the self, had opposed: mere examples of the species, identical to one another through isolation within the compulsively controlled collectivity.'[35] While the context of this passage concerns the destruction of experience as a 'new form of blindness', its source is clearly the work process insofar as it standardizes and makes fungible not just intellectual faculties but the workers themselves.

This all-encompassing mediation that constitutes bourgeois society as a totality becomes refined and restated in Adorno's *Negative Dialectics* as the 'exchange-principle, the reduction of human labor to an abstract universal concept of average labor-time'.[36] Here, Adorno indicates that the objective social basis of the 'fungibility of the individual' is to be found in the value character of capitalist production. To understand how such fungibility amounts to what I call the liquidation of 'actually-living individuals', we need to develop Adorno's insight with reference to Marx. From the perspective of the valorization process, the individual as wage worker is by definition absolutely fungible: the worker counts only as a source of labour-time, the expenditure of which can produce value. As Marx writes, the 'labor-time expressed in exchange-value is the labor-time of an individual, but of an individual in no way different from the next individual and from all other individuals in so far as they perform equal labor'. Indeed, Marx adds, 'it is quite immaterial *whose* labor-time it is' in the production of commodities.[37] As we will explore in the next section, what 'counts' or is 'valid' [*Geltung*] is the labour-time expended in production in abstraction from the concrete characteristics of labour and the labouring subject. Marx sums up the temporal basis of human fungibility as inherent in the production of value in his *Poverty of Philosophy*: '[O]ne should not say that one hour of a man is worth [*vaut*] one hour of another man, [but] a man of one hour is worth [*vaut*] another man of one hour.' As an appendage of the machine, the human being 'counts' only as a source of objectified time, or 'at most', a 'carcass of time' [*carcasse du temps*].[38]

II. Value validity, socially necessary labour-time and surplus population

Above, we examined the liquidation of the individual from the standpoint of its anthropological transformations as it adapts to the imperatives of the capitalist production process. The centrality of the form and organization of labour specific to capitalism, which undergirds these changes, turned our attention to the value-character of the fungibility of the individual as the third moment of its liquidation. In the section below, we continue to trace how the preponderance of labour-time over its human basis in the organization of capital begins to explain the ease at which fungibility passes over into superfluity. Although labour-time serves as the measure of the magnitude of value, not all expended labour-time is value producing; rather, it is only labour-time which 'proves' [*gilt*] to be 'socially necessary' that produces value. In fact, a great deal of labour-time expended in the production of material wealth can 'prove' to be 'wasted time' if it fails to valorize value. And insofar as the human being counts as a mere 'carcass of time', capital makes no distinction between wasted labour-time and human beings as waste. Within the logic of 'validating' labour-time as 'socially necessary', a surplus of labour-capacity appears as a surplus of human beings. The liquidation of the individual culminates in what I have called 'the liquidation of actually-living individuals', or what Marx theorizes as the 'surplus population'.

To understand how socially necessary labour-time functions as the heteronomous logic that distinguishes between necessity and superfluity, let us recall the peculiar differences Marx uncovers between wealth and value. Whatever its social form, use-value expresses 'the material content of wealth independent of the amount of labor required to appropriate its useful qualities'. The quantity and quality of use-values are neither necessarily a function of labour, nor measured by the amount of labour-time expended in their production.[39] Value, on the other hand, is the specific social form of wealth in capitalist society wherein its substance is labour alone (as abstract labour) and its magnitude is measured by socially necessary labour-time.[40] Therefore, value is not measured simply by the abundance and quality of useful things but solely by what Marx calls the expenditure of 'socially necessary labor-time'. By producing at rates faster than socially necessary, it is possible for individual producers to create 'in equal periods of time greater values than average social labor of the same kind'. The 'law of the determination of value by labor-time' – while appearing as the 'coercive law of competition… makes itself felt to the individual capitalist who applies the new method of production… by *compelling* him to sell his goods under their social value' and 'forc[ing] his competitors to adopt the new method'. Yet 'this extra surplus-value vanishes as soon as the new method of production is generalized'.[41] Since socially necessary labour-time is a rate which determines what 'counts' or is validated as socially necessary, it acts as a 'regulative law of nature' in determining the magnitude of value in the same way as does 'the law of gravity asserts itself when a person's house collapses on top on him'.[42]

Socially necessary labour-time measures not the time of individual producers but that of 'social labor'. However, what counts as social labour is neither predetermined, nor fully known by producers in advance. For the private labour expended in the production of commodities to be validated as social labour, it must prove to be a valid expenditure of labour-time that is socially necessary. A crucial moment of this validation occurs in exchange as the transformation of a commodity's value into a universal equivalent (the money-form). Prior to the sale, the value of the commodity as social labour-time exists 'in a latent state so to speak' because the 'point of departure is not the labor of individuals considered as social labor, but on the contrary, the particular kinds of labor of private individuals... which proves [*gilt*] that it is universal social labor'. Therefore, Marx adds: 'Universal social labor is consequently not a ready-made prerequisite but an emerging result.'[43] Therefore, what counts as 'socially necessary' is not a product of planning but determined '*post-festum*' whereby the surplus value expressed in the surplus product is transformed into the money-form.[44] While the transformation of the value congealed in a commodity into the money-form entails an exchange, value is not constituted by the act of selling a commodity for a price determined by market mechanisms in the sphere of circulation.[45]

According to Marx, that which exerts itself in the form of effective demand is ultimately the preponderance of the temporal determination of value itself. We can see this mechanism at work in the validation process. If a number of commodities remains unsold even though they were produced according to what had been anticipated as the time socially necessary for their production, this estimate can (and often does) prove to be wrong. The failure of these commodities to sell amounts to a failure of validation, which reveals, according to Marx, that too much labour time was expended on their production: 'If the market cannot stomach the quantity [of linen] at the normal price of 2 shillings a yard, this proves [*gilt*] that *too great a portion of the total social labor-time has been expended in the form of weaving*. The effect is the same as if each individual weaver had expended more labor-time on his particular product than was socially-necessary.'[46] In other words, the labour expended has proven to be socially *un*necessary, wasteful, and therefore redundant. If a commodity cannot be sold, it proves not to be a valid expenditure of social labour and therefore possesses no value despite absolutely no changes to its useful qualities as material wealth. Value is not 'embodied' within commodities simply because they are products of labour. Products of labour are embodiments of value only insofar as they are commodities: useful things produced to be sold. Only by exchange can these commodities prove [*gelten*] they embody value. Yet, exchange does not constitute value but validates [*gilt*] the allocation of already expended social labour time.

This process of validation yields a disturbing implication. Insofar as labour power (a commodity, after all) remains inextricably bound to actually living human beings, the persistence of mass under- and unemployment suggests that too much social labour time has been expended in the production of 'socially unnecessary' human beings. That the sale of labour power provides living individuals with their means of subsistence is in no way a concern for capital and the logic – the 'regulative law' – governing what counts as socially necessary. If their labour power remains unsold, such workers are summarily 'rendered superfluous' – that is, no longer 'necessary for the self-valorization of capital'.[47]

We can now understand that individuals face liquidation not only anthropologically, i.e. that the 'all-powerful identity-principle, the abstract commensurability of their social labour, drives them towards the obliteration [*Auslöschung*] of their personal identity'.[48] Moreover, capital threatens to liquidate actually living individuals when it no longer needs their labour-power. Those who find themselves among the intractably unemployed 'prove' to be unnecessary for capital accumulation. Along with expropriation and exploitation, exclusion crowns the trifecta of 'the monstrous objective power which social labor itself erected opposite itself as one of its moments'.[49] In other words, capitalist production increases by impoverishing human beings via economic exclusion.

Marx explains this contradiction with the concept of the 'changing organic composition of capital', which holds that capital can boost the productivity of labour by increasing its share fixed in means of production (e.g. machinery) by diminishing the share laid out in the purchase of labour power. On the one hand, capitalist production tends to massively increase the productivity of social labour; that is to say, 'constantly increasing the quantity of means of production may be set in motion by a progressively diminishing expenditure of human power' by applying machinery and large-scale industry to production. On the other hand, this increasing productivity (made possible by the increase in the means of production relative to labour power) makes it increasingly more difficult for workers to find or expect steady employment, i.e. to readily find a buyer for their labour-power.[50]

The implications of the organic composition of capital for the class forced to sell their labour-power are twofold. First, an increasing proportion of the working-class tends to be relegated to the 'industrial reserve army' as capital requires an ever-decreasing expenditure of living human labour for its accumulation. Secondly, the absolute population of the working-class swells despite an increasing proportion of whom are confined to the reserve army.

In the ceaseless thirst for surplus-value, capital drives down the proportion of necessary to surplus labour-time in the production process. This drive to reduce necessary labour-time explains the increase of the population amid the precariousness of waged-work because the reduction of overall necessary labour-time means that 'the *production of workers* becomes cheaper, more workers can be produced in the same time, in proportion as necessary labor-time becomes smaller or the time required for the production of living labor capacity becomes relatively smaller'.[51] In other words, the 'decrease of relatively necessary labor appears as increase of the relatively superfluous laboring capacities – i.e. as the positing of surplus population'.[52]

Although it appears as 'overpopulation', this surplus population is 'purely relative' in that its numbers are not determined by the availability of the means of subsistence as such but by the social forms of producing and distributing these means. Likewise, there is no 'absolute mass of means of substance' because 'the number and extent of his [the human-being] so-called necessary requirements, as also the manner in which they are satisfied, are themselves products of history'.[53] Despite the persistence of Malthusian assumptions up to the present day, there exist no 'natural' laws of human population and hence no 'overpopulation'. Rather, what appears as a 'surplus population' in capitalist society expresses a 'surplus of *labor capacities*' over and beyond those needed for capital.[54] We will return to the implications of this conflation in the conclusion. First we need to consider some of the shortcomings posed by the concept of surplus population.

III. The 'immiseration thesis' & the relevance of surplus population

Although Adorno and Marx provide the theoretical basis for the present argument – that the liquidation of the individual applies not only to the superfluity of bourgeois individuality as anthropological type but also to actually living individuals – we cannot simply reproduce without modification their respective treatments of the concept 'surplus population'. The term has been laden with the problems of the so-called 'immiseration thesis', which largely concerns the historical-empirical refutation of the prognosis of an ever-growing pauperization and inevitable collapse of capitalism. Alongside the development of capitalist production, Marx writes that 'the mass of misery, oppression, slavery, degradation, and exploitation grows; but with this there also grows the revolt of the working class… capitalist production begets, with the inexorability of a natural process, its own negation… the expropriators are expropriated'.[55] 'Against this argument', Adorno writes in the 1940s, 'all the statistics can be marshalled' – 'shorter working hours; better food, housing, and clothing; protection for family members and for the worker in his old age; [and] an average increase in life expectancy'.[56] Although it is debatable as to what degree such concessions were won by the threat of revolt or by the administrative contraception of one, ineluctable pauperization seemed empirically refuted by the mid-twentieth century. For Adorno, 'To speak of "relative immiseration" is ludicrous'.[57] Likewise, while the proletariat existed 'half-outside society' in Marx's time, their integration suggests that 'Marx's prognosis finds itself verified in an unsuspected way: the ruling class is so well fed by alien labour that it resolutely adopts as its own cause the idea that its fate is to feed the workers and "to secure for the slaves their existence within slavery" in order to consolidate their own'.[58]

While Adorno rightly emphasizes the process of proletarian integration as integral to the survival and transformation of twentieth century capitalism, his analyses are not immune to the limits of his own historical horizon. At times he suggests that the relations of production have superseded and neutralized the forces, the integration of the proletariat has irrevocably obliterated class consciousness, or, that the 'natural economic catastrophes' characteristic of the capitalism's liberal age appear to have been overcome by Keynesian state intervention.[59] With the advantage of writing some 50 years after Adorno's death in 1969, we too can marshal 'all the statistics' against these remarks, which seem to assume the perpetuity of what Marcuse in the mid-1960s coined the 'comfortable unfreedom'. Since the long downturn of the 1970s, it has become increasingly clear that the relative prosperity and high rates of employment in the rich countries of the post-war years were much more the exception to the rule of capitalist development.[60]

Much like those of Marx, the profundity of Adorno's analyses become evident when he glimpses tendencies that express the laws of motion specific to modern capitalist society even when they do not so readily appear. An example of such insight returns us to our main line of inquiry. Despite the relative abundance within the developed countries of the 1960s, Adorno continues to adduce strong indications of capital's tendency to render labour superfluous in the form of human beings. '[A] society which in its absurd present form has rendered not work, but people superfluous, predetermines, in a sense, a statistical percentage of people whom it must divest itself in order to continue to live in its bad, existing form'. Therefore, on the one hand, it appears that 'by continuing to live one is taking away that possibility from someone else, to whom life has been denied'. On the other hand, 'if one does live on, one has, in a sense been statistically lucky enough at the expense of those who have fallen victim to the mechanism of annihilation and, one must fear, will still fall victim to it'.[61] Likewise, Adorno could write in 1964:

> At bottom, I believe that domination … expresses itself despite prosperity; that all of us ultimately experience ourselves in this society in accordance with our labor as potentially superfluous. In a way, we only eke out an existence by the mercy of society … and that this deep feeling of superfluity ultimately underlies why our current condition can be generally described as one of malaise, precariousness, and the compulsion for security.[62]

Certainly, the 'prosperity' of the working-class in developed countries is no longer as it once was. Likewise, current forms of the superfluous labour seem to be calling into question the system's capacity to 'absorb the underlying population'.[63] Nevertheless, Adorno's analysis of the liquidation of the individual strongly anticipates what Honneth calls the 'social pathology' of individualization, which he describes as 'a number of symptoms of inner emptiness, of feeling oneself to be superfluous, and of absence of purpose'.[64] Yet, unlike Honneth, Adorno's commitment to the critique of political economy as critical theory provides a way to theorize these transformations in light of the possibility of emancipation, to which we will now turn.

IV. Emancipation from temporal domination

From the outset, this chapter has argued that the liquidation of the individual applies not only to the superfluity of bourgeois individuality as anthropological type but also to actually-living individuals. In reviewing the liquidation of the anthropological type, we linked its central components – self-effacement through self-preservation and the compulsion to conform – to the exigencies of finding a function within the division of labour, which most often takes the form of adapting labour-power to capital. In establishing the relevance of labour-power for the anthropological individual, we extended the thesis of the liquidation of the individual to 'actually-living' individuals as redundant or surplus labour-power. Such redundancy can be theorized as a failure of the validation of value, i.e. that the time expended by social labour to sustain the life of labour-power proves to be 'wasted' time. This redundancy of labour – i.e. the 'overproduction' of labour-capacity – expresses itself as the 'overproduction' of human beings, as a population relatively superfluous for capital. In this concluding section, we draw on Marx and Adorno to theorize how emancipatory moments continue to dwell in capital's otherwise dismal tendencies.

Despite capital's drive to reduce socially necessary labour-time, it cannot reduce labour-time expenditure as a whole. So long as the capitalist mode of production retains value 'as sole measure and source of wealth', living labour remains the lifeblood of capital despite its growing superfluity. Since the source of new value necessary for capital accumulation remains living labour, what is rendered superfluous for capital is not value-producing labour, but human beings who do not produce value. Living labour as labour power remains essential for the existence of capital but such labour power needs only to be 'at its disposal' [*disponibel Arbeitskraft*][65] but in a twofold sense: spendable or 'available for use' while simultaneously expendable, or 'able to be dispensed with'. As Marx writes, 'the most powerful instrument for reducing labor-time' for the production of material wealth 'becomes the most unfailing means for turning the whole lifetime of the worker and his family into labour-time at capital's *disposal* for its own valorization'.[66] Here, to be 'at capital's disposal' means 'over-work' for one part of the working-class and 'enforced idleness' for the rest condemned as surplus populations.[67]

However, toil and exclusion do not follow from the technical capacity to reduce labour-time within mass production but from its *social form* in capitalist society. As capital enlists the 'powers of science and of nature, as of social combination and of social intercourse', the quantity and quality of material wealth becomes increasingly divorced from the living labour-time expended in its production.[68] Marx suggests that if the specific social form of capitalist society was overcome, the technical basis of mass production could be retained to serve the individual instead of the opposite. Indeed, capital creates the material conditions of a post-capitalist society wherein the '*surplus labor of the mass* has ceased to be the condition for the development of general wealth'. Marx even countenances the emergence of a post-capitalist anthropological type wherein the individual would no longer be simply an appendage, but a living purpose – what Marx calls the 'social individual'. The dynamic of capitalist production prepares the grounds for this transformation because capitalism 'despite itself' is 'instrumental in creating the means of *social disposable time*, in order to reduce labor time for the whole society to a diminishing minimum, and thus to free everyone's time for their own development'.[69] According to Marx, the 'free development of individualities' requires that necessary labour time is reduced to the barest minimum. Hitherto such conditions have only been attainable by members of the ruling classes. In short, then, the abolition of class society requires that society be freed from a form of wealth based on the '*theft of alien labor time*'.[70]

This emancipatory horizon of a post-work society (i.e. one no longer ruled by 'alien labor time') is retained in Adorno's theory insofar as it recognizes that radical reductions in labour-time would constitute a world-historical shift in social organization. The germ of 'the possibility of change', writes Adorno, is the development of productivity capacity 'which will make human labor superfluous up to a point. The decrease in the quantity of work, which could theoretically be at a minimum even today, prepares the way for a new quality to come into society'. Indeed, 'given radically reduced labor-time', the horror of the precariousness and vulnerability that 'forms the individual through and through' could be overcome.[71]

To raise 'the question of individuality anew', as Adorno invites us to do, we considered the liquidation of the individual as a contribution to the critique of political economy. Unlike those of the second- and third-generation Frankfurt School, who emphasize a one-sided decline of the individual, the analysis given here uses the liquidation thesis to illuminate the contradictions of the individual in the process of its dissolution. Contradictions can reveal tendencies that point to immanently possible transformations conducive to emancipation. For instance, exchange as a 'social a priori' constitutes a real contradiction in that it possesses a 'real objectivity and is nevertheless objectively untrue' in that 'it violates its own principle, that of equality'.[72] By demonstrating that the exchange of commodities proceeds both equally and non-equally, Marx not only demystifies the source of surplus-value but also uncovers capital's immanent drive to increase labour-productivity to such heights that the measure of material wealth by labour-time becomes effectively obsolete. However, as explored above, so long as the reign of production for production's sake retains labour-time as the measure of value, the redundancy of labour-time expresses itself in the absurd form of the redundancy of human beings.

As with exchange, the fungibility and superfluity of the individual have 'real objectivity' that is nevertheless 'objectively untrue'. The fungibility of the individual obtains this real objectivity insofar as the products of labour-power count as congealed units of abstract labour-time. As labour-power, the individual is indeed absolutely fungible vis-à-vis the production of value. Indeed, the 'real objectivity' evinced by the fungibility of the individual is nothing other than the spectral-like objectivity of value as it 'haunts the space between the real and ideal'.[73] As Adorno explains, compared to 'bodily reality and all tangible data', the 'real conceptuality' of value may appear as 'illusion' [*Schein*]. Yet, given the preponderance of value in the organization of production, 'illusion dominates reality' as 'what is most real'.[74] In spite of the reality of the fungibility that value confers on the individual, it is also untrue. It is not human beings who are in themselves fungible – mutually interchangeable as identical instances of each other – but their labour-power. While untrue, such fungibility is nevertheless real. The conflation of labour-power and the human being is objectively rooted in the capitalist form and organization of labour, since living labour-power cannot exist apart from living human beings. Capital has no need of considering the human being attached to labour-power as anything other than a carcass of time. Yet, this fungibility of the actually-living individual, all too real, remains objectively untrue. According to Adorno, if fungibility entails 'the complete disposition [*Verfügung*] of all over all', it would prove incompatible with domination as 'the disposition of one over others', whether that 'one' would be the ruling class or the heteronomy of society over its captive membership. Indeed, Adorno suggests: 'Pure fungibility would destroy the core of domination and promise freedom'.[75] Along the same lines, Marx's critique of the concept of 'surplus population' reveals that it is not human beings who are superfluous but value-producing labour. As with exchange and fungibility, the very concept of superfluity retains an unredeemed promise in the untruth of its prevailing form. To be superfluous – not needed because there already exists more than enough – could only be achieved in a society of abundance, in which plentitude exists for the individual as a 'living purpose' instead of the opposite.

Notes

1   Theodor W. Adorno, 'Individuum und Organisation', in *Gesammelte Schriften* (Frankfurt: Suhrkamp, 2003), *Vol. 8: 450* My trans.

2   Theodor W. Adorno, *Minima Moralia: Reflections on a Damaged Life*,translated by Edmund Jephcott (New York: Verso, 2005), §97.

3   Theodor W. Adorno, *Notes to Literature*, translated by Shierry Weber Nicholsen (New York: Columbia University Press, 1991), Vol. 1: 106; Adorno, 'Individuum und Organisation', 451.

4   Ibid., 450.

5   For more nuanced accounts of transformation, see Dale Shin, 'The Precarious Subject of Late Capitalism: Rereading Adorno on the "Liquidation" of Individuality', in *Individualism: The Cultural Logic of Modernity*, edited by Zubin Meer (Lanham,

MD: Lexington Books, 2011), 203–18; Massimiliano Tomba, 'Adorno's Account of the Anthropological Crisis and the New Type of Human', in *(Mis)Readings of Marx in Continental Philosophy*, edited by Jernej Habjan and Jessica Whyte (Basingstoke: Palgrave Macmillan, 2014), 34–50.

6   Seyla Benhabib, *Critique, Norm, and Utopia: A Study of the Foundations of Critical Theory* (New York: Columbia University Press, 1986), 159ff; Tobias Ten Brink, 'Economic Analysis in Critical Theory: The Impact of Friedrich Pollock's State Capitalism Concept', *Constellations* 22, no. 3 (2015): 336; Axel Honneth, *The Critique of Power: Reflective Stages in a Critical Social Theory*, translated by Kenneth Baynes (Cambridge, MA: MIT Press, 1993), 72ff; Moishe Postone, 'Critical Theory and the Historical Transformations of Capitalist Modernity', in *The Palgrave Handbook of Critical Theory*, edited by Michael J. Thompson, Political Philosophy and Public Purpose (New York: Palgrave Macmillan US, 2017), 137–63.

7   Honneth, *The Critique of Power*, 72–83.

8   Adorno, *Minima Moralia*, §88.

9   Ibid., p. 18.

10 Ibid., §83.

11 Chris O'Kane, '"Society Maintains Itself despite All the Catastrophes That May Eventuate": Critical Theory, Negative Totality, and Crisis', *Constellations* 25, no. 2 (2018): 287–301; Dirk Braunstein, *Adornos Kritik der Politischen Ökonomie* (Bielefeld: transcript Verlag, 2011); Werner Bonefeld, *Critical Theory and the Critique of Political Economy: On Subversion and Negative Reason* (New York: Bloomsbury, 2014).

12 Adorno, *Minima Moralia*, §147.

13 Theodor W. Adorno, *The Jargon of Authenticity*, translated by Knut Tarnowski and Frederic Will (London: Routledge, 2002), 27.

14 Theodor W. Adorno, 'Society [1965]', *Salmagundi* 10–11 (1969): 151.

15 Theodor W. Adorno, *History and Freedom: Lectures 1964–1965*, translated by Rodney Livingstone (Cambridge, UK: Polity, 2006), 6.

16 Theodor W. Adorno, *Negative Dialectics*, translated by Dennis Redmond 2001, 258–61, http:// members.efn.org~dredmond/ndtrans.html.

17 Adorno, *Minima Moralia*, §147.

18 Theodor W. Adorno, 'On Popular Music', *Studies in Philosophy and Social Science* IX (1941): 25ff; Theodor W. Adorno, 'On the Fetish Character in Music and the Regression of Listening', in *The Essential Frankfurt School Reader*, edited by Andrew Arato and Eike Gephardt (New York: Continuum, 1982), 278ff.

19 Theodor W. Adorno and Max Horkheimer, *Dialectic of Enlightenment*, trans. Edmund Jephcott (Stanford: Stanford University Press, 2002), 21–2.

20 Ibid., 23.

21 Karl Marx, *Capital Vol. 1: A Critique of Political Economy*, translated by Ben Fowkes (New York: Vintage Books, 1977), 586.

22 Theodor W. Adorno, 'Late Capitalism or Industrial Society?', in *Can One Live After Auschwitz?: A Philosophical Reader*, ed. Rolf Tiedemann, translated by Rodney Livingstone (Stanford: Stanford University Press, 2003), 117.

23 Adorno, *Minima Moralia*, §147. It is no surprise that Adorno calls this transformation the 'changing organic composition of the human-being', the model of which is taken from Marx's analogous 'changing organic composition of capital'. We will explore this concept in the next section.

24 Adorno, 'Society [1965]', 145.

25 Karl Marx, 'Results of the Immediate Process of Production [1863–66]', in *Capital Vol. 1: A Critique of Political Economy*, trans. Ben Fowkes (New York: Vintage Books, 1977), 1019.

26 Adorno, *Minima Moralia*, §147.

27 Schweppenhäuser, *Ethik nach Auschwitz*, 167.

28 Adorno, *Minima Moralia*, p. 18 as explained by Hermann Schweppenhäuser, 'Das Individuum im Zeitalter seiner Liquidation: Über Adornos Soziale Individuationstheorie', *ARSP: Archiv Für Rechts- Und Sozialphilosophie / Archives for Philosophy of Law and Social Philosophy*, 57, no. 1 (1971), 93.

29 Theodor W. Adorno, *Prisms*, translated by Samuel Weber (Cambridge, MA: MIT Press, 1983), 115.

30 Adorno and Horkheimer, *Dialectic of Enlightenment*, 29.

31 Adorno, 'Society [1965]', 149; Adorno, *History and Freedom*, 211.

32 Adorno, *The Jargon of Authenticity*, 26.

33 For a discussion of the 'fungibility of the individual' as a crucial moment of identity, see Richard A. Lee, *The Thought of Matter: Materialism, Conceptuality and the Transcendence of Immanence* (London; New York: Rowman & Littlefield, 2015), 52ff.

34 On the individual's historical character, see: Giddens, *Modernity and Self-Identity: Self and Society in the Late Modern Age* Cambridge: Polity Press, 1991 and the entry on 'individual' in Raymond Williams, *Keywords: A Vocabulary of Culture and Society* (New York: Oxford University Press,1985).

35 Adorno and Horkheimer, *Dialectic of Enlightenment*, 29.

36 Adorno, *Negative Dialectics*, 149.

37 Karl Marx, *A Contribution to the Critique of Political Economy*, edited by Maurice Dobb, translated by S.W. Ryazanskaya (New York: International Publishers, 1970), 32 my emphasis.

38 Karl Marx and Friedrich Engels, *Marx Engels Collected Works, vol. 6: 1845–48* (New York: International Publishers, 1976), 127 Trans. amended.

39 Marx, *Capital*, 125–6.

40 Ibid., 131.

41 Ibid., 435–6, my emphasis.

42 Ibid., 168, cf. 129, 433ff.

43 Marx, *A Contribution to the Critique of Political Economy*, 45.

44 Marx, *Capital*, Vol. 1, 202.

45 'The forms which stamp [*stempln*] products of labor into commodities ... are therefore presupposed by the circulation of commodities', *Capital*, I, 168 [trans amended].

46 Marx, *Capital*, Vol. 1, 202, my emphasis.

47 Ibid., 557.

48 Adorno, 'Society [1965]', 148 trans. corrected.

49 Karl Marx, *Grundrisse*, translated by Martin Nicolaus (New York: Penguin, 1973), 831.

50 Marx, *Capital*, Vol. 1, 798.

51 Marx, *Grundrisse*, 400; Marx, *Capital*, Vol. 1, 433ff.

52 Marx, *Grundrisse*, 608–9.

53 Ibid., 608; Marx, *Capital*, Vol. 1, 275.

54 Marx, *Grundrisse*, 608. We should note that being rendered superfluous for capital does not necessarily entail unemployment if the capitalist class can hire 'unproductive' servants, which itself has limits. For an extended discussion of productive and unproductive labour, see Marx, 'Results', 1038–49.

55 Marx, *Capital*, Vol. 1, 929.

56 Theodor W. Adorno, 'Reflections on Class Theory', in *Can One Live After Auschwitz?: A Philosophical Reader*, edited by Rolf Tiedemann (Stanford: Stanford University Press, 2003), 103.

57 Adorno, 'Late Capitalism or Industrial Society?', 112.

58 Adorno, 'Reflections on Class Theory', 105.

59 Adorno, 'Late Capitalism or Industrial Society?', 112. For a discussion, see Stefano Petrucciani, 'Adorno's Criticism of Marx's Social Theory', in *Critical Theory and the Challenge of Praxis* (New York: Routledge, 2015), 19–32.

60 For nearly 40 years, OECD countries have been attended by a persistent decline in the rate of economic growth, and equally persistent increases in overall indebtedness as well as inequality in terms of income and wealth. Wolfgang Streeck, 'How Will Capitalism End?', *New Left Review* 87 (June 2014).

61 Theodor W. Adorno, *Metaphysics: Concepts and Problems*, translated by Edmund Jephcott (Stanford: Stanford University Press, 2001), 113.

62 Adorno, *Philosophische Elemente*, 99. My trans.

63 For a recent literature review, see Nick Bernards and Susanne Soederberg, 'Relative Surplus Populations and the Crises of Contemporary Capitalism: Reviving, Revisiting, Recasting', *Geoforum*, 2020, 10.1016/j.geoforum.2020.12.009

64 Axel Honneth, 'Organized Self-Realization: Some Paradoxes of Individualization', *European Journal of Social Theory* 7, no. 4 (1 November 2004): 467.

65 Marx, *Capital*, Vol. 1, 798.

66 Ibid., 531–2. My emphasis.

67 Ibid., 789.

68 Marx, *Grundrisse*, 704–8.

69 Ibid., 158 and 708, my emphasis.

70 Ibid., 708.

71 Adorno, *Negative Dialectics*, 272–5.

72 Ibid., 190.

73 Lee, *The Thought of Matter: Materialism,* 43.

74 Theodor W. Adorno, 'Sociology and Empirical Research', in *The Positivist Dispute in German Sociology*, translated by David Frisby and Glyn Adey (London: Heinemann, 1976), 80.

75 Theodor W. Adorno, *Prisms*, trans. Samuel Weber and Shierry Weber (Cambridge: MIT Press, 1983), 105.

8

Society as real abstraction: Adorno's critique of economic nature

Charles Andrew Prusik

In a time punctuated by crisis, the alternatives to capitalism appear as remote as ever. Why does the movement of speculative financial flows, of money, and of market prices appear to govern us like laws of nature? Although Theodor W. Adorno did not live to see the neoliberal revolution of the 1970s–1980s, his critical theory can provide a framework for theorizing the naturalization of the contemporary neoliberal turn of capitalist society.[1] This chapter develops Adorno's concepts of exchange and real abstraction to criticize economic concepts and categories, focusing on Marx's dialectical approach to 'natural history' as the key to an immanent critique of economic theory. Adorno's revitalization of Marx's concepts of natural history, as well as the related concepts of commodity fetishism and real abstraction, can be developed to demystify the ideological function of the epistemological turn in neoliberal economic theory. The liberal concept of a free market society that arises through the spontaneous, competitive actions of individuals has returned in neoliberal theory, particularly in the work of Friedrich von Hayek, whose theory holds that the free market is a 'superior information processor', and the absolute horizon of all rational economic action.[2] This chapter returns to Adorno to critique neoliberal society in its ideological appearance as a self-regulating, evolving order that asserts itself as an independent economic logic. I argue that Adorno's dialectics reveals how the abstract and impersonal relations of capitalism are generative of reified forms of thought in social science, and how these forms of thought become ideological moments in the social world they reinforce. By conceptualizing society as a process of 'subject-object' mediation, Adorno's dialectics can recover the genesis of economic concepts in their constitution by the practice of commodity exchange. Through a reconsideration of Adorno's critique of positivism, social science, and subjective economics, I argue that the neoliberal free market can be grasped as an ideological form of thought that belongs to the structuring relations of capitalist society. In what follows I delineate Adorno's critical theory of society by focusing on the related concepts of exchange, society as second nature, and real abstraction as the key to grounding the ideological function of economic thought in the neoliberal present.

Real abstraction and identity thinking

Adorno's critical theory argues that value in capitalism is a socially constituted abstraction. Social reality is abstract because individuals relate to each other through commodity exchange. This understanding of society is grounded in Marx's critique of the 'fetish-character of the commodity', a theory which suggests that capitalism is organized by isolated producers who only realize the social character of their labour through exchange.[3] Adorno similarly maintains that the fundamental principle of capitalist society is the exchange abstraction, the principle of mediation that unconsciously synthesizes society as an objective whole. 'What really makes society a social entity, what constitutes it both conceptually and in reality, is the relationship of exchange, which binds together virtually all the people participating in this kind of society.'[4] Exchange is the 'all-around mediator' that connects individuals through abstract commodity relations.[5] The exchange abstraction is thus an 'objective abstraction' that is prior to the individual's cognitive abstractions: 'The first objective abstraction takes place, not so much in scientific thought, as in the universal development of the exchange system itself; which happens independently of the qualitative attitudes of producer and consumer, of the mode of production, even of need, which the social mechanism tends to satisfy as a kind of secondary by-product. Profit comes first.'[6]

What does it mean to say that society is really abstract? According to Adorno, abstraction is present in every act of commodity exchange, because in the exchange commodities are reduced to a principle of unity: socially necessary labor.[7] Through the exchange of commodities we 'abstract' from concrete reality through an unwitting reduction to unity. Adorno remarks: 'In this exchange in terms of average social labour time the specific forms of the objects to be exchanged are necessarily disregarded; instead, they are reduced to a universal unit.'[8] In commodity exchange we equate qualitatively different, heterogeneous things to each other by reducing them to quantities of money. This practice not only relates non-identical things to an abstract form of equivalence in money, it also isolates value from its genesis in society's relations of production.

This practice of exchange-based abstraction is connected to Adorno's concept of 'natural history', because exchange systematically generalizes throughout society, transforming relations between individuals into a universal context of abstract determinacy. As the exchange abstraction extends through every sphere of life, society petrifies into an object that appears to reproduce – and posit – itself independently of the individuals who constitute it. The capitalist relations of society thus appear automatic and immutable, a congealed whole that Adorno calls 'second nature'. By second nature, Adorno means that social practice presents itself in a manner that appears to be 'first nature' – that is, as an external and alien objectivity that seems to govern individuals independently of their own action.[9] This production of society as a second nature lends capitalist relations the quality of fated necessity. That society appears as a second nature is attributable to the fetishized law of exchange-value: 'The law is nature-like due to the character of its inescapability under the dominating relationships of production.' [10] The exchange abstraction seems to be a law-like – or fated – principle of socialization that binds all individuals to the necessity of capital accumulation: 'The law which determines how the fatality of mankind unfolds is the law of exchange.' [11] This naturalization of exchange is a function of the commodity abstraction, or, the condition that social relations appear indirectly in the form of value, of abstract quantities between commodities: 'The concept of commodity fetishism is nothing but this necessary process of abstraction. By performing the operation of abstraction, the commodity no longer appears as a social relation but seems as if value were a thing-in-itself.' [12] The fetish-character of exchange, according to Adorno, is not a subjective illusion, but belongs to the objective relations of capitalist society: 'the fetish-character of commodities is not chalked up to subjective-mistaken consciousness, but objectively deduced from the social a priori, the process of exchange'.[13] The relations of capitalist society reproduce themselves through an objective illusion, namely, that economic laws govern society as if they were natural laws. And yet the objective illusion of value is also a reality; individuals in capitalism really do act and relate to each other through the medium of exchange. Exchange value 'dominates human needs and replaces them; illusion dominates reality. To this extent, society is myth and its elucidation is still as necessary as ever. At the same time, however, this illusion is the most real thing of all, it is the formula used to bewitch the world'.[14] The fetish character of exchange arises from the peculiar character of the mediated relations of capitalist society, a system of production organized by isolated producers who do not relate to each other directly, but only realize the value of their social labour indirectly through exchange. Value is realized in an unconscious, unwitting manner in capitalist society. Through the objective and mediated relations of society, exchange imposes a static claim on individuals and things: by reducing non-identical things to a principle of unity – value – these things are assumed to remain identical during their comparison in markets.

An economic thing, such as money or a price signal, is the manifestation of a social relation, a fetishized form that exerts power over individuals. The movement of money is, as Adorno puts it, the power by which 'the life of all men hangs by'.[15] This blind and automatic movement of exchange reproduces society in a quasi-mythological manner, because individuals experience the movement of society in the form of an abstract, independent movement of value. Adorno calls this abstract context of exchange a 'secular logic of things', an autonomously self-moving whole that attributes social power to commodities and objectifies individuals as bearers of exchange-value.[16] The interdependence of the whole that synthesizes individuals through exchange is predetermined by the end of capital as the automatic subject. This externalization of social relations and practices in things is a part of natural-history, of the passage of historically produced forms into the appearance of nature. The socially constituted 'second nature' of capitalism asserts itself through the exchange abstraction: 'What is self-made becomes the In-itself.' [17] This process of exchange-based socialization inverts means and ends, reducing individuals to functions of capital accumulation in the form of a 'fatal mischief (*Unwesen*) of a world arranged so as to degrade men to means of their *sese conservare*[.]'[18] Rather than acting as the subject of its own social world, the individual in capitalism is ruled by the autonomous movement of abstractions, by the law of value which they create behind their backs as if by force of nature.

One area that differentiates his critical theory from Marx's critique of political economy is the key role Adorno attributes to subjectivity in the reproduction of society. Although he grounds the dialectical accounts of exchange, abstraction and natural history in Marx's critique of value, Adorno also suggests that Marx 'went rampaging through the epistemological categories like the proverbial bull in the china shop.' [19] Focusing on the inner-connection between the exchange abstraction, naturalization and subjectivity, Adorno's approach conceptualizes the constitution of epistemological categories by the objective relations of society. The cognizing subject, according to Adorno, is not merely a passive object of exchange, but is equally a necessary moment in the reproduction of society. The real abstracting practices of commodity exchange are not only constitutive of economic forms, but also forms of thought that condition the naturalization of value. Adorno names the prevailing mode of thinking in capitalist society 'identity thinking'. Identity thinking is any mode of cognition that represents reality through conceptual predication; identification is classificatory and subsumptive. According to Adorno, identity thinking is instrumentalizing and dominating because it reduces particulars to functions of universals. In *Negative Dialectics,* Adorno is at pains to point out the inadequacies of identity, revealing the non-identical moment that is cut out of subjectivity: 'the name of dialectics says no more, to begin with, that objects do not go into their concepts without leaving a remainder'.[20] Identity thinking, according to Adorno, is pervasive in logic, formal reasoning, science and positivism. It is the mode of cognition that is as dominating as the social world it reflects. His materialist claim suggests that there is a concealed link between identity thinking and the exchange abstraction:

> The exchange-principle, the reduction of human labor to an abstract general concept of average labor-time, is Ur-related to the identification-principle. It has its social model in exchange, and would not be without the latter, through which non-identical particular essences and achievements become commensurable, identical. The spread of the principle constrains the entire world to the identical, to totality.[21]

Here Adorno points to an affinity between identity and exchange as principles of synthesis; the resemblance between identity and exchange lies in the act of abstraction. If the exchange abstraction is the principle of socialization that equalizes and reduces different use-values to labour-value, then the cognitive act of abstraction similarly reduces different, particular objects to universal concepts through identification. Adorno thus frequently refers to an 'exchange principle', and an 'identity principle', to illuminate their inner-connection. This convergence of thought and practice belongs to the mediations of capitalist society in general, as each principle reinforces the other, compelling subjects to adopt identity as the paradigmatic form of cognition and validity. Thinking therefore, in capitalist society, is necessarily mediated by the form of the commodity and the real abstraction of exchange, and exchange is mediated by the form of thinking.

In articulating an inner-connection between thought and practice that converges in the exchange abstraction, Adorno's critical theory can grasp the constitution of forms of thought by the objective relations of society in a manner that is both self-reflexive and immanent to its context. Its critical intent is to reveal the non-conceptual in the concept, the relations of sensuous practice that appear as an abstract relation between values. Adorno's epistemological critique of identity thinking reveals the implicit non-identity in every identification. This critique of identity belongs to his critique of liberal society and its ideal notions, of the concept of a social whole that arises through the free and spontaneous actions of individuals.[22] Insofar as the compulsory drive to master reality through identity always falls short, the social totality is similarly disunited in its unity, it is a 'negative totality' that reproduces itself through the class antagonism between capitalist and wage-labourer.[23] Concealed within the appearance of society as an abstract movement of values lies the antagonistic relation between the class of capitalists and the class of wage-labourers who must sell their labour power as means of subsistence. 'The class relationship makes up the objective motor of the production process which the life of all men hangs by, and the primacy of which has its vanishing point in the death of all.'[24] This antagonistic relation between capital and labour disappears in the appearance of the exchange abstraction, individuals exist as 'personifications' of economic categories, bearers of particular class interests, 'character masks' who act as functions of the objective relations of production.[25]

To further delineate the connection between exchange and identity, Adorno conceptualizes society as a dialectical process of 'subject-object' mediation, a double-sided totality that reproduces itself through practice. Individuals within the class-relation unconsciously reproduce society though the exchange abstraction, a process of objectification that constitutes society as a 'mediating conceptuality', compelling subjects to reproduce society in a manner that conceals domination.[26] 'Society as subject and society as object are the same and not the same.'[27] Society is subjective because it depends on subjects, on human practice. 'Society is subjective because it refers back to the human beings who create it.'[28] Society does not reproduce itself independently of practice; society can only maintain itself and reproduce itself through subjects. The social totality 'does not lead a life of its own over and above that which it unites'.[29] Society, however, is also objective, because, 'on account of its underlying structure, it cannot perceive its own subjectivity'.[30] The concept of society as the simultaneous subject–object is connected to Adorno's claim that exchange naturalizes capitalist relations, because in exchange individuals externalize their practice in abstract relations between things, in commodity values, in prices that seem to lead a life of their own. Adorno's claim that society is systematically 'false' can be understood in terms of this inversion of subject and object: the social world of capital that appears to be governed by economic laws is the world that subjects make. Society is simultaneously 'blind nature and yet mediated by consciousness'.[31]

Unlocking the constitution of the invisible principles that govern society in the form of abstract value is the pivot of Adorno's critique of domination, as well as the reified forms of thought that systematically fail to grasp the ideological character of society's autonomization from those who make it.

Positivism and the science of economic nature

What are the implications of this inversion of society as subject and object for the social scientist who studies it? Many of Adorno's post-war reflections on social science, instrumental reason and positivism are an attempt to answer this question. One consequence of the inversion of subject and object is that the subject appears in this inverted reality as the agent of her own sociability. Positivist social science, according to Adorno, fails to recognize the inverted reality of the subject's social world. As Adorno puts it:

> The notions of subjective and objective have been completely reversed. Objective means the non-controversial aspect of things, their unquestioned impression, the façade made up of classified data, that is, the subjective; and they call subjective anything which breaches that façade, engages the specific experience of a matter, casts off ready-made judgments and substitutes relatedness to the object for the majority consensus of those who do not even look at it, let alone think about it – that is, the objective.[32]

By placing the dialectic of society as subject–object at the centre of his critical theory, Adorno recovers the genesis of the disciplines of sociology and economics in the relations of society. Positivism represents a particularly insidious case of identity thinking; in social science, positivist methods grant priority to 'what is at hand, what is given as fact', without conceptualizing the mediation of facts by the totality.[33] Positivist approaches to social science apply a reified method to their object, reducing society to empirical data without recognizing the reified character of the social object.

In addition to the undialectical methods Adorno attributes to empiricist social science (e.g., classification, statistical analysis, opinion polls), his main objection to the positivist tradition lies in its 'primacy of method', that is, its refusal to recognize the objectivity of mediation, of a social essence that appears in inverted form.[34] This critique can be seen in his debate with Karl Popper in the *Positivist Dispute in German Sociology* (1962), where Adorno synthesizes his claims about the question of method, as well as the fragmentation of social science into isolated disciplines. Insofar as positivism refuses to conceptualize society as an internally contradictory object that is not immediate, but mediated, it can only register the surface appearances of social phenomena. Observing this one-sided primacy of method in the abstractly isolated disciplines of sociology and economics, Adorno names positivism 'reified thinking', and locates its genesis in the real movement of the social object: 'Scientific mirroring indeed remains a mere duplication, the reified apperception of the hypostatized, thereby distorting the object through duplication itself. It enchants that which is mediated into something immediate.' [35] By collapsing the social essence with its forms of appearance, positivism cannot grasp the objectivity of reification – it merely reflects it through a primacy of method that treats society as 'nothing but the average value of individual modes of reaction'.[36] Cut off from the economic categories of exchange, value, and labour, sociology tends to study subjective attitudes and opinions without theorizing their objective mediation.[37] By the same token, the discipline of liberal, 'subjective' economics reduces the totality to the law-like movement of putatively objective, or natural economic laws, while failing to grasp the genesis of these laws in society's relations. Both sociology and economics, according to Adorno, are positivist methods that fetishize the identifiable facts and figures of reality, and ignore the socially constituted character of their form of appearance. 'Positivism is so blinded by society that it regards second nature as first nature and identifies the data of society with the data of natural science.'[38] The absence of any determinate concept of society in positivism means that sociology and economics are ill-equipped to grasp non-empirical relations and tendencies, such as the reality of class antagonism, or the persistence of general crises of capital accumulation.[39] All empirical research devoid of theory, according to Adorno, is blind to the fundamental 'conceptuality which holds sway in reality (*Sache*) itself', and is doomed to function as a moment in the reproduction of the totality.[40]

If positivist sociology fails to grasp the economic form of society's relations, economic theory is similarly one-sided in its reduction of society to economic laws. Adorno invariably names the tradition of liberal bourgeois economics, 'subjective economics', and criticizes its failure to recognize the 'congealed human relationships' that manifest in economic things.[41] To review the background briefly, subjective economics began in the context of the 'Marginalist Revolution' – a body of research that developed a scientific model for formalizing economic laws. Similarly originating within the wider context of the 'Methodenstreit' in social science, Marginalist economics resembled the positivist methodologism of sociology in its prioritization of scientific validity.[42] Rejecting the classical liberal tradition and its objective labour theory of value, Marginalists like William Stanley Jevons, Leon Walras and Carl Menger introduced a subjective theory of value that focused on the individual's 'utility' as the foundation of market equilibrium.[43] This neoclassical approach turned away from the classical considerations of production in political economy, focusing on consumption and rational economic behaviour. The subjective turn in neoclassical economics holds that the individual's evaluations of commodity prices are the true cause of market equilibrium. The master concept of 'utility' refers to the degree of satisfaction derived by individuals in consumption, a principle of subjective rationality that finds its ideal representation in the figure, '*homo economicus*'.[44] Despite the neoclassical departure from Smith and Ricardo's labour theory of value, the neoclassical school can rightly be interpreted as a political revival of the liberal ideal of individual freedom. To neoclassicals, supply and demand find equilibrium through the evaluations of individuals in free markets, and laissez-faire returns as the ideal form of political organization.[45]

Adorno's critique of subjective economics suggests that its scientific validity is merely a description of marketized relations: 'Subjective economics is essentially an analysis of market processes in which established market relations are already presupposed.' [46] The formal models of neoclassical theory describe the movement of quantitative economic things without comprehending the social constitution of value relations. To neoclassicals, prices represent nothing but the abstract movement of an independent economic rationality that individuals possess in relations of competition. In its one-sided fixation on prices and market equilibria, neoclassicism attributes subjective power to a sui generis economic nature. By relinquishing Marx's distinction between value and price, subjective economics 'fails to translate the economic laws back into congealed human relationships'.[47] The theory's blindness to the question of social constitution is most acute in its naturalization of need, a category which, in the hands of neoclassicals, is reduced to the static principle of 'utility'. This naturalized vision of a market society is a part of the inverted world of capital. The exchange abstraction, as Adorno claims, is not simply an immediate transaction between atomized individuals that express value preferences – exchange is the universal principal of mediation that envelopes the movement of social reproduction in an abstract totality. Exchange cannot be detached from value as the social form of wealth that valorizes value through abstract labor.[48] Subjective theory is blind to the manner in which the exchange-principle prevails in things, shaping the whole sphere of social need according to the compulsory ends of capital accumulation. By reifying need as a static principle of optimization, neoclassical theory idealizes market relations according to a mythically formal, homogeneous and static conception of market self-regulation.

Against this universal, quasi-scientific concept of value as utility, Adorno reminds us of the historically specific relations of production in capitalist society, and suggests that the regulation of consumption is itself something mediated by the antagonistic class relation between capital and labour.[49] Subjective economics, he claims, is essentially the 'apology' of liberal bourgeois society.[50] Economics is akin to the positivist methods of sociology insofar as it reifies the putatively objective facts of society (in the form of prices), without recognizing the 'problem of constitution', that is, the historical process that generated all mediation as value-relations.[51] This scientific turn in economics isolates the movement of quantitative things in a manner that mirrors the sociological reduction of inter-personal relations to empirical facts. 'As for economics itself, however, it will have no truck with anything – whether it be history, sociology or even philosophy – which does not take place within the context of the developed market economy and which cannot be calculated, mathematized, according to the schemata of current market relationships[.]'[52] Positivist sociology and subjective economics are opposite sides of the same false coin. Both disciplines fail to grasp the contradictory movement of society in its unity as subject–object. The isolation of both disciplines, Adorno suggests, 'sets aside the really central interest of both disciplines'.[53] Neither grasps the fundamental inversion of capitalist society: the movement of a world where the material relations between people manifest as an abstract movement of economic things amongst themselves. Instead, sociology objectifies interpersonal relations, and economics subjectifies things. By fixating on the appearance of society in statistical facts or prices, positivist social science fails to grasp the manner in which society's essence disappears in its form of appearance. Society is a process of mediation, subject and object are dialectically caught up in an ongoing inversion of 'subjectivity into objectivity', and vice versa.[54] Misrecognizing second nature for first nature, the traditional theories of sociology and economics conceptualize the movement of markets in their appearance as natural laws. Such an approach describes marketized phenomena without comprehending the historical production of society's relations. This scientific model of society loses the perspective that could grasp the processes of domination that are immanent to liberal society, affirming what has been constituted as mythically prearranged.

Neoliberal theory: Markets think too

The ascent of neoliberalism in the 1970s revived the dream of a free market society. Breaking from the neoclassical framework of market equilibrium, neoliberals transformed subjective economics by conceptualizing markets as 'superior information processors', instruments of an economic rationality that knows more than individuals.[55] The origins of neoliberal economics are multiple: Carl Menger and Ludwig von Mises of the 'Austrian School' are key players, but the most decisive thinker of this tradition was Mises's student, Friedrich Hayek, who would play a major role in building the Mont Pelerin Society in 1947, a closed society of economists, philosophers and business elites committed to forming a 'new liberalism'.[56] With training in biology, brain science and psychology, Hayek transformed economics by shifting its conceptual framework to epistemology. This epistemic grounding of markets was first formulated during the 'Socialist Calculation Debate', where Hayek departed from the neoclassical emphasis on resource allocation, and reconceptualized markets as instruments of communication. This shift can be seen in his influential essay, 'The Use of Knowledge in Society' (1945): 'The economic problem of society is thus not merely a problem of how to allocate "given" resources [...] it is a problem of the utilization of knowledge not given to anyone in its totality'.[57] Hayek's argument is that free markets are necessary because the data individuals need to evaluate goods is 'dispersed', 'subjective', and therefore fallible.[58] This concept of dispersed information decentres the rational economic agent, *homo economicus*, and turns away from the concept of utility to a vision of markets as aggregators and conveyers of incomplete fragments of information. According to Hayek, the free movement of prices both reflect and shape the beliefs and plans of individuals. As he insists, 'It is more than a metaphor to describe the price system as a kind of machinery for registering change, or a system of telecommunication.'[59] Against the neoclassical ideal, which grounds the invisible movement of markets in the economic rationality of individuals, Hayek insists upon the fragmentary, partial and misleading status of the individual's knowledge, while affirming the superior rationality of markets.

In something of an ironic twist, Hayek's theory is forced to decentre the standpoint of the economist who purports to understand economic data, because his theory holds that no economist can rival the superior information of the free market itself.[60] After a brief period of hostility to the use of scientific methods and categories in economics, Hayek later turned to the sciences of cybernetics and systems theory to elaborate the distributed character of information in market self-regulation. (This return to scientific method for economic theory was crucially influenced by Mont Pelerin society member and interlocutor, Karl Popper).[61] Hayek's efforts to translate cognitive processes into market principles led to another wave of naturalized concepts and categories in neoliberal theory.[62] This shift from the traditional theory of marginal utility brought a corresponding transformation to foundational liberal concepts: knowledge became 'information', competition became 'discovery', and freedom became 'order'.[63] In addition to cybernetics, Hayek also turned to biology and systems theory, developing a cultural evolutionary framework that would ground his concept of the free market. In his mature work, Hayek frequently names the free market a 'spontaneous order', an emergent whole that has evolved through the competitive rules human beings have acquired over the course of civilization's development. As he remarks in his final text, *The Fatal Conceit* (1988): 'the extended order is perfectly natural: in the sense that it has itself, like similar biological phenomena, evolved naturally in the course of natural selection'.[64] The spontaneous order emerges through the unconscious behaviours of individuals, and through the selection of competitive 'rules' that facilitate market activity.[65]

Hayek's theory is not merely the apologia of a capitalist class perspective; it has its truth-content. Capitalist society reproduces itself through exchange; the relations between individuals appear in abstract form as a quantitative movement of things. The exchange process is not only the objective principle of socialization, it has also played a key role in the historical production of the individual, understood as spontaneous, autonomous and free. Hayek's epistemology of the free market approaches the border of the dialectic of subject and object, and it recognizes the secret identity of exchange and thought. However, it does not ask the question: why does society appear in the form of an autonomous movement of abstractions? Society forms itself as system of communication in exchange, but this system is not a function of the immediate decisions of individuals, rather, it is a function of the fundamental inversion of a social world where human relations vanish in their commodified appearance. Hayek's theory attributes the determination of the free market's information to the value preferences of individuals without recognizing the objective social form of value. His theory remains caught in the subjective moment of the social totality. This neoliberal concept of the free market affirms the incomprehensibility of economic quantities as if the abstract movement of society was the movement of an independent economic nature. But this autonomization of society belongs to the law of exchange that socializes individuals within an immanent context of value that is valorized through labour. The reproduction of the social totality is the fated movement of a real abstraction. Individuals experience this alien world of finance capital through the convergence of chance and necessity. As Adorno remarks: 'What chance and necessity have, lethally in common, is what metaphysics refers to as *fate*.'[66] In capitalism, chance is 'the form taken by freedom under a spell', by the expulsion of all moments of reality by the identity principle, by the rule of abstractions over life. That society can only take the form of this identity is illusion, socially necessary illusion. This mythological appearance of society as fate is a moment of the naturalization of exchange, of the independence of exchange-value that circulates and returns in abstract isolation from productive relations.[67] This real metaphysics of capital is the neoliberal 'secular logic of things', the blind movement of prices which individuals confront as economic predetermination. The mythological appearance of fate belongs to the real abstracting practices of individuals who are not the subject of their social world. The individual in neoliberalism lives in relation to the immediacy of market prices, of apparently self-determining fluctuations that conceal the mediated opacity of value. Hidden within the appearance of society as a free and equal exchange of spontaneous individuals is the silent compulsion of capital, the automatic subject that must accumulate more capital. The appearance of society as a free and spontaneous movement is a reality and illusion. As Adorno points out, the 'illusion signifies that within this society laws can only be implemented as natural processes over people's heads, while their validity arises from the form of the relations of production within which production takes place'.[68] Neoliberal theory is so blinded by the abstract identity of the exchange principle that it cannot grasp the socially constituted nature of the fated economic nature it affirms.

This concept of a free market society fails to extricate itself from its positivist legacy – it cannot comprehend the antagonistic unity of society's appearance and essence, of subject and object. Hayek's concept of information is a type of identity thinking, it sees only equivalence between things amongst themselves, but it does not enquire into the social basis of this identity. Considered as a part of natural history, the neoliberal dream of returning the world to an invisible law of economic nature betrays the need of a society to actualize a directly social world that was never realized. The free market fundamentalism of neoliberal thought asserts the primacy of economic nature as if it were first nature, ontologizing the sphere of the market as the only possible site of freedom. In a brief moment of speculation in *Negative Dialectics*, Adorno questions the natural basis of society's origins, the famed '*principle of homo homini lupus*', of liberal contract theory. Perhaps for a time in prehistory – he suggests – humanity was compelled by scarcity to live through violent acts of 'power-seizure'.[69] (He doubts that such prehistory is knowable). That the whole of human history appears as natural history, as the prolongation of domination, is a piece of ideology that belongs to capitalist modernity. The standpoint of domination in the present conditions the appearance of history as mere natural history: 'Human history, progressive domination, continues the unconscious one of nature, of devouring and being devoured'.[70] To the extent that liberal theory derives the origins of bourgeois social institutions from the putatively natural unity of progress and domination, theory naturalizes the antagonism of the capitalist totality. Adorno's point regarding natural history is that the unity of progress and domination is semblance, socially necessary illusion. In the final analysis, he suggests, 'Marx was ironically a social Darwinist'.[71] What the social Darwinists praised – natural conflict – is in truth the social negativity of a false world that reduces individuals to means, to a form of wealth that exploits labour for the valorization of value. The social subject in capitalism exists through objectification, through an immanent compulsion that prolongs history as mere preservation. This form of compulsion, Adorno suggests, is not a necessary fact of nature: 'The inescapable spell of the animal world is reproduced in the brutal domination of a society, still caught up in natural history. But one should not apologetically conclude from this that compulsion is immutable'.[72]

The neoliberal idea of a market society eternalizes what has been historically produced: the inverted world of capital that attributes social power to things. In the present conditions of financial and political crisis, the independent movement of abstract value now threatens to capture the whole of planetary nature in the exchange-principle. As the automatic subject, capital 'ruthlessly compels humanity towards production for production's sake'.[73] That social reproduction still occurs through compulsion is betrayed by the neoliberal push to marketize ecological crises, swallowing nature in carbon markets and speculative commodity futures.[74] Ruled by the abstract movement of flows of speculative finance capital, the contemporary neoliberal order confronts us as if it were an independent economic logic of nature, rather than the result of human practice. For Adorno, the key to critical theory that could demythologize society as a second nature does not reside in an alternative science of economics, but in recovering the historical process underlying the universal extension of the exchange principle. The disappearance of history from society is the basis of society's reproduction as second nature: 'The more relentlessly the process of societalization spins its web around every aspect of immediate human and interpersonal relations, the more impossible it becomes to recollect the historical origins of that process and the more irresistible the external semblance of something natural.'[75] Unlocking the riddle of society as second nature requires deciphering the human relations and practices that appear in abstract things. Understanding the present's relations as socially constituted is the key to breaking the appearance of capital as the automatic fetish of capitalist wealth, of money that appears to generate more money through its own movement.

Conclusions

Adorno's contribution to critical theory can continue to illuminate forms of social domination in today's neoliberal order. The potentials of his theory for resistance to neoliberal capitalism do not consist in an alternative science of economics, but turns on a 'conceptualized praxis' that reveals the nature of economy as a socially produced nature.[76] Such a praxis moves through the concepts and categories of a society ruled by value, revealing the relations of human practice that appear in reified form. Faced with the ongoing realities of rising inequality, austerity and the concentration of private wealth, contemporary criticism of neoliberalism often demands a more just and equal distribution of the social product. The absence of any clear capacity by capital to resolve its crises of accumulation has led to the recent wave of right-wing, populist and racist movements, each demanding a return to a mythological past. This fascist critique of neoliberalism is a personalized critique of individuals, of tangible and concrete representatives of capital. The critique of politicians, financiers and immigrants is the reaction formation of a disempowered resistance to abstract domination. Such a fetishized critique of capitalism only identifies the capitalist as a force of corruption and manipulation without recognizing the capitalist as the personified function of capital.

Adorno's critical theory is a useful alternative to such a fetishized perspective. His critical theory targets the dependence of all individuals on the social world that they make. Rather than demanding more of the social product for the worker in a world that remains hostile to the subject, Adorno criticizes the capitalistically arranged relations that reduce practice to the ends of profit. His critical theory suggests that freedom from need and domination requires the abolition of the class relation and the exploitation of labour: 'the absolutization of labor is that of the class relationship: a humankind free of labor would be free of domination'.[77] Rather than affirming an alternative economics that would expose the inequality of financialized wealth, critical theory would do well to refuse all sciences of economic nature. All theory that is critical, Adorno suggests, illuminates the law of value as socially necessary illusion. The critique of society's appearance as second nature points to the abolition of the law as the horizon of freedom: 'That the assumption of natural laws is not to be taken à la lettre, least of all ontologized in the sense of a however stylized draft of so-called humanity, is confirmed by the strongest motive of Marxist theory of all, that of the potential abolition of those laws. Where the realm of freedom had begun, they would no longer apply.'[78] The critique of neoliberalism does not find its resolution in the return to a more equally distributed, comfortable liberal society, but in the abolition of the class-divided form of society that valorizes value through labour, of the antagonistic social object that 'only needs all'.[79]

Notes

1   For an account that explores the transition from state managed capitalism to neoliberalism, see Charles Andrew Prusik, *Adorno and Neoliberalism: The Critique of Exchange Society* (London: Bloomsbury, 2020).

2   There are of course differences amongst neoliberals regarding the meaning of free markets, market societies and self-regulation. While the 'Chicago School' still remains methodologically committed to fundamental neoclassical principles, Hayek's framework represents a major break from this tradition. For a detailed overview of the myriad strands of neoliberal theory, see *The Road from Mont Pelerin: The Making of the Neoliberal Thought Collective*, edited by, Philip Mirowski and Dieter Plehwe (Cambridge: Harvard University Press, 2015). For an analysis of the ordoliberal tradition that focuses on Hayek's role in the development of an anti-democratic, free market society, see Werner Bonefeld, *The Strong State and the Free Economy* (London: Rowman & Littlefield, 2017).

3   For accounts of Adorno's development of Marx's theory of fetishism, see Gillian Rose, *The Melancholy Science: An Introduction to the Thought of Theodor W. Adorno* (London: Verso, 2014), and Riccardo Bellofiore and Tommaso Redolfi Riva's 'The *Neue Marx-Lektüre*: Putting the Critique of Political Economy Back into the Critique of Society', in *Radical Philosophy* 189 (January/February 2015), 24–36.

4   Theodor Adorno, *Introduction to Sociology*, translated by Edmund Jephcott (Stanford: Stanford University Press, 2002), 31.

5   Adorno, *Negative Dialectics*, translated by Dennis Redmond. Retrieved 20 December 2018, from http://members.efn.org/~dredmond/ND2Trans.txt, 328.

Note that the Redmond translation is not paginated, all paginations refer to the German original.

6   Adorno, 'Society', translated by Frederic Jameson *Salmagundi* 3, no. 10–11 (1969–1970): 148.

7   Adorno, *Introduction to Sociology,* 31–2. Note that the notion of real abstraction was introduced to Marxian theory by economist Alfred Sohn-Rethel. Adorno praised Sohn-Rethel's theory of real abstraction and applied it to his own critique of epistemology. As Adorno writes, 'Sohn-Rethel was the first to point out that in the latter, in the general and necessary activity of the Spirit, inalienably social labor lies hidden', *Negative Dialectics,* 178. For an account of the differences between Adorno and Sohn-Rethel's approach to real abstraction, see Frank Engster, 'Subjectivity and Its Crisis: Commodity Mediation and the Economic Constitution of Objectivity and Subjectivity', *History of the Human Sciences* 29 (2016): 1–19.

8   Adorno, *Introduction to Sociology,* 32.

9   For an account of the use of the concepts first and second nature in Adorno's work, see Stefan Breuer's, 'Adorno's Anthropology', translated by John Blazek, *Telos* 64 (1985): 15–31.

10   Adorno, *Negative Dialectics,* 347.

11   Adorno, 'Sociology and Empirical Research', in *The Positivist Dispute in German Sociology*, translated by Glyn Adey and David Frisby (London: Heinemann Educational Books, 1977), 80.

12   Adorno, 'Marx and the Basic Concepts of Sociological Theory: From A Seminar Transcript of the Summer Semester 1962', translated by Verena Erlenbusch-Anderson and Chris O'Kane, *Historical Materialism* 26, no. 1 (2018), 6.

13   Adorno, *Negative Dialectics,* 190.

14   Adorno, 'Sociology and Empirical Research', 80.

15   Adorno, *Negative Dialectics,* 314.

16   Ibid., 313.

17   Ibid., 339.

18   Ibid., 164.

19   Ibid., 206.

20   Ibid., 17.

21   Ibid., 149.

22   For an account that analyses Adorno's critique of liberalism in the context of his theory of integration, see Jakob Norberg's, 'Adorno's Advice: *Minima Moralia and the Critique of Liberalism*', *PLMA* 126 (2011): 398–411.

23   Adorno, *Negative Dialectics,* 21.

24   Ibid., 314.

25   Adorno, 'Society', 148.

26   Adorno, 'Sociology and Empirical Research', 80.

27 Adorno, 'Introduction', in *The Positivist Dispute,* 34.

28 Ibid., 33.

29 Adorno, 'On the Logic of Social Sciences', in *the Positivist Dispute,* 107.

30 Adorno, 'Introduction', 33.

31 Adorno, 'On the Logic', 107.

32 Adorno, *Minima Moralia: Reflections on a Damaged Life,* translated by E.F.N. Jecphcott (London: Verso, 2005), 69–70.

33 Adorno, 'Einleitung zu Emile Durkheim', *Soziologische Schriften I,* Band 8 (Frankfurt: Suhrkamp, 2018), 246–7.

34 For an analysis of Adorno's critique of methodologism, as well as the details regarding its neo-Kantian context, see Rose's *Hegel Contra Sociology* (London: Verso, 2009), 2–38, and Matthias Benzer, *Adorno's Sociology* (Cambridge: Cambridge University Press, 2011).

35 Adorno, 'Sociology and Empirical Research', 75–6.

36 Adorno, *Negative Dialectics,* 197. Note that Adorno is referring to the neoclassicism of Vilfredo Pareto. See also his critique in *Introduction to Sociology,* 11.

37 'In other words, sociology [...] disregards the social production and reproduction of the life of society as a whole. And if anything is a social relationship it is precisely that totality'. *Introduction to Sociology,* 141.

38 Adorno, 'Marx and the Basic Concepts', 3.

39 See Adorno, 'Introduction', 37.

40 Adorno, 'Sociology and Empirical Research', 80.

41 Adorno, *Introduction to Sociology,* 143.

42 For background and discussion regarding the origins of neoclassical economics that analyses its relation with sociology, see Simon Clarke's, *Marx, Marginalism, & Modern Sociology* (London: Macmillan, 1991), and Janek Wasserman, *The Marginal Revolutionaries: How Austrian Economists Fought the War of Ideas* (New Haven: Yale University Press, 2019).

43 The individual's utility preferences render goods commensurable and valuable in markets rather than labour. See Clarke, *Marx, Marginalism,* 182–206.

44 For an historical analysis of the neoclassical revolution that focuses on the utility concept as being analogous with proto-energetics physics, see Mirowski's, *More Heat than Light: Economics as Social Physics: Physics as Nature's Economics* (Cambridge: Cambridge University Press, 1999). For a critique of this scientism of economics in neoclassicism which mobilizes Adorno's subject–object dialectic, see Hans-Georg Backhaus, 'Between Science and Philosophy: Marxian Social Economy as Critical Theory', in *Open Marxism,* vol. 1, edited by Werner Bonefeld, Richard Gunn and Kosmas Psychopedis (London: Pluto Press, 1992), 54–92.

45 See ibid., 193–241.

46 Adorno, 'Marx and the Basic Concepts', 10.

47 Adorno, *Introduction to Sociology*, 143

48 See Clarke, *Marx, Marginalism*, 219.

49 Adorno, 'Marx and the Basic Concepts', 9.

50 Ibid., 10.

51 Ibid. Adorno also cites Marx's concept of 'primitive accumulation' as the historical process in which exchange relations dissolved traditional social ties. See *Negative Dialectics*, 328.

52 Adorno, *Introduction to Sociology*, 142.

53 Ibid., 144.

54 Backhaus, 'Between Science and Philosophy', 60.

55 For an historical analysis of the multiple concepts of information in neoliberal theory, see Mirowski and Edward Nik-Khah, *The Knowledge We Have Lost in Information: The History of Information in Modern Economics* (Oxford: Oxford University Press, 2017).

56 See Plewhe, 'Introduction', *Road from Mont Pelerin*, 1–39.

57 Friedrich Von Hayek, 'The Use of Information in Society', *American Economic Review* XXXV, no. 4 (1945), 519.

58 For an extensive analysis of Hayek's subjectivism, see Bruce Caldwell, *Hayek's Challenge: An Intellectual Biography of F.A. Hayek* (Chicago: The University of Chicago Press, 2004), 205–31.

59 Hayek, *Individualism and Economic Order* (Chicago: Gateway, 1972), 87.

60 For a time, Hayek's opposition to rational economic planning and expertise brought about an 'anti-scientism' phase in his work, particularly in his 'Abuse of Reason' project, a text devoted to criticizing socialist planning and the 'slavish imitation of the method and language of Science'. His target was primarily Keynesian regulation, but his critique of scientism and positivism also took aim at the failure by social scientists to conceptualize the subjective, or 'dispersed', information possessed by individuals. For details on this change in Hayek's work, see Mirowski, 'On the Origins (at Chicago) of Some Species of Neoliberal Evolutionary Economics', in *Building Chicago Economics: New Perspectives on the History of America's Most Powerful Economics Program*, edited by Robert Van Horn, Philip Mirowski and Thomas A. Stapleford (Cambridge: Cambridge University Press, 2013), 260–6.

61 For details regarding Karl Popper's influence on Hayek, see Malachi Haim Hacohen, *Karl Popper: The Formative Years, 1902–1945: Politics and Philosophy in Interwar Vienna* (Cambridge: Cambridge University Press, 2000), 449–95.

62 In addition to developments in information theory, Hayek plundered the science of cybernetics to further elaborate the priority of information in economic activity. Cybernetics, which enjoyed numerous waves of development since its origins in the famed 'Macy Conferences' of 1941, is a trans-disciplinary theory that analyses the properties of living and non-living systems. Hayek praised a number of elements

of cybernetic theory and systems theory, particularly its reduction of cognition to mechanism. For details see Mirowski's, *Machine Dreams: Economics Becomes a Cyborg Science* (Cambridge: Cambridge University Press, 2002); Quinn Slobodian, *Globalists: The End of Empire and the Birth of Neoliberalism* (Cambridge: Harvard University Press, 2018); Stephen Beckett, 'Knowledge Conditioned by the Void: On Complexity and the Design Problem', *Design Issues* 36, no. 2 (Spring 2020): 6–17.

63 See Slobodian, *Globalists,* 224–40.

64 Hayek, *The Fatal Conceit: The Errors of Socialism*, edited by W.W. Bartley III (Chicago: University of Chicago Press, 1988), 19.

65 Ibid., 11–47.

66 Adorno, *History and Freedom: Lectures 1964–1965*, edited by Rolf Tiedemann (Cambridge: Polity Press, 2006), 97.

67 Adorno, 'Marx and the Basic Concepts', 8.

68 Adorno, *History and Freedom*, 118.

69 Adorno, *Negative Dialectics,* 315.

70 Ibid., 349

71 Ibid.

72 Adorno, 'Introduction', 64. Translation modified.

73 Adorno, *Negative Dialectics*, 301.

74 For an account that uses Horkheimer and Adorno's critique of reification to theorize the domination of nature in the context of ecological crisis, see Harriet Johnson, 'The Reification of Nature: Reading Adorno in a Warming World', *Constellations* 26 (2019): 318–29.

75 Adorno, *History and Freedom*, 121.

76 For an analysis that draws from Alfred Schmidt's notion of Adorno's conceptual praxis, see Bonefeld, 'Negative Dialectics and the Critique of Economic Objectivity', *History of the Human Sciences* 29, no. 2 (2016): 60–76.

77 Adorno, *Hegel: Three Studies*, translated by Shierry Weber Nicholsen (Cambridge: The MIT Press, 1999), 26.

78 Adorno, *Negative Dialectics*, 347.

79 Max Horkheimer and Theodor Adorno, *Dialectic of Enlightenment: Philosophical Fragments*, translated by Edmund Jecphcott (Stanford: Stanford University Press, 2002), 42.

9

'Society reproduces itself despite the catastrophes that may eventuate': Critical theory, negative totality, and permanent catastrophe

Chris O'Kane

It is a common place to say that the 2008 crisis has led to a revival of interest in Marx, of critical theory with capitalism, and with it the revitalization of socialism. Prominent Marxists and Critical Theorists – such as Leo Panitch, Jason E Moore, Wolfgang Streeck and Nancy Fraser – have argued that the period from 2008 to the present is a crisis of Neoliberalism, or a crisis of neoliberal hegemony, or a general systematic crisis affecting all of the domains of capitalist society. These thinkers have also developed accounts of how these crises provide opportunities for advancing socialism.

This chapter criticizes these traditional Marxist and Habermasian critical theory accounts of the emergence of Neoliberalism, the 2007 crisis, and its aftermath from a perspective that draws on an Adornian approach to critical theory and the critique of political economy. In distinction to the prevalent interpretations of Adorno by traditional Marxists and Habermasian critical theorists, the chapter also develops a critique of these phenomena that draws on Adorno's critique of negative totality and permanent catastrophe.

Part One provides a critical overview of contemporary traditional Marxist and Habermasian critical theory approaches to the emergence of Neoliberalism, the 2007 crisis and its aftermath focusing on Nancy Fraser's synthetic 'crisis critique of capitalism'. Here I show that Fraser's 'crisis critique of capitalism' as

The following substantially revises and updates Chris O'Kane, 'Society Reproduces Itself Despite the Catastrophes That May Eventuate: Critical Theory, Negative Totality and Crisis', *Constellations* 25, no. 2 (2018): 287–301.

an 'institutionalized social order' conceives of the accumulation regimes of 'state managed capitalism', 'financialized capitalism' and their crises as symptomatic of the progressive development of capitalism as a contradictory mode of distribution. According to Fraser, these crises can be resolved by progressive struggles that seek to remedy maldistribution on the road to building a democratic socialist type of distribution.

Since Fraser's theory exemplifies the presuppositions of traditional Marxist and Habermasian Critical Theory, the rest of the chapter turns to developing an Adornian critique of 'Keynesian', 'Neoliberalism' and its aftermath by reconstructing and drawing on his ideas of negative totality and permanent catastrophe. The conclusion uses the Adornian perspective that I have developed to criticize the approaches Fraser exemplifies, arguing that the analysis of Neoliberalism and crises that proceed from traditional Marxist and Habermasian assumptions pass over the regressive development of history while promoting the perpetuation of negative totality and permanent catastrophe. I conclude by considering Adorno's 'pessimism' in an emancipatory light.

I

Time and space prevent a thorough recapitulation of the reception of Marx from 2007 to the present and of the crisis theories associated with this Marx reception.[1] This is also true of critical theories of capitalism and crisis that were developed following the crisis. Nonetheless I will contend that the early reception of Marx and critical theory around 2008, Occupy, the UK student movement, and the movement of the squares drew on secular crises theories to promote spontaneous revolutionary uprisings in reaction to then unfolding social and economic dimensions of the crisis.[2] Following the ebb of this cycle of struggles, and the displacement of bank bailouts into austerity, this reception of Marx and critical theory was superseded by a traditional interpretation of Marx and the development of a number of social democratic and Habermasian theories of crisis that are premised on traditional theoretical presuppositions. Coupled with the pressing issue of climate change, this set the stage for a number of theories of capitalism and crisis that drew on and extended Marx and Polanyi to conceive of Neoliberalism as a 'disembedded' variety of capitalism, profiting from finance, debt and privatization that was instigated by non-democratic market fundamentalist states.[3] Wolfgang Streeck, George Caffentzis, Diane Elson and others drew on this interpretation of Neoliberalism to conceive of the crises of democracy, reproduction and nature that were created by the neoliberal accumulation regime.[4] Others, such as Jason E. Moore, developed synthetic theories of the multiple crisis-tendencies in all of these spheres.[5] Noted critical theorist Nancy Fraser's democratic socialist 'crisis-critique' of capitalism brings together and exemplifies these Marxist and contemporary critical theory interpretations.[6]

Fraser's 'crisis critique' offers an 'expanded' theory of capitalism as an 'institutionalized social order' on a theoretical and historical level. On a theoretical level, capitalism is characterized by a 'foreground' and 'background' relationship between the capitalist economy and reproductive labour and nature. This 'institutionalized social order' is facilitated by the state and results in profits. Yet this process of profit making is also 'crisis prone'. The pursuit of profit is limitless, but the background spheres profits rely on are limited. There is then an inherent tendency for the process of accumulation to impinge upon and destabilize these background spheres, resulting in crises. Crises lead to class and boundary struggles between progressive and regressive forces over how and where the relationship between the foreground and background should be delineated premised on the norms in each of these spheres.[7]

According to Fraser, such a 'crisis prone' accumulation dynamic has unfolded historically in successive 'regimes of accumulation'. Fraser defines a 'regime of accumulation' as 'a relatively stable institutionalized matrix in which the accumulation dynamic is shaped and channelled by a specific organization of its background conditions'.[8] Since, as we have seen, accumulation is premised on a 'contradictory' and 'crisis prone' relationship between capitalism's 'foreground' and 'background' spheres, this means that each 'accumulation regime' consists in historically unique contradictory relationships between the 'foreground' and 'background' spheres. The historically unique contradictory 'foreground' and 'background' relationships in these accumulation regimes have in turn resulted in particular crises in each sphere, which have culminated in 'systematic crises' of each 'accumulation regime'. These systematic crises have led to progressive and regressive class and boundary struggles, which have resulted in the creation of new regimes of accumulation.

Fraser defines the 'accumulation regime' that arose following the Second World War as 'state managed capitalism'. In this 'accumulation regime', the states of the Global North managed their economies, reproductive spheres and regulated nature, resulting in stability, affluence and legitimacy. Starting in the late 1960s, the contradictory relationship between the foreground and the background that typified 'state managed capitalism' culminated in economic, political, reproductive and ecological crises. This led to the systematic crisis of 'state managed capitalism', and a period of struggles, typified by the New Social Movements and the New Right, that resulted in the new 'accumulation regime' of 'financialized capitalism'.

'Financialized capitalism' profited from globalization, financialization and debt. This 'accumulation regime' was created by undemocratic transnational forms of governance. 'Financialized capitalism' was premised on the two-family wage, household debt and the financialization of nature. This contradictory relationship between the 'foreground' and the 'background', which typifies 'Financialized Capitalism', resulted in economic crises, crises of legitimacy in the political sphere, a crisis of care in the reproductive sphere, and the ecological crisis. Taken together, all of these separate crises have culminated in the 'general crisis of financialized capitalism'. According to Fraser, 'the general crisis of financialized capitalism' led to the rise of regressive Neoliberalism exemplified by Trump. Fraser further holds that 'regressive Neoliberalism' should be contested by a progressive alliance of productive and reproductive workers, who pressure the state, on the basis of sphere specific norms and the balance of class forces to enact more democratic types of governance and equitable distribution, overcoming these crises, on the road towards building an 'expanded' conception of socialism.

My contention is that the Marxist and Habermasian theories of capitalism, crisis, and socialism that Fraser draws on and exemplify rely on traditional interpretations of Marx and critical theory. This is because, as I have indicated, these theories of capitalism, crisis and socialism essentially amount to a critique of capitalism as a mode of distribution from an expanded standpoint of labor.[9] Productive and reproductive labour creates all the wealth. Crises are caused by the progressive historical development of the contradiction between production and distribution. While productivity has continued to develop, the capitalist maldistribution of the proceeds of labour has taken place in different historical configurations that have led to crises. The current systematic crisis of 'financialized capitalism' (or Neoliberalism) is a conjunctural expression of these contradictions. Yet this general crisis also provides an opening and should be resolved in a progressive manner by struggles that are intended to tip the balances of forces so that the state is compelled to issue fairer distributive policies on the road to building a democratic socialist type of distribution. While such a democratic socialist type of distribution would undoubtedly be more equal than ours, such a notion of capitalism, crisis and socialism imply the perpetuation of capitalist society on the basis of these traditional theoretical ideas.

II

These Marxist and Habermasian theories raise the question whether an approach to critical theory and Marx that follows Adorno could critique 'Keynesianism', 'Neoliberalism', and its aftermath on the basis of a critical theory of capitalist crisis that doesn't rest on traditional theoretical presuppositions that unwittingly promote the perpetuation of capitalist society. Surprisingly, apart from the work of Fabian Arzuaga, Charles Prusik, Carl Casegaard and Christos Memos, such an option has either been discounted or dismissed by the Marx revival and contemporary critical theory.[10] This is no doubt due to one of the shibboleths prevalent in the Anglophone literature on Adorno; that *Dialectic of Enlightenment* marked the point when Adorno discarded the Marxian foundation of his critical theory of society for a trans-historical theory of instrumental reason in which a totally administered state capitalist society had overcome capitalism's crisis tendencies, leading to a pessimistic one-dimension social theory with no emancipatory basis.[11] This line of interpretation certainly leads Anita Chari[12] and Amy Kim,[13] in their works on critical theory, capitalism, and crisis, to the conclusion that, at the very least, Adorno would have little to say about the 2008 economic crisis, or to the stronger claim that his account of Keynesian stability and integration is anachronistic to Neoliberalism.

There is some evidence to support this interpretation of Adorno's late critical theory. Comments in the *Dialectic of Enlightenment*, coupled with the noted absence of Marxian crisis theory, can be seen as drawing on Pollock's analysis.[14] Moreover, as Adorno's work on the culture industry and administration attests his critical theory of mid-twentieth-century capitalist society certainly consisted in criticizing the state management of the economy, culture and the integration of classes into mass society. Finally, Adorno's equivocal comments about 'proto-comical' immiseration, Marx's theory of final crisis, and 'the direction of economic processes… passing into the hands of political power',[15] in 'Late Capitalism or Industrial Society?' can be read as abandoning Marx's theory of crisis and following Pollock's analysis of state capitalism nearly thirty years later.

Yet there is also a strand of Adorno's work that cuts against this interpretation. As James Schmidt[16] Deborah Cook[17] and Adorno himself in 'Reflections on Class Theory'[18] point out, Adorno never agreed with Pollock's contention that capitalism's crisis tendencies had been overcome. Moreover, as Hans-Georg Backhaus and Werner Bonefeld have shown,[19] Adorno developed an interpretation of the critique of political economy in the 1960s that was distinct from traditional Marxism, and was central to his critical theory of this era.

Finally, the discussions of Adorno's abandonment of crisis theory refrain from discussing the notions of 'negative universal history', 'permanent crisis', and 'permanent catastrophe' Adorno developed that were intended to capture the trajectory of the historical development of the negative totality of capitalist society from the emancipatory perspective he is alleged to have abandoned.

In what follows, I reconstruct Adorno's late critical theory of negative totality and permanent catastrophe and adapt such a critical theory to critique 'Neoliberalism', the 2007 crisis and its aftermath. I begin by focusing on how Adorno's critical theory is premised on an interpretation of the critique of political economy that is distinct from classical Marxism and Lukács. I then draw on Adorno's interpretation of the critique of political economy to reconstruct Adorno's critical theory of negative totality and permanent catastrophe. This leads me to show how Adorno's critical theory of negative totality and permanent catastrophe are at the heart of his critique of late capitalism. Finally, I draw on Adorno's critical theory of negative totality and permanent catastrophe to critique 'Neoliberalism', the 2007 crisis, and our present moment.

III

Classical Marxism, following Engels, believed that a dialectical process of progressive development linked society and nature. Once again following Engels, Classical Marxism placed the origins of class society in the creation of private property, the ensuing production of surplus by the propertyless and the appropriation of surplus by the property owners. Classical Marxism further held that history was characterized by the contradictory development of the forces and relations of production, which progressed through successive historical stages. In capitalism these contradictions would come to a head, culminating in an emancipatory final crisis. The development of the productive forces would create the collective worker yet immiserate proletarians who would band together, rise up, and seize the means of production, instituting the dictatorship of the proletariat and replacing the capitalist mode of exploitative distribution with the socialist mode of distribution.[20]

The final crisis predicted by classical Marxism did not come about. Instead classical Marxism itself fell into crisis after the splintering of the Second International and worker's support for their nations in the First World War. Lukacs's theory of reification, which synthesized classical Marxism with the Hegelian conception of consciousness and totality, was intended to overcome this crisis of class consciousness.[21] According to Lukács, the proletariat created the social totality. But the proletariat was separated from the totality they created due to the capitalist process of appropriation. This process of appropriation was veiled by the anarchy of the market. However, the privileged epistemological standpoint of the proletariat would allow them to pierce this reified veil. On this basis, the proletariat would grasp themselves as the subject and object of history and the creators of totality. This would lead to the revolutionary seizure of totality and the supplanting of the capitalist mode of distribution with the socialist mode of distribution.

Adorno's interpretation of Marx was premised on a critique of classical Marxism and Lukács. In contrast to classical Marxism, Adorno held that the antagonistic organization of society had emerged for historically contingent reasons and was premised on the domination of external and internal nature. Rather than escaping from natural history, humanity had become imprisoned in second nature. The development of the productive forces and the persistence of class antagonism through the different stages of history were not necessary for the emergence of socialism. Nor was the final crisis of capitalism, necessary or inevitable. The historical development of society was tantamount to a natural history of social domination. Society's further development consisted in regression rather than progress.

Moreover, in contrast to Lukács, Adorno held that capitalist society is a negativity totality. Society is object and subject rather than the proletariat. Hence, dialectics does not disclose the emancipatory standpoint of labour. Rather negative dialectics discloses how object and subject reinforce each other due to the antagonistic organization of capitalist society, resulting in the perpetuation of capitalist society. Consequently, in contrast to classical Marxism and Lukács, Adorno's critical theory deciphered natural history as a negative universal history culminating in the negative totality of capitalist society with the aim of breaking the identification of subject and object and awakening a global subject that would spontaneously negate negative totality.[22]

It is from this vantage point that we can reconstruct Adorno's interpretation of the critique of political economy, crisis theory, capitalism as a negative totality and history as permanent catastrophe.

IV

This is because the constitution and reproduction of capitalist society as a negative totality is articulated on the basis of Adorno's interpretation of the critique of political economy. Society is 'subjective because it refers back to the human beings who create it'.[23] 'Society is objective because, on account of its underlying structure, it cannot perceive its own subjectivity, because it does not possess a total subject and through its organization it thwarts the installation of such a subject.' [24] Society's 'underlying structure' is created by the aggregate activity of production for profit carried out by the antagonistic capital relation within the capitalist social division of labour who collectively create the emergent phenomena of the exchange abstraction. Consequently, as Adorno states, since 'society is a system in the sense of a synthesis of an atomized plurality' the 'shabby permanency in the constitution of society itself' is 'the universal development of the exchange system' which 'largely endows the system with a mechanical character'.[25] The 'objective rationality of society, namely that of exchange'[26] also requires 'everyone to respect the law of exchange if he does not wish to be destroyed, irrespective of whether profit is his subjective motivation or not'.[27] This objective coercive reality thus 'reduc[es] humans into agents and bearers of commodity exchange'.[28]

Adorno further characterizes the dynamic of this process of reproduction on the basis of his understanding of Marx's theories of accumulation and crisis. For, a 'dialectical theory of society concerns itself with structural laws... tendencies, which more or less stringently follow the historical constitution of the total system. The Marxist models for this were the law of value, the law of accumulation, the law of economic crisis.'[29] Thus, as Adorno states, 'Whether or not capitalist society will be impelled towards its collapse, as Marx asserted... is one of the most important questions with which the social sciences ought to concern themselves.'[30] However, Adorno's answer to this question distinguishes him from the classical Marxist and Lukácsian emancipatory theory of crisis, while also further going against the dominant interpretation of his later critical theory. For, as he states in regard to the importance of the exchange abstraction for critical theory, the model of a dialectical concept of a general law of social reproduction

> would be Marx's law of crisis – even if it has become so obscured as to be
> unrecognizable – which was deduced from the tendency of the rate of profit to
> fall. Its modifications, for their part, should also be derived from it. The efforts
> to ward off or postpone the system immanent tendency are already prescribed
> within the system.[31]

Crucially, as this implies, Adorno conceived of these system immanent tendencies as inherent to his interpretation of the critique of political economy and his conception of capitalist society as an objective–subjective negative totality.

Accordingly, for Adorno, contra traditional Marxism, the exchange abstraction is not a distributive veil created by the anarchy of the market. Not is capitalism a mode of maldistribution. Rather the antagonistic organization of society necessarily appears in the exchange abstraction, which is objective and subjective and possesses socially objective and supraindividual properties that mutually mediate the other spheres of capitalist society, compelling individuals and shaping subjectivity. Following Adorno, such a negative totality is

> understood a sort of linking structure between human beings in which everything and everyone depend on everyone and everything; the whole is only sustained by the unity of the functions fulfilled by all its members, and each single one of these members is in principle assigned such a function, while at the same time each individual is determined to a great degree by his membership in this total structure.[32]

Consequently, there is a 'negative unity of society in unfreedom'. The economy, state, law, administration and the family are moments in capitalist society that mutually mediate exchange, and individuals are compelled and socialized by it so that 'totality is pre-established for all individual subjects' leading them to 'obey its "contrainte" even in themselves'. In this purview, since capitalist society, 'is just as much founded' in the subject 'as it comprehends and constitutes them'[33] the reduction of individuals to 'character masks', following the imperative of 'self-preservation', is reflected in the formation of 'maimed' subjectivity. Hence 'The society based on domination has not simply robbed itself and human beings – its compulsory members – of dignity, but rather it has never permitted them to become ... emancipated beings.'[34] Instead, the overwhelming majority of individuals not only 'tolerate relations of domination' but 'identify themselves with them and are motivated towards irrational attitudes by them'.[35] Consequently, their 'real impotence' and reliance on the system is 'consciously realized in an authoritarian mental attitude'.[36] In moments of crises, rather than negating the system, individuals thus tend to support strong leaders and the state who act to reinforce the system and perpetuate negative totality.

Yet such an interpretation of capitalism did not lead Adorno to abandon an emancipatory theory. Rather Adorno's interpretation of capitalism informed his negative dialectical alternative to crisis theory, which he termed 'negative universal history', 'permanent crisis' or 'permanent catastrophe'. As we have seen, for Adorno contra traditional Marxism, historical development was not progressive but regressive. Rather than leading to an emancipatory final crisis, the development of the productive forces had led to domination, integration,

authoritarian subjectivity and the perpetuation of capitalist society. On
this basis, Adorno held that 'the crucial contribution to a theory of history
is to be found in the idea that mankind preserves itself not despite all the
irrationalities and conflicts, but by virtue of them'.[37] Consequently, 'universal
history should be construed and denied'[38] as that of a permanent crisis or
the catastrophic 'teleology' of 'suffering'[39] due to the perpetuation of the
antagonism and domination that has culminated in the negative totality of
capitalist society. However, in contrast to what prominent Adorno scholars
contend, the construal of such a negative universal history was not intended
to affirm pessimism, nor discard an emancipatory basis, but to espouse one.
By construing the development of capitalism as that of a permanent crisis and
catastrophe, Adorno intended to demonstrate that it is not maldistribution,
or moments of crisis, that typify the suffering capitalism incurs, but its very
organization. In so doing, Adorno hoped to break 'the spell' of second nature,
demonstrating how the negative objectivity of society was perpetuated by
antagonistic subjectivity, in the hopes of awakening the 'global subject' that
would negate such a society.

As this demonstrates, rather than abandoning the critique of political
economy, Adorno's conceptions of negative totality and permanent catastrophe
are grounded on his interpretation of Marx.

V

Adorno's critical theory of negative totality and permanent catastrophe, in
turn informs Adorno's critical theory of historical development, which can be
seen in his critique of late capitalism. Here mirroring his critical theoretical
interpretation of Marx, Adorno held that 'modifications' to the historical
dynamic of accumulation had counteracted crises, leading to the perpetuation
of capitalist society as a negative totality. Yet such an analysis of late capitalism
does not lead Adorno to abandon emancipation, but informs his emancipatory
critique of the perpetuation of capitalism as that of permanent catastrophe.

Adorno's critique of late capitalism thus held that the transformations in mid-
twentieth-century industrial society – amounting to Fordist mass production and
the 'Keynesian' state management of the economy – derive from and modify the
process of accumulation and reproduction leading to stability and integration,
counteracting immiseration and crises. For, as Adorno goes on to state, 'the
resources that capitalism had discovered to postpone economic collapse' were
numerous and primarily consisted of what he terms 'industrial society'. Chief

among these were the large labour force required by 'Fordist' models of mass production coupled with the state's management of the economy, which acted as what he called 'the system-immanent embodiment of self-defense' against crises by assuring an adequate level of effective demand. The Fordist model of mass production thus assured unprecedented levels of mass employment and high wages. Moreover, the state management of the economy not only consisted of the welfare state, policies of full employment and price fixing, but also the military Keynesianism of the Cold War, which helped maintain the relations of production without 'the apocalyptic earthquake of renewed economic crises' by assuring that an inordinate and unsaleable share of the social product not met by the aforementioned welfare policies was dedicated to 'the production of the means of destruction'.[40] Finally, Adorno states that exploitative international relations between the industrial nations and developing countries were a displaced political realization of class struggle.

From this it follows that Adorno characterizes late capitalist economy and industrial society as elements of the objective–subjective exchange mediated reproduction of negative capitalist totality. For the 'the all-penetrating ether of society' consists in 'the exchange-relationships, the objective abstractions, which belongs to the social life-process' of accumulation. Hence 'The economic process continues to perpetuate domination over human beings' because '[p]roduction goes on today just as it did before, for the sake of profits'.[41] Consequently, on the objective level:

Society has developed itself into a [negative] totality due to the fact that modes of procedure, which resemble the industrial ones, are extending by economic necessity into the realms of material production, into administration, the distribution-sphere and that which we call culture.[42]

Therefore, on the subjective level, the power of the exchange 'abstraction over humanity is far more corporeal than that of any single institution, which silently constitutes itself in advance according to the scheme of things and beats itself into human beings' so that 'The objects of such are no longer merely the masses, but also the administrators and their hangers-on'.[43]

From this it follows that:

[i]f the theory of immiseration was not borne out of à la lettre [to the letter], then it certainly has in the no less frightening sense, that unfreedom, one's dependence on the consciousness of those who serve an uncontrollable apparatus, is spreading universally over humanity… like in mythology, it confronts them as fate [Schicksal].[44]

Consequently, revolutionary class-consciousness had not arisen. Instead in adapting 'themselves to the constitution of the machines which they serve' individuals have been 'compelled to assume the roles of the social mechanism and to model themselves on such, without reservation, on the level of their most intimate impulses'.[45] Consequently, individuals 'are as little as ever autonomous masters of their lives'. Rather, the maiming of subjectivity inherent to this subjective–objective dynamic means 'the kernel of individuation is beginning to come apart', as is 'the rationality of the fixed, identical ego'.[46] Hence rather than developing class consciousness, late capitalism has resulted in the formation of the 'authoritarian mental attitude' and the possibility of authoritarianism arising from within democratic societies above, in which '[s]ubjective regression favors once again the regression of the system'.[47]

As a result, Adorno's critical theory of late capitalism does not promote the further development of the productive forces, nor of increased distribution on the road towards socialism. Rather since everything is 'equally close to the midpoint'[48] in the negative totality of capitalist society, and history has developed in a regressive manner, this would promote the further domination and misery, the perpetuation of integration, and the reproduction of negative totality as a permanent catastrophe. Instead Adorno points towards reducing social objectivity to the antagonistic relations that perpetuate it, in order to break 'the spell' of integration, and awaken a 'global subject' that will negate negative totality.

Rather than a pessimistic one-dimensional theory of instrumental reason, Adorno's late critical theory thus consists in an emancipatory critique of capitalism as permanent catastrophe that draws on his interpretation of the critique of political economy. On this basis his critique of late capitalism does not consist in a one-dimensional trans-historical theory of instrumental reason with no emancipatory basis but of an emancipatory critique of the perpetuation of the negative totality of capitalist society as permanent catastrophe. This raises the possibility that, contra the prevalent interpretation of Adorno, Adorno's thought could critique 'Neoliberalism'. However, for this to be the case it would still need to be shown that Adorno's theory is compatible with the transformations that purportedly separate 'Keynesianism' and 'Neoliberalism' as distinct accumulation regimes, which serve as the premise for relegating Adorno's critical theory to the former.

VI

Luckily, showing that Adorno's critical theory can critique these 'Neoliberal' transformations as the continuation of permanent catastrophe is not as formidable as it sounds. In the first place, it should be noted that Adorno stated in the introduction to *The Positivist Dispute* that it 'is by no means certain that' that the 'efforts' detailed in 'Late Capitalism' 'to ward off or postpone the system immanent tendency' to crisis, efforts which 'are already prescribed within the system', are 'possible indefinitely', for 'such efforts' also 'enact the law of crisis against their own will'.[49] At this point in 1968, he even went so far as to suggest that 'writing on the wall suggests a slow inflationary collapse'.[50] In the second place, Adorno gestured towards a dialectic development of 'disintegration through growing integration'.[51] He also tied these incipient objective and subjective socio-economic developments to the growing support for right-wing parties.[52] Here Adorno argued that fears of inflation, automation, and unemployment were leading to an impending sense of superfluity in people with petit bourgeois structures of subjectivity. Yet in a regressive inversion of 'Marx's theory of collapse', he argued that such a sense of impending 'social catastrophe' and 'doom', led to the embrace of right-wing parties who reinforced the system, the scapegoating of socialism and antisemitism, and resentment against those who do not conform. Taking these comments together with my reconstruction of Adorno's critical theory, I will thus sketch an Adornian critique of Neoliberalism, not as a distinct accumulation regime, but as the perpetuation of negative totality and the continuation of permanent catastrophe, resulting from the 'modifications' that 'derived' from and 'counteracted' the crisis prone historical dynamic of capital accumulation.

In this light, the very technological developments Adorno discussed in 'Late Capitalism' led to overaccumulation and the inflation he indicated, laying the groundwork for an economic slowdown in the early 1970s, which, following ineffective government intervention marked the end of the 'Keynesian' golden age. The ensuing efforts to revive the global economy meant that late capitalism's counteracting modifications – technology, state policy, and relations between the Global North and South – took on new roles in the process of valorization and the ensuing trajectory of accumulation. A state-led attack on unions coupled with the introduction of lean technology in the Global North, outsourcing, and waves of primitive accumulation in Asia lead to declining wages, the emergence of surplus populations, the generation of waves of profits, and the subsequent rapid and pronounced polarization of wealth. These state-administered economic policies were coupled with the transformation of welfare provisions and tax laws. These developments and policies were able to revive profits, but they also led to the unintended consequence of the increased importance of debt and 'speculative investment channeled through the world's financial institutions'[53] for insuring accumulation and reproduction.

However, while the roles of technology, state policy, and global relations were qualitatively different from Adorno's account of late capitalism, they were still in line with my reconstruction of Adorno's critical theory of negative totality insofar as they were derived from this process of capitalist reproduction, counteracting crises tendencies and reproducing capitalism albeit in a time in which cycles of boom and bust have reasserted themselves. In other words, these 'Neoliberal' modifications much like their 'Keynesian' forefathers were indeed efforts that derived from the system, warding off and postponing the system-immanent tendency to crisis until they culminated in another crisis against their own will.

Moreover, just like 'Keynesianism', 'Neoliberalism' could not overcome the crisis tendencies of accumulation. The last several decades have been marked by boom-and-bust cycles that have engendered rising inequality and increased levels of debt. The 2007 crisis did not rupture these tendencies; it only magnified them. Bailouts laid the foundations for an official recovery, yet austerity measures led to pronounced misery and a decade of weak and uneven recovery.

Yet these crises were not the grounds of progressive struggles or emancipation, but led to further state measures to revive the economy, declining standards of living, the further embrace of right-wing populism and the perpetuation of domination and misery. Certainly, as we have seen, the 2007 crises led to contentions that Neoliberalism was in crisis and that Marx (and maybe even socialism itself) was back. Indeed, the erosion of the material conditions of so many and the wave of progressive populist anti-austerity movements in the West in the wake of the 2008 (such as Occupy) lent these analyses credibility. So did the ascendance of Syriza, Corbyn, Sanders and democratic socialism. Yet the class-in-itself never became the class-for-itself; Syriza quickly embraced Neoliberalism, Corbyn and Sanders lost. Here, as Adorno anticipated, it does indeed seem to be the case that the maiming of individual subjectivity he analysed as inherent to the dynamic of 'disintegration through growing integration' fostered reliance on the very processes that maimed it. At the same time, in the regressive inversion of 'Marx's theory of collapse' those with a petit bourgeois structure of subjectivity, who felt threatened by the social catastrophe of restructuring and automation embraced strong leaders that promised to reinforce the system rather than do away with it. Hence the flowering and electoral success of right-wing populist movements that advocated reinforcing the former, in its 'Neoliberal' form, while holding socialism and marginalized scapegoats to account for its miseries. Profits were thus restored by the persistence of 'neoliberal policies' that exacerbated inequality and misery and scapegoating migrants rather than through radical democratic process of reform.

As a consequence, an Adornian critical theory of negative totality and permanent catastrophe does not understand 'Keynesianism' and 'Neoliberalism' to be antithetical, nor even distinct types of capitalism. Instead, both are understood to be ways in which negative totality counteracted capitalism's crisis-ridden dynamic of accumulation and reproduction. The former may have achieved a higher standard of living for some, but it does not represent a golden age to which we ought to aspire. Nor was the latter an elite-driven market-fundamentalist policy of deregulation. Rather, 'Keynesianism' represented one failed attempt to overcome capitalism's crisis-ridden dynamic, 'Neoliberalism' another. In both cases, domination, antagonism and misery persisted. Hence rather than forming distinct accumulation regimes, that reflect different balances of class forces, 'Keynesianism' consisted in the integration and depoliticization of the worker's movement, 'Neoliberalism' consists in continued integration in the context of a disintegration in living standards, leading to left and right efforts to remedy disintegration via integration. Thus rather than their crises marking opportunities for progressive struggles, Keynesianism, Neoliberalism and their crisis exemplify the permanence of catastrophe.

Conclusion

The 2008 crisis may have led to a revival of Marxism, critical theories of capitalism and the left. Yet despite the proliferation of crisis theories premised on the former and the latter, right-wing authoritarian populism has succeeded where the socialist alternative has failed.

This chapter has offered a critique of these crisis theories as premised on traditional Marxist and traditional theoretical conceptions of capitalism, crises and historical development. It has also provided a reconstruction and development of an Adornian critical theory of negative totality and permanent catastrophe. Part One focused on the theoretical and historical components of Nancy Fraser's synthetic 'crisis critique' of capitalism as an 'institutionalized social order'. Here it was shown that on a theoretical level Fraser draws on an array of traditional Marxist and Habermasian critical theorists to provide an expanded conception of the crisis prone dynamic of accumulation and emancipatory struggles. It was also demonstrated how Fraser drew on this theoretical framework to conceive of the contradictory but progressive historical development of accumulation regimes and systematic crises, with 'state managed capitalism' being supplanted by 'financialized capitalism' leading the general crisis of our contemporary moment as an opening to advance the struggle for an expanded idea of democratic socialism. The second half of the paper turned to developing an Adornian conception of the negative totality of capitalist society and of its historical development as one of permanent catastrophe. Despite the revival of interest in Marx and the critical theory of capitalism such a perspective has been largely eschewed due to a number of shibboleths in the influential secondary literature on Adorno, eradicating the centrality of his interpretation of the critique of political economy and his emanciaptory notion of permanent catastrophe from his critical social theory, relegating Adorno to a pessmistic Weberian critic of Fordism. Yet my ensuing reconstruction of Adorno's late critical theory demonstrated how he drew on the critique of political economy to conceive of the negative totality of late capitalist society, and how his idea of permanent catastrophe drew on his modified interpretation of Marx's crisis theory. Finally, I showed how these Adornian ideas were reflected in his analysis of late capitalism and could be extended to our present.

This leaves us with two distinct approaches to Marx and to critical theory. The traditional Marxist and Habermasian approach exemplified by Fraser conceives of crises as caused by the maldistribution of the proceeds of labour due to the contradictory capitalist organization of the relationship between the productive and distributive spheres of modern society. Yet these approaches also see crises as contradictory opportunities to restore profitability in a progressive manner via the balance of class forces that will drive history towards the democratic socialist organization of distribution. In this perspective crisis critique entails a critique of the maldistribution of the proceeds of labour from the perspective of their just distribution. The Adornian approach, on the other hand, conceives of the antagonistic organization of capitalist society as a negative totality replete with domination and suffering. Rather than viewing history as the progressive contradictory development of the productive forces, it sees historical development as a negative universal history. Rather than viewing crises as stemming from the contradictory capitalist process of distribution, it conceives of the perpetuation of capitalism as permanent catastrophe. In this perspective, crises do not provide openings for socialism through their resolution via class struggle. Rather their resolution tends to promote authoritarianism. But even if crises lead to progressive measures, they nonetheless reproduce negative totality. Consequently, the class struggle should not be advanced towards the socialist configuration of modern society, for this would merely prolong capitalism.

Instead, negative critique seeks to break the spell of progress by construing and denying universal history and awakening a global subject that will abolish negative totality. Only this will lead to the escape from nature and the beginning of progress.

From this perspective, the current crisis being bandied about as a crisis of capitalism, a crisis of Neoliberalism, or a crisis of neoliberal legitimacy is a contest over the way in which the state should manage the world economy. Democratic socialism and right-wing authoritarianism are simply different ways to manage the crisis-ridden process of accumulation and reproduction. The former is certainly more desirable than the latter. But even, against all odds, if democratic socialism somehow manages to achieve electoral success worldwide, it will do so by co-opting a progressive social movement. If it likewise, against further odds, is able to drive a government agenda and implement successful redistributive and regulatory policies, this will also broaden the scope of the state and diminish people's autonomy and solidarity. What is more, it will not abolish exploitation, antagonism or domination. Nor will it be effective. Even if the current crisis were to be resolved, another crisis will arise. More importantly the permanent catastrophe will continue.

Such a picture of society and historical development will no doubt seem pessimistic to those who follow the new interpretations of Marx and critical theory and advocate for democratic socialism. Pessimism is indeed the classic charge against Adorno's critical theory. Yet an important distinction has to be made between pessimism and negativity. For the critical theory of society would not be critical of society if it simply held this is the way things are and will continue to be. That would simply be a fatalistic theory of human nature, which would certainly lead to pessimism. But fatalism and pessimism are different than a theory that accentuates the negativity of our capitalist society. In fact, they are the opposite. Negative critique aims to liberate us from a society in which we are fated to work, to suffer, to be miserable, to revile, instrumentalize and act antagonistically towards others, nature and ourselves in order to merely survive. Negative critique does so by showing how the social relations and institutions that make up our present society manifest themselves in this manner. In so doing, negative critique points to the necessity of the emancipatory abolition of these social relations and institutions in order to end the fate that befalls us in this social reality of permanent catastrophe and holds that this process can happen at any time. For a society premised on freedom and human flourishing will not come about by democratically redistributing the proceeds of toil and misery of our unfree society. That is a pessimistic vision of socialism and liberation and it points to the validity of critical theory in a time when 'humanity must and will, certainly *will*, continue to be oppressed until the question of material needs has been resolved' this 'will be decided solely by the avoidance of a calamity through the rational organization of society as a whole in a manner befitting humanity'.[54]

Notes

1   For an overview of the different Marxian explanations of the 2007 crisis, see Riccardo Bellofiore and Giovanna Vertova (ed.), *Contradictions of Contemporary Capitalism* (London: Edward Elgar, 2014) and David Bailey, Mónica Clua-Losada, Nikolia Huke and Olatz Ribera-Almandoz, *Beyond Defeat and Austerity: Disrupting (the Critical Political Economy of) Neoliberal Empire* (London: Routledge, 2018).

2   Notable examples of these ideas in Marxist theory include *Endnotes*, Paul Mattick, Jr., *Business as Usual: The Economic Crisis and the Failure of Capitalism* (London: Reaktion Books, 2011) and Nick Dyer-Witherford, *Cyberproletariat: Global Labour in the Digital Vortex* (London: Pluto Press, 2015). In Critical Theory these notions of crisis and spontaneity were reflected in Amy Kim, 'The Vicissitudes of Critique: The Decline and Reemergence of the Problem of Capitalism', *Constellations* 21 (2014): 366–81 and Anita Chari, *A Political Economy of the Senses: Neoliberalism, Reification, Critique* (New York: Columbia University Press, 2015).

3   See David Harvey, *The Enigma of Capital: And the Crisis of Capitalism* (New York: Oxford University Press, 2011); Greg Albo, Sam Gindin and Leo Panitch, *In and Out of Crisis: The Global Financial Meltdown and Left Alternatives* (Berkeley: PM Press, 2010); Wolfgang Streeck, *Buying Time: The Delayed Crisis of Democratic Capitalism* (London: Verso, 2017).

4   See Wolfgang Streeck, *Buying Time: The Delayed Crisis of Democratic Capitalism* (London: Verso, 2017); George Caffentzis, 'On the Notion of a Crisis of Social Reproduction: A Theoretical View', *The Commoner* no. 5 (Autumn 2002): 1–22; Diane Elson, 'Social Reproduction in the Global Crisis: Rapid Recovery or Long-Lasting Depletion?', in *The Global Crisis and Transformative Social Change*, edited by Peter Utting, Shahra Razavi and Rebecca Verghese Bucholz (London: Springer, 2012); Jason E. Moore, 'The Capitalocence, Part I: On the Nature and Origins of our Ecological Crisis', *The Journal of Peasant Studies* 44 (2017): 594–630.

5   Jason E. Moore, *Capitalism in the Web of Life: Ecology and the Accumulation of Capital* (London: Verso, 2015).

6   Fraser's theory is synthetic and exemplary of these Marxian and Habermasian Critical theories of capitalism and crisis for a number of reasons: (1) Fraser's theory mirrors and synthesizes the Marxian and Habermasian theories of capitalism

that are being developed by figures such as Moore and Honneth by drawing on and synthesizing the work of prominent Marxist scholars and approaches (such as Immanuel Wallerstein, Jason E. Moore, Ellen Meiksins Wood, David Harvey, Silvia Federici and Maria Mies) and Habermasian critical theorists (such as Jurgen Habermas, Wolfgang Streck and James O'Connor). (2) Fraser has also developed her theory in Marx and Habermasian critical theory publications (such as *New Left Review*, *Socialist Register*, and Polity). In addition, Fraser's latest formulation of crisis-critique were put forward in books co-authored with leading figures from these discourses and pitched to these different audiences; *Capitalism: a Conversation in Critical Theory* was co-authored with Rahel Jaeggi, *Feminism for the 99 %* was co-authored with leading Marxist theorists Cinzia Arruzia and Tithi Bhattacharya, and *The Old Is Dying and the New Cannot Be Born* consists in a conversation with the publisher of *Jacobin*, Bhaskar Sunkara.

7   For a detailed reconstruction and critique of Fraser's theory see Chris O'Kane, 'Critical Theory and the Critique of Capitalism: an Immanent Critique of Nancy Fraser's Crisis-Critique of Capitalism ass an Institutionalized Social Order', *Science & Society* 85, no. 2 (2021): 207–35.

8   Nancy Fraser and Rahel Jaeggi, *Capitalism: A Conversation in Critical Theory* (Cambridge: Polity, 2018), 65.

9   See Chapter 5 in this volume.

10   Fabian Arzuaga, 'Socially Necessary Superfluity: Adorno and Marx on the Crises of Labor and the Individual', *Philosophy and Social Criticism* 45, no. 7 (2018): 819–43.; Charles Prusik, *Adorno and Neoliberalism: The Critique of Exchange Society* (London: Bloomsbury, 2020); Carl Cassegård, *Toward a Critical Theory of Nature: Capital, Ecology and Dialectics* (London: Bloomsbury, 2021); Christos Memos, *Global Economic Crises as Social Hieroglyph: Genesis, Constitution and Regressive Progress* (London: Palgrave Macmillan, 2021).

11   Chari rightly deems such an account 'familiar' as it repeated by leading scholars in the field. See Jürgen Habermas, *Theory of Communicative Action*, vol. 1 (Boston: Beacon Press, 1985) (particularly chapter 4 339–403) *Theory of Communicative Action*, vol. 2 (Oxford and Cambridge: Polity, 1992) (particularly chapter VI 113–99 and VIII) 301–405); 'Excursus on the Obsolescence of the Production Paradigm and The Entwinement of Myth and Enlightenment: Max Horkheimer and Theodor Adorno', in Jürgen Habermas, *Philosophical Discourse of Modernity: Twelve Lectures;* Perry Anderson *Considerations on Western Marxism* (London: Verso, 1976); Martin Jay, M*arxism and Totality: The Adventures of a Concept from Lukács to Habermas* (Berkeley, CA: University of California Press, 1984); Martin Jay, *Adorno* (Cambridge, MA: Harvard University Press, 1984); Ralf Wiggershaus, *The Frankfurt School: Its History, Theory and Political Significance*, New ed. (Cambridge: Polity Press, 1995). Andrew Arato and Eike Gephardt Ed, *The Essential Frankfurt School*

Reader (London: Continuum, 1997). Andrew Feenberg, *The Philosophy of Praxis: Marx, Lukács and the Frankfurt School*, Revised ed. (Brooklyn: Verso, 2014).

12 Chari's interpretation of Adorno's late critical theory in tandem with her periodization of neoliberalism as historically distinct from Fordism leads her to presuppose the irrelevance of Adorno's theory of Fordist capitalism, and by extension, his critique of capitalist society, for neoliberal capitalism.

13 Kim notes early critical theory's account of capitalism and crisis in regard to its analysis of fascism. However, due to her reading of Habermas and Postone's work as responses to *Dialectic of Enlightenment's* trans-historical theory of instrumental reason, in accordance with her secular reading of the crisis, she forecloses the possibility of turning to Adorno's later work.

14 See, for instance, the statement that 'the conscious decisions of the company chairmen execute capitalism's old law of value' (Max Horkheimer and Theodor W. Adorno, *Dialectic of Enlightenment* (London: Continuum, 1969), 30.

15 Theodor W. Adorno, *Late Capitalism or Industrial Society?* (1968). D. Redmond (trans.). Retrieved from https://www.marxists. org/reference/archive/adorno/1968/late-capitalism.htm

16 As Schmidt puts it: 'Adorno was unconvinced by Pollock's vision of a society that, having transformed the crises that plagued earlier forms of capitalism into "mere problems of administration," could hold out "the promise of security and a more abundant life for every subject who submits voluntarily and completely." Though he conceded that Pollock might be correct in his pessimistic assessment of the ubiquity of political domination throughout history, he rejected what he characterized as Pollock's optimistic belief that the new order would be any more stable than the one it replaced. He saw such a conclusion as resting on the "undialectical assumption that in an antagonistic society a non-antagonistic economy would be possible." What Pollock had produced struck him as an inversion of Kafka: "Kafka presented the hierarchy of bureaucrats as Hell. Here Hell transforms itself into a hierarchy of bureaucrats." James Schmidt, Racket, monopoly, and the *Dialectic of Enlightenment* (2016). Retrieved from http://nonsite. org/ the-tank/max-horkheimer-and-the-sociology-of-class-relations

17 Deborah Cook, 'Adorno on Late Capitalism', *Radical Philosophy* 89 (1998): 16–26.

18 Theodor W. Adorno, 'Reflections on Class Theory', in *Can One Live after Auschwitz?: A Philosophical Reader*, edited by T.W. Adorno and R. Tiedemann (Stanford, CA: Stanford University Press, 2003), 93–110.

19 See Hans-Georg Backhaus. 'Between Philosophy and Science: Marxian Social Economy as Critical Theory', *Open Marxism*, 1 (London: Pluto, 1992), 54–92; Hans-Georg Backhaus, *Dialektik Der Wertform: Untersuchungen zur Marxschen Ökonomiekritik* (Freiburg: Ça ira, 1997); Werner Bonefeld, 'Negative Dialectics and

the Critique of Economic Objectivity', *History of the Human Sciences* 29 (2016): 60–76.

20   See Friedrich Engels, *Anti-Dühring* in *Marx and Engels Collected Works*, vol. 25 (Moscow: Progress Publishers, 1987) and *The Origin of the Family, Private Property and the State*, in Marx and Engels Collected Works, vol. 26 (Moscow: Progress Publishers, 1990); Simon Clarke, *Marx's Theory of Crisis* (Basingstoke: Macmillan, 1994).

21   See Chris O'Kane, 'Reification and the Critical Theory of Contemporary Society', *Critical Historical Studies* 8, no. 1 (2021): 57–86.

22   See particularly Theodor W. Adorno, *History and Freedom: Lectures 1964–1965*, 1st ed. (Cambridge: Polity, 2006); Theodor W. Adorno, *Negative Dialectics* (London: Routledge, 1990); Adorno, Positivist.

23   Ibid., 33.

24   Ibid.

25   Ibid., 37.

26   Ibid., 15.

27   Ibid., 13.

28   Theodor W. Adorno, 'Society', *Salmagundi* 10–11, no. 144–53 (1969): 148–9.

29   Adorno, Late Capitalism.

30   Adorno, *Positivist*, 42.

31   Ibid., 37.

32   Institut Für Sozialforschung, *Aspects of Sociology* (Germany: Frankfurt am Main,1973), 16.

33   Adorno, *History and Freedom*, 42.

34   Adorno, *Positivist,* 42.

35   Ibid., 47.

36   Ibid., 58.

37   Adorno, *History and Freedom*, 50.

38   Adorno, *Negative Dialectics*, 320.

39   Ibid.

40   Adorno, Late Capitalism.

41   Ibid.

42   Ibid.

43   Ibid.

44   Ibid.

45   Ibid.

46   Ibid.

47   Ibid.

48   Adorno, *Negative Dialectics,* 'on the crisis of causality'.

49   Adorno, *Positivist*, 37.

50 Ibid.

51 The terms are used together in Theodor W. Adorno, *Philosophical Elements of a Theory of Society* (Cambridge: Polity, 2019) and capture Adorno's discussion of these topics between then and his untimely death.

52 Theodor W. Adorno, *Aspects of the New Right-Wing Extremism* (Cambridge: Polity, 2020)

53 Simon Clarke, *Keynesianism, Monetarism and The Crisis of the State* (Cheltenham: Edward Elgar, 1988), 89.

54 Adorno, *History and Freedom*, 144.

Part Three

Subjectivity and Pseudo Practice: On Social Praxis

10

Conceptuality and social practice

Werner Bonefeld

Introduction

The concerns of this chapter can best be summarized by the following quotation from Adorno's 1941 publication 'Spengler Today':

> They [the adherents of dialectical materialism] did not challenge the ideas of humanity, liberty, justice as such, but merely denied the claim of our society to represent the realization of these ideas. Though they treated the ideologies as illusions, they still found them illusions of truth itself. This lent a conciliatory splendour, if not to the existent at least to its 'objective tendencies'... Ideologies were unmasked as apologetic concealments... [and] were rarely conceived as powerful instruments functioning in order to change liberal competitive society into a system of immediate oppression... Above all the leftist critics failed to notice that the 'ideas' themselves in their abstract form, are not merely images of the truth that will later materialize but that they are ailing themselves, afflicted with the same injustice under which they are conceived and bound up with the world against which they are set.[1]

In this passage, Adorno also praises Georg Lukács as the dialectician who asked how society can be changed by those who are its victims. Adorno's endorsement is surprising. Lukács's Leninist conception of the vanguard party as the locus of revolutionary practice was anathema to Adorno. For Adorno, Lukács was important because of his theory of reification. According to Adorno, 'the metamorphosis of labour-power into a commodity has permeated men through and through and objectified each of their impulses as formally commensurable variations of the exchange relations'.[2] Social reproduction, he argued, is possible only on the condition that the living have been replaced by the dead, that is, every social activity is always already what Marx called the activity of personifications of economic categories. He seems to suggest that the reified world allows only reified activity. Although it was 'time for a praxis that fights barbarism',[3] 'whatever one does, it is false'[4] and 'everything is the same'.[5]

In the context of war and terror, dispossession, violence, environmental destruction and desperate class struggles to make ends meet, discussion of Adorno's conception of praxis might appear quaint. Here we have modern forms of barbarism and there we have the theoretician who denounced '1968' as a pseudo-praxis.[6] Adorno's negative dialectics is important. It challenges us to think what it means to say 'no'. To say no to something is simple. But to say what the no is, is difficult. For one, the no is not external to but operates within that same society which it opposes. Like Marx's summons of class struggle as the motor of history, the no belongs to the negative world. It is its dynamic force.[7] Furthermore, to say what the no is compromises the no insofar as it becomes positive in its affirmative yes to something that has no valid content except the negative totality of bourgeois society itself. The no is immanent to capitalist society; it belongs to it and gives it its dynamic.

As pointed out by Hans-Jürgen Krahl, conceptuality [*Begrifflichkeit*] is one of the most important elements of Adorno's negative dialectics.[8] In fact, it is key. What is the concept of the concept [*Begriff*], and what is the conceptuality of praxis in the capitalist social relations? Regarding the critique of reification, reified social relations entail the 'reification of consciousness', and what therefore is the basis for a critique of reification and how does one protest against and indeed overcome the reified social relations?[9]

Chris Arthur rightly commends Adorno for having understood that capitalism has a specific conceptuality, and that its conceptuality 'holds sway in reality (*Sache*) itself'.[10] Conceptual thinking 'aims at the thing itself'.[11] It amounts to theoretical 'digging' into things and thinking out of things to determine what is active in them and what therefore imbues them with an independent will that asserts itself behind the backs of the acting individuals. Negative dialectics is meant to '[strip] the blindfold from our eyes'. It is to '[extinguish] the autarky of the concept', which makes the 'things in being' seem to exist as if by their own nature and volition. Reification is real. Yet, what is reified and what appears in reification? 'That the concept is a concept even when dealing with things in being does not change the fact that on its part it is entwined with a non-conceptual whole.'[12] Reified social objectivity does not exist regardless of the social relations. Rather, social objectivity is the objectivity of historically specific social relations. The 'objective conceptuality' of the capitalist institutions and forces appears as natural and inevitable because of the 'prevailing relations of production'.[13] The chapter expounds Adorno's 'concept of the concept' in broad terms. The aim is not to regurgitate Adorno's argument, but to map it out as an exploration of Marx's critique of commodity fetishism, and to appreciate its subversive cunning in the eye of the storm. The argument returns to the difficulty of saying no without affirmation of the existing relations in section IV and in the Conclusion.

I

Adorno's critical theory holds that 'concepts are moments of the reality that requires their formation. All concepts refer to non-conceptualities'.[14] For a critical social theory, therefore, conceptualization does not mean the expounding of meta-theories, which, by means of infinite regress, finishes up akin to the doctrine of the invisible hand with deist conceptions of social existence, whether in their religious or secularized forms – the so-called logic of things. Instead, it grounds the existence of invisible and ontological principles in the historically specific human social relations and argues that it is these that produce their own enslavement to the invisible, whether in its religious or secularized forms. Conceptuality does also not entail the explanation of one thing by reference to another. Such thought moves from one thing to another in an attempt to render its term coherent by means of external reference. The state is explained by reference to the economic, and the economic by reference to the state. By means of vicious circularity, then, explanation becomes tautological. Further, conceptuality does not mean the positing of natural laws, like, for example, the natural propensity of Man to barter, as Adam Smith alleged. That Man has to eat says nothing about her mode of subsistence and the social necessities that a mode of subsistence entails – so-called social laws.

To conceptualize means to bring the thing to its concept [*die Sache auf den Begriff bringen, der Begriff der Sache*]. Conceptuality has to do with the recognition of reality – not with the analysis of concepts. Concepts are required to render reality intelligible, to grasp and comprehend the reified relations and to understand the power of compulsion that issues from them. Conceptualization goes beyond the immediate perception of reality in order to comprehend what is hidden in its immediacy or immediate appearance. What is appearance an appearance of, and what appears in appearance? 'Why [has] this content [human social relations] assumed that particular form [the form of capital]?'[15] This also means that thought's critical quality does not rest on the answers it gives, but on the questions it asks.

The comprehension of the social things is not the same as their definition *qua* identification, or indeed 'registration in a system governed by, for example, ideal-types'.[16] The conceptual comprehension of a thing means to perceive its individual moment in its connection *not* with other things but *in and through* them.[17] Thinking by means of definition or identification is quite able to say what something comes under, what it illustrates, exemplifies or represents. It does not, however, say what it is. Thinking, as Adorno saw it, is essentially the negation of things in their immediacy. Immediacy feeds the perceptions and points of view of scientific prejudice, which holds that there is nothing more to see here since the facts speak for themselves. In contrast, conceptualization means to dissolve the immediate appearance of things to recognize their mediated immediacy [*vermittelte Unmittelbarkeit*]. Conceptualization melts what appeared at first hard and solid, factual and real, like a certain economic quantity that can be expressed with mathematical accuracy in relationship to all other economic quantities, without once asking what it quantifies. Its first impulse is not to ask 'what things represent on the market' but 'what these things actually mean for people'.[18] Every act of conceptualization implies this initial effort of asking about the meaning of things for people. Their validity is a social validity. Money does not mind whether it deflates or inflates. People do, and they do so because it means something for them in their daily struggle to either make ends meet or conquer the world of wealth to avoid bankruptcy.

Conceptualization is an act of revolt against immediacy. It does not bow to things. It is not social statistics nor is it a formal method of analysis. It wants to know what the things are, and what they are is within them. It thus does not pretend that the immediate appearance of things is unreal; nor does it simply negate the world of appearances as if it were no more than a veil that hides the supposedly real human beings who are drawn into the system at ever greater cost of alienation and suppression of existential impulses. Such arguments, as can be found, for example, in Jaeggi, and in Marcuse too, are a mere gesture of social critique that, in a different context, Adorno rightly dismisses as 'abstract negativity'.[19] The critique of reification is critique of the social relations that objectify themselves in, and thus assume, the form of a relationship between things. Conceptuality is about the recognition of 'the existent'[20] for what it is: 'the human being itself in its social relations', however perverted their objectification in the form of reified things.[21] Reification does not make them less 'human', as if the reified world were a world apart. Reification is not something objectively 'given'. Nor is it founded on some nature, like Smith's natural propensity to truck and barter. It is an historical generated, social product and its nature is a social nature. However reified the world of things and however hostile its manifestation especially towards the propertyless, mere human material enlisted to produce surplus value and discharged into unemployment without further ado, it remains a human world. The immediacy of things is thus real as objective illusion [*gegenständlicher Schein*]. Conceptualization is required to decipher this illusion, demystifying it through the comprehension of the human social practice that validates and imbues the social objectivity with an independent will to the point of destruction.

Conceptualization does thus not mean 'thinking' *about* things. Rather, it means thinking *out of* things.[22] If it were really *about* things, then conceptualization would be external to its subject matter. Thought would thus relate to its world as a tool that can be applied to society like a (Descartesian) instrument. The social world is here presupposed as something external to thought, and vice versa, as if they really belonged to different worlds. For example, instead of the critical notion that 'concepts are moments of the reality that requires their formation', concepts are treated as generally applicable scientific instruments, which are capable of dissecting and analysing every society at all times and places as an historically specific overdetermined manifestation of universal, abstract social laws. This view suggests a radical separation between thought and reality. Haug articulates this view most clearly when he proclaims that the mastery of Marx was 'the discovery of thought independent from empirical conditions'.[23]

Alex Callinicos argues similarly.[24] He advocates that the Marxist method of analysis amounts to a sophisticated version of the science of knowledge, which hypothesizes society as an 'as if' of theoretical construction. Theoretical knowledge appears as a hypothetical figure of speech, an 'as if', which is corroborated by empirical analysis that falsifies or verifies the proposed theory of society. This approach is, however, deceitful in that the real world is mirrored in its theoretical hypothesis. That is, the science of knowledge posits the scientific idea that the real world is, say, regulated by a competitive market structure and then applies this idea to capitalist markets, with conclusive effect, though questions remain as to whether the freedom of competition has in reality not trans-morphed into a freedom of monopolies.

Similarly, the sociology of knowledge does not touch reality by thought either. It argues that consciousness is the product of reality and from this it concludes that reality is experienced differently from the competing (class) perspectives. From the standpoint of the labourer, capitalism is experienced quite differently than from the standpoint of the capitalist. Capitalism simply means different things to different people. According the Georg Lukács, the standpoint of labour is allegedly privileged because of its ontological privilege as the revolutionary class.[25] In contemporary Marxism, the relativism of sociology of knowledge is turned into a positive theory of relationalism according to which the social institutions, like the state, are essentially determined by the character of the wider social relations in which it is situated, especially the balance of social forces. The concrete materiality of social institutions manifests thus the shifts and changes in the balance of the social forces that act upon them. Within this analytical frame, 'the power of the state is the power of the forces acting in and through the state'.[26] The dialectics of structure and agency gives dialectics a bad name. It depends on dogmatic immediacies and moves in vicious circles as it hops from structure to agency, and back again, from agency to structure; and instead of comprehending what they are, each is presupposed in a tautological movement of thought; none is explained. Thought that does not go into its object does not recognize its object. Such thought is able to name and analyse things in the immediacy of the given social situation, but it does not grasp them, nor does it comprehend the logic that holds sway in them. Relativism does not recognize the power of society in the form of the economic object. It merely pacifies its contradictions.

Thinking *out of* things aims at discovering what is active in them. For instance, does 'price of labour amount to a yellow logarithm' or is £10 an hour just and fair?[27] Whatever the fairness or unfairness of a £10 an hour wage, analytical thinking does not bring the thing to its concept. It presupposes its veracity, and, dismayed by the meagre income level of the poor, demands higher wages. Why has social labour acquired the form of a commodity? And what laws of necessity exist in a society whose social labour power is a saleable property? What is its value? Are the interests of the sellers and buyers of labour power the same, and how and with what consequence do they converge in the form of a labour contract, and who sets down and enforces the rules of the game of a trade in labour power? Once it has been traded, what has been acquired, what anyhow is the purpose of the acquisition and how is labour power consumed; and what has been relinquished and why, and what happens to its seller once its buyer starts consuming the acquired commodity to achieve his own purposes and is the seller not dependent for her own subsistence on the profitability of her labour, enriching its buyer as the condition of the sustained employment of society's dispossessed surplus value producers? If labour power is not traded, what can be traded instead to make a living – how much for a kidney, how many for prostitution? Reification entails human suffering as the vanished premise of its concept. That is, reification, which for Lukács was the one category of enquiry, is really just an 'epiphenomenon'.[28] What is reified, what is reification a reification of, and what is active within it and how is it that it has a consciousness and a will? The labour market trade in exploitable human material entails suffering as the premise of the concept of the freedom of contract. The law of value presupposes the force of value, which is experienced as economic compulsion.

Marx's critique of religion argues that God requires no explanation. This is not because God cannot be explained on the basis of power and fear but because the explanation of God rests on the comprehension of the social relations that bring God to the fore as an objective abstraction that controls and cows those same social relations from which it springs. Equally, the comprehension of reified things rests on the understanding of the social relations that exist in the mode of the reified object and that thus disappear in reification only to reappear in it as agents of their own reified existence and its compelling force. Humanity is not a category of economic objectivity. It is however governed by its cold conceptuality, which is fed by 'active humanity'. For example, money as the form of value represents 'the socially valid character of wealth'.[29] Yet, it does not recognize hardship, nor does it know mercy and the human need for housing, welfare, education, affection and human dignity, nor does know anything about the struggle to make ends meet.[30] However, the money form of wealth does not create the coldness of capitalist society. It represents it and, as such, it presents it to the social individuals, requiring them to generate money for the sake of more money in order to sustain the strength of their link to the 'world of social wealth'.[31] It is a truly abstract power. Man (*Mensch*) does not eat money. However, without money she does not eat. Profit is primary. For the sake of making a living, money needs to be made, that is, it has to 'yield living offspring', for the sake of expanded social reproduction and on the pain of ruin.[32]

The *reducio ad hominem* that for Adorno characterizes the critical intent of Marx's work does not entail the replacement of the object by the subject.[33] It means the comprehension of the object as social mode of the subject. Just as the idea of objectivity without the subject is a nonsense, subjectivity without the object is nothing. In order to understand society in the form of a relationship between things, one has to be within them. Hegel's notion of the work of the concept [*die Arbeit des Begriffs*] entails an internal connection between concept and thing, experience and substance, human endeavour and the logic of things. The concept, of course, does not work. We do. The work of the concept thus means to be led by thought without fear of where it might take us. The work of the concept means recognizing the interior life of the economic object, to engage in its contradictions and to comprehend the sheer unrest of life as the vanished premise of its conceptuality, and thus to understand not only the necessity of its movement, but also its capacity for violence and for inflicting social misery. What belongs to the constituted conceptuality of, say, the form of the state? What is it capable of? What lies within its concept? What is the logic of the matter? Revealing the conceptuality of the social things entails understanding the necessity of their mode of motion [*Bewegungsweise*], force and power [*Macht*], means and ends, not as arbitrary coincidences that come about because of the social forces that act through the state but as definite forms of life that belong to definite social relations.

Conceptualization thus means articulating what is active in things, deciphering their social constitution, and comprehending the formative violence, that is the violence of the original, primitive or *ursprüngliche*, act of dispossession, as the hidden secrete of the civilized appearance of, say, the labour market as the institution of trade between 'moneybags' (Marx) and dispossessed producers of surplus value.[34] This, however, also means that conceptualization – the work of the concept – works against its own tendency. Its critical intent is to demystify the fetish character of the economic object. However, to conceptualize means to identify. Identification does not crush the fetish; it affirms it. Conceptualization is thus itself contradictory – it has to think against itself. In order to bring the thing to its concept [*Sache auf den Begriff bringen*] it has to articulate more than the logic of society as objectified thing, and this 'more' has also to be within the thing, as its 'nonconceptual' secret (Adorno) or its 'secrete history' (Marx). The conceptualization of social things entails the recognition of the non-conceptual as their constitutive premise. There is, say, no price mechanism without the social relations that carry the price tag on their forehead; and there no law of value without the force of law making and law preserving violence. The law of value contains the historical creation of the doubly free labour in its concept.

II

'All social life is essentially practical.' This, from Marx's *8th Feuerbach* thesis, includes thinking. Thinking is part of social life and all social life is essentially practical. The thesis continues: 'All mysteries which lead theory to mysticism find their rational explanation in human practice and in the comprehension of this practice.'

The thesis is clear and at the same time most difficult. Thought is able to demystify reality, and demystification depends on the comprehension of human practice. Human practice is thus deemed essential, and thought's purpose is a subversive one: it is to reveal the hidden secret of all mysteries in human social practice. For thought to be thought it has to demystify the economic forces as the forces of definite forms of human social practice. And here the difficulties start. What human practice has Marx in mind? How can it be revealed and where might it be found? The appearance of human practice in the world as we know it does not show directly the human practice whose comprehension alone is said to explain the relations between things. If it were, there would be no need for demystification as essence and appearance would coincide. Marx's thesis suggests that human practice needs to be discovered by thought in order to comprehend its mysterious appearance in forms that deny it. What sort of human practice do we have to comprehend for demystification to occur in a valid sense? Can its validity be tested by means of verification or falsification, or is a different 'test' required? Is it valid on the condition that it is true in practice? What does it mean to say that something is true in practice? And this in a society where the 'living have been replaced by the dead' and where the 'denial of all will to live' is the condition of social existence.[35]

Marx's thesis that the understanding of all mysteries depends on the comprehension of human social practice implies that this practice is constitutive. However, this formulation is full of dangers, too. It presupposes a definite resolution to the stated problem: If social practice is constitutive can it remain innocent in the mysterious world that it has created? Negri says that capital is a 'bewitching force' whose power is such that the constitutive subject is, as it were, sucked into capital.[36] In this argument, the constitutive subject is merely an alleged subject. The real power, it seems, is not the constitutive but the constituted subject. Concepts do indeed live a dangerous life. As Debord puts it: 'in a world which really is topsy-turvy, the true is a moment of the false'.[37] Truth appears thus to exist in the mode of being denied – an existing untruth that is, however, true all the same. That is, however reified the social world in the form of the economic object, of capital as the automatic social subject, there would be 'nothing without individuals and their spontaneities'.[38] The reified world is a world of reified forms of human social practice and it therefore remains a human world.

III

'All science would be superfluous if the outward appearance of things and the essence of things directly coincided.'[39]

Essence and appearance do not coincide directly, nor do they belong to distinct realities. As Marx put it in an earlier work, the 'separation between in-itself and for-itself, the substance of the subject, is abstract mysticism'.[40] The essence of things is human practice in the mode of the object. Essence must appear. If it does not, then it is not essence; conversely, appearance must be the appearance of essence or it is nothing. There is only one reality – a reality in which society's surplus value producers struggle to make ends meet against the background of an ever-increasing pile of material wealth, and therefore also a reality of disunion, contradiction, fissures, struggles and antagonism. The distinction between essence and appearance exists within the things themselves in the form of irreconcilable, antagonistic, restless relations of a coerced and coercive sociability as unity of things, as negative ontology of ghost walking economic quantities. The bourgeois relations of abstract equality, one hundred pounds of this is the same as one hundred pounds of that, render the difference between this and that commensurable in the form of an abstract identity, which is 'the actual mask of death'.[41] What appears in abstract identity is the ghost-walking reality of economic quantities, the subject's disenchantment in her own world. Distinction, the sheer quality of this and that and the human needs that could be satisfied by either, is coerced to appear indifferent to itself in the form of value, that is of money. In the form of money, qualitative differences vanish and the products of labour assume the form of a certain amount of money. This or that, useful things of definite qualities, only count if they assume the opposite form of a certain quantity of money. If they fail to express themselves as such, this and that are nothing. The social validity of distinct material things appears in the form of abstract quantities of money. It does not appear in the form of satisfied human needs. In fact, products of concrete labour that cannot be transformed into money represents a socially invalid expenditure of labour, and thus a loss on the investment into that labour. Exchangeability for money, measurability through money, counts. What cannot be transformed into money is burnt. It is within the concept of abstract identity, commensurability of social qualities in the form of a quantity of money, a 100 pounds of this is the same as a 100 pounds of that, in its internality and immanence, that the non-coincidence of essence and appearance manifests itself. The non-coincidence strains the concept of society, forcing it, torn by contradiction and in antagonistic battle, to sustain its essence, which is 'the life process of society', by positing C as capital, ΔC as investment, and living labour as the means of valorisation. On the one hand, workers might 'have more to lose than their chains',[42] on the other, the 'poor chew their words to fill their bellies'.[43]

Hegel's notion that essence has to appear does not mean that the human subject makes an appearance by asserting itself in and against the world of things – say, in terms of a conception of class struggle as a force that, from the outside, breaks into the capital relation during periods of crisis and unrest. Hegel's notion that essence has to appear means that essence cannot choose not to appear. What makes essence essential, subsists in appearance, however inhospitable its world in the form of the economic object. Its appearance is thus at the same time its disappearance. The law of essence is its appearance *qua* disappearance. In the 'enchanted and perverted' world of capital[44] essence appears not only in the form of 'a thing'.[45] It also appears as human suffering and as struggle to overcome suffering. Following on from Charlotte Baumann's contribution to this volume, human suffering is the non-conceptual foundation of the economic concept of society. Conceptuality holds sway in the logic of things and that it is to say, it 'expresses the fact that, no matter how much blame may attach to the subject's contribution, the conceived world is not its own but a world hostile to the subject'.[46]

I have argued that reification arises 'from the social relations of production themselves'.[47] Therefore, the immediacy of the objective world is not really an immediacy of things but 'the forms of appearance of essential relations'.[48] That is to say, '[e]ssence passes into that which lies concealed beneath the façade of immediacy, of the supposed facts, and which makes the facts what they are'.[49] The circumstance that the 'appearance of things hides their genesis',[50] entails a programme of critique that deciphers the 'mysterious' forms' of capitalist society as forms 'assumed by human relations'.[51] That is, essence appears in and subsists through mysterious forms. Negative dialectics is about the comprehension of essence in its appearance, that is, its appearance in disappearance. The force of value disappears in the law of value. It also appears in it as economic compulsion 'to dodge the freedom to starve' through the production of surplus value, which is the condition of wage-based employment.[52] The separation of labour from the means of subsistence passes into the free labourer as both trader in labour power and producer of surplus value. The free labourer is 'bound by invisible threads' and her 'economic bondage' appears as the precise opposite as a relationship characterized by the freedom of exchange between equals before the law, each and every one endowed with 'the innate rights of man', pursuing their ends in liberty from each other as independent utility seekers.[53] In this appearance, 'the actual relations [are] invisible, and indeed present to the eye the precise opposite of that relation'.[54] The abstract identity of 'moneybags' and free labourer as equal partners of contract, and the civility of their exchange, is as real as the same old 'activity of the conqueror, who buys commodities from the conquered with the money he has stolen from them'.[55]

I have argued that the essence of the topsy-turvy world of economic quantities is mischief. Capitalism hurts. Crisis and destruction is the ever-present nightmare of the capitalist mode of social reproduction:

> Society suddenly finds itself put back into a state of momentary barbarism; it appears as if famine, a universal war of devastation had cut off the supply of every means of subsistence; industry and commerce seem to be destroyed; and why? Because there is too much civilisation, too much means of subsistence; too much industry, too much commerce. The productive forces at the disposal of society no longer tend to further the development of the conditions of bourgeois property; on the contrary, they have become too powerful for these conditions, by which they are fettered, and so soon as they overcome these fetters, they bring disorder into the whole of bourgeois society, endanger the existence of bourgeois property. The conditions of bourgeois society are too narrow to comprise the wealth created by them. And how does bourgeois society get over these crises? On the one hand by enforced destruction of a mass of productive forces; on the other, by the conquest of new markets, and by the more thorough exploitation of the old ones.[56]

This commentary by Marx is not a brilliant anticipation of things to come, which after all turned out to be far too optimistic. Rather, it conceptualizes the social object and, in doing so, shows what lies within it. What lies within the concept are its constituted necessities. Creation *qua* destruction is a valid necessity of the capitalist social relations – it belongs to its conceptuality [*Begrifflichkeit*). Amidst an accumulation of great wealth, capitalist reproduction, suddenly and without warning, cuts a whole class of surplus value producers off from access to the means of subsistence, making them redundant. Man vanishes in her own world and exists against herself as a personification of economic categories – an 'alienated subject' that, in order to make a living, sacrifices her living being on the altar of abstract wealth, money as more money, to the point of madness.[57]

In sum, the 'domination of exchange value over human beings, which, *a priori*, prevent subjects from being subjects, degrades subjectivity itself to a mere object and convicts the universal principle which claims to establish the predominant status of the subject as its untruth'.[58] The meaning of objectivity excludes the possibility that it can also be a subject. However, to be an object is part of the meaning of subjectivity. Subjectivity means objectification. The circumstance that objectification exists in a reified mode does not imply that there is an as yet undiscovered, and indeed undiscoverable, logic that lies solely within the thing itself. Only as a socially determinate object can the object be an object. Reason exists – but in irrational form, in the form of a 'ghost-like' economic object. The irrational world is a rational world – of maddening abstractions.

IV

Adorno conceives of his negative dialectics as follows: 'Negative dialectics thinks the power of the whole which is at work in every individual determination not merely as a negation of that individual determination but also as itself the negative – in other words, as the untrue, as that which thwarts reconciliation.'[59] Adorno's notion that 'dialectics is the consistent sense of non-identity' is about the existing untruth of things.[60] To think dialectically is to think 'nonidentity through identity'.[61] Definite social relations assume the form of a relationship between things and appear in their appearance as personifications of the economic categories. The identity of their social nature appears in the form of a movement of measurable abstract economic quantities and it manifests itself in a form that does not belong to their measurable self-identity, that is, it manifests itself in the form of a daily struggle to make ends meet. This struggle belongs to the conceptuality of the economic object but it does not belong to its identity as calculable quantity. Yet, it is this struggle for the sake of social reproduction that endows the economic categories with a will. By itself, the identity of a coin is metal. What gives this metal an economic identity of overwhelming power are the social relations, a definite relation between individuals, that assume the form of a relationship between economic things, by which they governed according to a logic that holds sway in their reified identity.[62] On the pain of ruin, money has to beget more money. Suffering is the weight of objectivity upon the subject. Therefore, to think dialectically means to think 'in contradictions, for the sake of the contradiction once experienced in the thing, and against that contradiction'.[63] It means to think of man not as a metaphysical distraction to the science of economic matter but rather as the untruth of that matter. What appears identical in the money form of wealth is non-identity under the aspect of identity – one-hundred pounds for this is the same as one-hundred pounds for that – and yet, this and that are not the same. They are articles of different qualities. Negative dialectics is 'suspicious of all identity' and hinges on this 'turn towards nonidentity'.[64] That is to say, variable capital does not go on strike, humans do, and they do so at the same time that they really exist as personifications of variable capital. Fetishism is real, but its concept contains more than it reveals; that what is non-identical to the concept drives the concept. There is no secret reality outside reification, nor is there an external vantage point from which to launch the assault. Reality is divided within itself. The resolution to the dialectical context of immanence is that context itself.

Adorno's concept of the concept is emphatically practical. It holds that reification remains a form of human practice. Helmut Reichelt makes this point well when he argues that 'human sensuous practice subsists through its supersensible existence in the autonomization of society as both the object and subject of its perverted social practice'.[65] Adorno's 'concept of the concept' is distinct. According to Lukács the worker can resist reification because, as long has he rebels against it consciously, 'his humanity and his soul are not changed into commodities'.[66] That for Lukács, the soul of the worker-in-resistance is the party is of no interest here. What is important, however, is that reification does not affect the soul of the worker, as if the soul is not of this world but of divine issue. Lukács's position is a paradox. He derives the revolutionary subject, he calls it the totality of the proletarian subject represented by the party, from something that is and remains external to its reified existence. Ernst Bloch conceived of the unreified within reification as the 'inner transcendence of matter'; and Oskar Negt and Alexander Kluge conceived of it as 'materialist instinct'.[67] And Adorno? The very idea that there is a world out there that has not yet been colonized by the logic of things is nonsensical. Instead of a concept of society, their differentiations of society into system and soul or transcendent matter or materialist instinct, separates what belongs together. Indeed, whichever formulation is favoured, they all insist on a subject that is conceived in contradistinction to society. Leaving aside Adorno's despair – 'he allows himself to hope only on the condition that all hope has disappeared'[68] – his conception of bourgeois society does not allow for externalities. There is only one world and that is the world in which we live.

The demand that thought is adequate to its subject matter entails more than it bargains for. Its adequacy cannot be established by means of falsification or verification. There is no verifiable 'it is'. To say that something 'is' already casts doubt on the proclaimed identification of the 'it' and it also casts doubt on the normative idea that 'it' ought to be more civilized in its conduct. Like Marx's critique of political economy, Adorno's negative dialectics mocks those who depict socialism as the realization of the ideals of bourgeois society. As Marx put it:

[W]hat divides these gentlemen from the bourgeois apologist is, on the one side, their sensitivity to the contradictions included in the system; on the other, the utopian inability to grasp the necessary difference between the real and the ideal form of bourgeois society, which is the cause of their desire to undertake the superfluous business of realizing the ideal expression again, which is in fact only the inverted projection [*Lichtbild*] of this reality.[69]

Or in Adorno succinct formulation, the 'whole is false'.[70]

Conclusion

I have argued that negative dialectics is not a formal procedure or method applied to society in the form of the economic object. Rather, it thinks out of the economic object as 'the very essence of the subject'.[71] It is also not a self-perpetuating triad where the thesis confronts its anti-thesis, reconciling the two by means of synthesis, only for the synthesis to result in a new thesis. Rather, it thinks the disunited unity of the social object. Its 'attempt to arrive at truth through the form of its own untruths'[72] is about the understanding of the social relations in and through their 'apotheosized' social forms.[73] Although the ghostly movement of reified things manifests itself behind the back of the social individuals, it remains their world.

The critique of political economy amounts fundamentally to a critical social theory. It rejects the perception of society as founded on economic nature as the necessary ideology of the existing social relations. Instead of 'natural economic laws', it recognizes the social relations as the hidden secret of the economic categories. Contrary to traditional rejections of critical theory as a retreat from practice, it does not substitute thought for practice. Rather, negative dialectics amounts to a conceptualized praxis of the capitalist society relations and it musters thought as a preventative against a false practice. It brushes society against the grain so that the negative reason of human emancipation does not become 'a piece of the politics it was supposed to lead out of'.[74]

On the one hand, there is the preponderance of the object – society as a real abstraction that manifests itself behind the backs of the acting social subject – and, on the other hand, there is the spontaneity of society as subject – a subject of its own objective dialectics of the forces and relations of production, which might bury us all, but a subject, nevertheless. Society as object does nothing. It does not maim and kill. "'It is man, rather, the real, living man who does all that," and in so doing, bestows society as object with a deadly will.[75] The truth contents of the 'the real life-activity' of reified society are the wounds that the struggles to make ends meet leave behind.[76] These struggles may lead to new forms of repression in reified society or they may resist the logic of reification, breaking its façade to allow a glimpse of what might be. The prospect of emancipation lies in these 'breaks' in its logic and in the gaps in the systematic unity of reified society. These 'cracks', as Holloway refers to these breaks in reification, disclose 'traces' of utopia already experienced in the present. Only in these 'traces', is there 'hope of ever coming across genuine and just reality'.[77] Those who demand human emancipation and, for the sake of a better politics in reified society, simultaneously battle against the concrete utopia of the society of human purposes, contradict themselves.[78]

Notes

1 Theodor W. Adorno, 'Spengler Today', *Zeitschrift für Sozialforschung* 9, no. 1 (1941): 305–25, here 318f.

2 Theodor W. Adorno, *Minima Moralia. Reflections from Damaged Life*, translated by Edmund Jephcott (London: Verso, 2005), 229.

3 Theodor W. Adorno, 'Marginalien zu Theorie und Praxis', in Theodor W. Adorno, *Stichworte. Kritische Modelle* 2 (Frankfurt: Suhrkamp, 1969), 169–91, here 179. Quotations from German sources have been translated by the author. For an interpretation of this text, see Marcel Stoetzler in this volume.

4 Theodor W. Adorno, *Einleitung zur Musiksoziologie* (Frankfurt: Suhrkamp, 1962), 30.

5 Theodor W. Adorno, *Soziologische Schriften, Gesammelte Werke*, vol. 8 (Frankfurt: Suhrkamp, 1972), 369.

6 Adorno, 'Marginalien zu Theorie und Praxis', 169–91. On Adorno's notion of pseudo-praxis, see Marcel Stoetzler's contribution to this volume.

7 On this point, see Klaus Heinrich, *Versuch über die Schwierigkeit nein zu sagen* (Marburg: Stroemfeld/Roter Stern, 1982).

8 Hans-Jürgen Krahl, *Konstitution und Klassenkampf* (Frankfurt: Verlag Neue Kritik, 1971).

9 Theodor W. Adorno, *Philosophical Elements of a Theory of Society*, translated by Wieland Hobas, edited by Tobias Ten Brink and Marc Phillip Nogueria (Cambridge: Polity, 2019), 45.

10 Chris Arthur, *The New Dialectic and Marx's Capital* (Leiden: Brill, 2004), 243.

11 Theodor W. Adorno, *Negative Dialectics*, translated by E.B. Ashton (London: Routledge, 1990), 205.

12 Ibid., 12.

13 Adorno, *Negative Dialectics*, 245. Translation amended.

14 Ibid., 11.

15 Karl Marx, *Capital*, vol. 1, translated by Ben Fowkes (London: Penguin, 1990), 174.

16 Adorno, *Negative Dialectics*, 25.

17 See ibid., 149.

18 Adorno, *Philosophical Elements of a Theory of Society*, 45.

19 Rahel Jaeggi, *Alienation*, translated by Frederick Neuhouser (New York: Columbia University Press, 2016). Herbert Marcuse, *Eros and Civilisation* (London: Routledge, 1987). Theodor W. Adorno, *Lectures on Negative Dialectics*, translated by Rodney Livingstone, edited by Rolf Tiedemann (Cambridge: Polity, 2008), 25.

20 Adorno, 'Spengler Today', 318.

21 Karl Marx, *Grundrisse*, translated by Martin Nicolaus (London: Penguin, 1973), 712.

22 Adorno, *Negative Dialectics*, 33.

23 Wolfgang Fritz Haug, *Vorlesungen zur Einführung ins 'Kapital'* (Hamburg: Argument Verlag, 2005), 150. See also Louise Althusser, *Lenin and Philosophy*, translated by Andy Blunden (New York: Monthly Review Press. 1971), 71–2.

24 Alex Callinicos, 'Against the New Dialectic', *Historical Materialism* 12, no. 2 (2005): 41–59.

25 See Georg Lukács, *Marx's Basic Ontological Principles*, translated by David Fernbach (London: Merlin, 1978) and Georg Lukács, *Lenin: A Study in the Unity of his Thought*, translated by Nicholas Jacobs (London: Verso, 1997). On standpoint critique in Marxism, see Michael Heinrich, *Introduction to the Three Volumes of Capital*, translated by Alexander Locasio (New York: Monthly Review Press, 2012). For a critique of Lukács along the lines suggested here, see Joe Fracchia (2013), 'The Philosophical Lenin and Eastern "Western Marxism" of Georg Lukács', *Historical Materialism* 21, no. 1 (2013): 69–93, and Vasilis Grollios, 'Dialectics and Democracy in Georg Lukács Marxism', *Capital & Class* 38, no. 3 (2014): 563–81.

26 Bob Jessop, *State Power* (Cambridge: Polity, 2007), 270.

27 Karl Marx, *Capital*, vol. 3 (London: Lawrence & Wishart, 1966), 818.

28 Adorno, *Negative Dialectics*, 190.

29 Martha Campbell, 'The Objectivity of Value versus the Idea of Habitual Action', in *The Constitution of Capital: Essays on Volume I of Marx's Capital*, edited by Riccardo Bellofiore and Nicola Taylor (London: Palgrave, 2004), 63–87, here 85.

30 For further argument on this point, see Sergio Bologna, 'Money and Crisis', *Common Sense* nos. 13 and 14 (1993), https://commonsensejournal.org.uk/tag/sergio-bologna/

31   Marx, *Capital*, vol. 1, 739.

32   Ibid., 255.

33   Theodor W. Adorno, 'Zur Logik der Sozialwissenschaften', in *Der Positivismusstreit in der deutschen Soziologie*, edited by Theodor W. Adorno, Hans Alberts, Ralf Dahrendorf, Jürgen Habermas, Harald Pilot and Karl R. Popper (Munich: DTV, 1993), 125–43, here 143.

34   Capitalist accumulation contains the violence of primitive accumulation in its concept. It is its secret history. See Marx, *Capital*, esp. chapter 26. For an exposition, see Werner Bonefeld, 'Primitive Accumulation and Capitalist Accumulation', *Science & Society* 75, no. 3 (2011): 379–99.

35   Adorno, *Minima Moralia*, 229.

36   Antonio Negri, 'Interpretation of the Class Situation Today', in *Open Marxism*, vol. 2, edited by Werner Bonefeld, Richard Gunn and Kosmas Psychopedis (London: Pluto Press, 1992), 69–105, here 89.

37   Guy Debord, *Society of the Spectacle* (London: Rebel Press, 1987), para 9.

38   Adorno, *Negative Dialectics*, 304.

39   Karl Marx, *Capital*, vol. 3, 817.

40   Karl Marx, *Kritik des Hegelschen Staatsrechts*, MEW (Berlin: Dietz, 1966), 265.

41   Theodor W. Adorno, *Gesellschaftstheorie und Kulturkritik* (Frankfurt: Suhrkamp, 1975), 60.

42   Theodor W. Adorno, *Philosophical Elements of a Theory of Society* (Cambridge: Polity, 2019), 50.

43   Adorno, *Minima Moralia*, 205.

44   Marx, *Capital*, vol. 3, 830.

45   Marx, *Grundrisse*, 157.

46   Adorno, *Negative Dialectics*, 167.

47   Ibid., 677.

48   Ibid.

49   Adorno, *Negative Dialectics*, 167.

50   Theodor W. Adorno, 'Einleitung', in *Der Positivismusstreit in der deutschen Soziologie*, edited by Theodor W. Adorno, Hans Alberts, Ralf Dahrendorf, Jürgen Habermas, Harald Pilot and Karl R. Popper (München: DTV, 1993), 7–79, here 25.

51   Marx, *Capital*, vol. 1, 186.

52   Theodor W. Adorno, *Introduction to Sociology*, translated by Edmund Jephcott (Cambridge: Polity, 2000), 201.

53   Marx, *Capital*, vol. 1, 719, 723, 280.

54   Ibid., 680.

55   Ibid., 728.

56   Karl Marx and Friedrich Engels, *The Communist Manifesto* (London: Pluto, 1997), 18–19.

57 See Hans-Georg Backhaus, 'Between Philosophy and Science: Marxian Social Economy as Critical Theory', in *Open Marxism*, vol. 1, edited by Werner Bonefeld, Richard Gunn and Kosmas Psychopedis (London: Pluto Press, 1992), 54–92, for an account of 'alienated subject'.

58 Theodor W. Adorno, *Ontology and Dialectics* (Cambridge: Polity, 2019) 246.

59 Adorno, *Ontology and Dialectics*, 241.

60 Adorno, *Negative Dialectics*, 5.

61 Ibid., 189.

62 See Marx, *Grundrisse*, 293.

63 Adorno, *Negative Dialectics*, 145.

64 Ibid., 12.

65 Helmut Reichelt, 'Social Reality as Appearance: Some Notes on Marx's Concept of Reality', in *Human Dignity*, edited by Werner Bonefeld and Kosmas Psychopedis (London: Routledge, 2017), 31–68, here 65.

66 Georg Lukács, *History and Class Consciousness*, translated by Rodney Livingstone (London: Merlin, 1971), 172.

67 Ernst Bloch, *Logos der Materie* (Frankfurt/am Main: Suhrkamp, 2000). Oskar Negt and Alexander Kluge, *Public Sphere and Experience*, translated by Peter Labanyi, Jamie Owen Daniel and Assenka Oksiloff (Minneapolis: University of Minnesota Press, 1993).

68 Frank Böckelmann, 'Die Möglichkeit ist die Unmöglichkeit. Die Unmöglichkeit ist die Möglichkeit. Bermerkungen zur Autarkie der Negativen Dialektik', in *Die neue Linke nach Adorno*, edited by Wilfried F. Schoeller (Munich: Kindler, 1969), 17–37, here 22.

69 Marx, *Grundrisse*, 248–9.

70 Adorno, *Minima Moralia*, 50.

71 Adorno, *Ontology and Dialectics*, 248.

72 Theodor W. Adorno, *Introduction to Dialectics*, translated by Nicholas Walker, edited by Christoph Zimmermann (Cambridge: Polity, 2017), 214.

73 Marx, *Capital*, vol. 1, 494, fn. 4.

74 Adorno, *Negative Dialectics*, 143.

75 Ibid., 304, quoting Karl Marx and Friedrich Engels, *Die heilige Familie*, MEW 2 (Berlin: Dietz, 1980), 98.

76 Karl Marx and Friedrich Engels, 'The German Ideology', in *The Marx–Engels Reader*, edited by Robert C. Tucker (New York: W. W. Norton, 1978), 146–201, here 154.

77 Theodor W. Adorno, *Die Aktualität der Philosophie, Gesammelte Werke*, vol. 1 (Frankfurt: Suhrkamp, 1973), 325. John Holloway, *Crack Capitalism* (London: Pluto Press, 2010).

78 This point paraphrases Johannes Agnoli, 'Destruction as the Determination of the Scholar in Miserable Times', in *Revolutionary Writing*, edited by Werner Bonefeld (New York: Autonomedia, 2003), 25–37. The political outlook of critical theory

is geared towards that sort of radical change, whose passing Max Horkheimer, 'Authoritarian State', in *The Essential Frankfurt School Reader*, edited by Andrew Aarato and Eike Gebhard (London: Continuum, 1985) 95–117, bemoaned in 1942 and whose actuality Oskar Negt, *Keine Demokratie ohne Sozialismus, kein Sozialismus ohne Demokratie* (Frankfurt: Suhrkamp, 1976), 462, sought to reclaim in the 1970s: 'if there was anything in the twentieth century akin to a concrete utopia, that was the utopia of the councils'.

11

Non-identity, critique of labour and pseudo-praxis: Extra-marginal palinlegomena on the dialectics of doing

Marcel Stoetzler

This chapter is a gloss (a *Marginalie*) on one of Adorno's last manuscripts, 'Marginalien zu Theorie und Praxis', the second part of 'Dialektische Epilegomena' which is an appendix to *Stichworte. Kritische Modelle 2*.[1] Adorno notes that the 'Dialectical Epilegomena' belong in the context of *Negative Dialektik* and were drafted as notes for a lecture that was interrupted by student protesters and abandoned. The chapter attempts to find pleasure in the vertigo of the hard graft of the critique of labour, of the incessant praxis that is needed to create a world where all are free to float on water like Baloo the Bear, as much as they like. It follows the structure of the fourteen sections of Adorno's text, in turns paraphrasing, glossing, expanding, exaggerating and having fun with. It is an Adorno play for one actor: *Adorno's Last Tape*, as it were.[2] It aims to demonstrate the ethics and the method of Adorno's style: the object, which is here the text, is to be embraced and loved (because it is lovable). Adorno's text demands to be heard out, and the demand is granted, in a posture of *solā scripturā*, as if Adorno could never be wrong. The actor does have second thoughts, though [mostly added in square brackets, as inner dialogue]: *could Adorno be wrong?* What about those sects, tribes and affinity groups who turn *solā theoriā* into an instrument of occult and esoteric identity-building? Aren't they just as annoying as the obsessive-compulsive doers? 'Marginalien' is arguably Adorno's definitive statement on theory and praxis, but one could be forgiven for thinking that he is being somewhat narcissistic treating this crucial problem only with a view to (his own) students. [Were they that important? Was he hurt? Is this an act of theory revenge? Was he not at all aware of other forms of praxis current at the time – migrant workers squatting factories, here, there and everywhere? Did it really escape his attention that there almost was another French Revolution?] The marginal notes on the marginal notes aim to transport this not-so-popular document into the present without adapting it too much, like one of those strange objects one finds on, or under, a beach. It might be useful to those who try not to turn the critique of labour into anything carrying the signature of labour.[3]

#1: Don Quixote won't listen

Modernity is the dictatorship of the subject, and dictatorship makes stupid. For the practices of modern industry, the world is pure matter, material without qualities. The processing of the material is motivated, organized, legitimized by the market, which is constituted by the subjects and their social relationships: the materials have no say in it. Praxis in modern society is self-referential and locked into its own bubble: it directs itself at random and exchangeable objects like a deranged dictator. The subjects alone (or rather, the relationships between the subjects) constitute meaning; matter does not matter. Such dictatorship is pseudo-praxis. It is violent: it violates the objects. In pseudo-praxis, subjects rule the world like idiots.[4] They don't care. Praxis properly understood, by contrast, would receive its meaning as much from the objects as from the subjects. Proper praxis reconciles subject and object: what I as a subject want from the world is meaningfully related to and dependent on what the world is, which requires that I make a serious effort to understand the world.

The practical types, the *machers*, don't listen – they cannot be reached by words of reflection, like the original modern Man of Praxis, the don of all doers, Don Quixote. They live in the bubble of their own subjectivity which they deem sovereign, their obsessive urge to do stuff, to imprint themselves on an otherwise meaningless world. They try to create a world in their own image which they can rule more easily. The demand that theory ought to be 'useful for practice' locks theory into the existing, blindly subject-centred conception of praxis. Usefulness can only be measured by the criteria of the existing world, the criteria of the existing subjects who, as personifications of its constituent forces, constitute and rule the existing reality. Mephistopheles, that is, the devil, tells a deliberate lie when he claims that 'the tree of life is green': it is not green, especially not when it is measured in gold. Nor is all theory grey, though: only to the extent that it stands in the service of a grey reality is theory grey.

The modern individual is born from hesitation, as illustrated by Hamlet, one of its prototypes: becoming an individual means de-automation, the overcoming of reflexes by reflection. It means not being a machine anymore. As such individuality is an impediment to praxis. Here is the rub, in the dialectic between on the one hand, the automated activist's monomaniac assertion of subjectivity, shooting from the hip, making history, obsessed with giving form to a shapeless world, and on the other hand, the destruction of subjectivity, the elimination of the hesitation to act. The activist *macher* asserts a subjectivity that eats itself. Hesitation to do things, though, might result from the sense that being a doer makes us commensurate with a world of grey and dull things.

The rationality of the ever-same leads to the loss of experience and furthermore to the loss of the *ability* to make experiences. This damages praxis while it increases our longing for praxis. The less we are capable of it, the more we overvalue and fetishize praxis. The process of rationalization destroys spontaneity and produces an ever more abstract subjectivity. Practice appears the more important the more standardized it is, the more it follows a script that gives it legitimacy, the more exchangeable and representative it is, repeated and repeatable performance. Pseudo-praxis is closely related to pseudo-thinking. The delusional realities of some political mass movements of the twentieth century illustrate this: starting out from the demand that something needs to be done, false political practice reinforced false practices of perception, and pseudo-realities became bloody real. When thinking is reduced to practical, pragmatic reasoning in the service of a world-making subject, the question of reason stops being 'what is reasonable?', i.e. what does reason, imagined as an objective authority, command here, and becomes instead 'what is, from the subjective perspective of my individual interests, the rational, i.e. the most advantageous thing to do?' Reason thus diminished is condemned to making nothing more than images of the world as it is and to serving the attempt to keep it as it is, albeit on an expanded level. Although bourgeois society loves to celebrate the autonomy of the subject, its hostility to theory, that is, to sustained hesitancy in the form of reflection, undermines the subject. The strict conceptual separation of theory and praxis makes the latter arbitrary and the former powerless and irrelevant. Thinking is a practice: it is part of a particular, specific reality. No theory ever existed in a parallel universe: as it cannot, there is no need neurotically to emphasize that it does not do so. The *demand* that theory be practical maintains the delusion that theory *could* not be a practice, that it could exist outside the dirty world of praxis. It cannot. The question is whether theoretical practice is allowed to do its awkward, unpopular job within praxis, within the world, or whether it is banished from it.

#2: Theory is the praxis of freedom

Reflection, contemplation and hesitation interrupt action. Uninterrupted action is liable to become manic and blind, naïve and inhuman. The dialectic of theory and practice is not exclusively a problem of modernity: 'Whoever does not want to romanticize the middle ages must trace the divergence of theory from practice back to the earliest separation of manual from mental labour,'[5] that is, to the beginnings of civilization. Praxis evolved from labour. The concept of praxis emerged with human society, that is, when labour became more complex and included the production of the conditions of production. All praxis labours heavily from its descent from labour. Praxis is marked by unfreedom and renunciation. The pleasure principle and the longing for freedom are opposed to praxis. Art speaks truth to the extent that it constitutes a critique of praxis as unfreedom – it anticipates, as a glimpse, true praxis, liberated praxis. An image of the opposite extreme is that of the ant or the bee: they are horrifyingly serious about a practice they have not chosen to engage in. Emancipation begins when labour assumes an aspect of play and playfulness. Like ants and bees, actionists lack humour [except the collectivist Homeric group-laughter that is in fact a form of aggression].[6] Lack of reflection is the signature of fetishized praxis that becomes the barricade preventing it from reaching its goals. Only praxis, though, can break the spell that praxis has put on humans, which is the real reason why fetishized, anti-theoretical praxis is such bad news: it ruins our attempts at non-fetishizing praxis. [If we could change the world through intense contemplation, we could simply ignore the actionists, sit back, focus our minds on the hostile real–abstractions that govern us, and chillax. The fact that theorists go to the effort of writing and rewriting long complicated essays on theory and praxis suggests that this is not an available option, unfortunately.] As the means are not neutral with respect to the ends, freedom cannot be won by entirely un-free means; therefore theory is a placeholder of freedom in the state of unfreedom – not unlike art. [The obverse is true, too, though: when art and theory are practical representations of freedom, then only practices that represent freedom can count as art and theory. This disqualifies most of the trash that currently goes by those names, from the pedantic-scholastic to the happy-chatty-networky.]

#3: Theory is labour, albeit labour of negativity

The practical types seem to think that theory makes too much work. They have a point: it requires the laborious praxis of resistance to the mainstream of thinking. The refusal of theory constitutes therefore some kind of a commitment to the pleasure principle, albeit a regressive and deformed one. Those who avoid the labours of theory are taking it easy. Their vibes earn them extra coolness kudos from their comrades. Those who relinquish their critical autonomy and join the coalition of the willing are saluted as advanced human beings. Contemporary political activists are moralistic: good intentions, being of good will is what matters to them. They replicate in this kind of moralizing thinking the eighteenth-century attitude of Kant who wrote an ethics pivoted on the intentions and volition of individuals. Already Hegel's critique of Kant signalled that under the condition of increasingly closed totality, such an ethics is ever more irrelevant. Political reflection matters more than good intention. [Adorno seems to say here also that politics matters more than the praxis of the individual, which would include the praxis of autonomous reasoning by the individual against the collective. Section three seems to override individual autonomy by the emphasis on politics, albeit the former remains in place as the *raison d'être* of reflective, more-than-individualist politics. Means and ends are here not quite the same, except that the society that the individuals constitute always already inhabits them.] It is not enough to be a bunch of good, well-meaning individuals: to fight developed capitalism we need to be smart and well-studied.

As soon as praxis becomes the praxis of politics, though, repression of the individual by the generic becomes a real possibility. The praxis of the collective must not therefore scorn the individual. A higher form of praxis will have to overcome the dialectic of the two principal poles of bourgeois consciousness, Kant's moral philosophy and Hegel's philosophy of right. The discovery of such praxis requires theoretical reflection, not least the rational analysis of the situation, aiming to identify moments that might allow transcendence of, rather than adaptation to, reality. Through such reflection, theory becomes a practical productive force that has the capacity to change reality. Although the thinking individual may not be aware of it, thinking about anything that matters always starts from a practical impulse: a want, a need, pain, suffering. Those who think they live in the best possible world, or even just in one that is good enough, will not bother with thinking – why would they? In this general sense, all thinking is negative: no-one engages in any thinking (beyond the mere ordering of data) without a practical *telos*, a goal that aims to negate some negative reality. This does not imply, though, the unity of theory and praxis: neither can praxis tell theory what its practical *telos* ought to be nor the other way round, just as the subject cannot order the world of objects not to be different from the subject. 'True praxis' challenges domination that aims to impose identity on the world. Praxis that fails to do so is pseudo-praxis, assimilation to domination: passivity dressed up as praxis. [This seems to be a gloss on Hegel's notion that 'what is actual', *das Wirkliche*, is reasonable, whereas not everything that just happens to be in existence necessarily deserves the name of *Wirklichkeit*, actuality. Conversely, this also means that what is reasonable should, and sooner or later will, exist, whereas the unreasonable parts of what currently exists are just inconsequential stuff that will disappear. Reality that is not reasonable is pseudo-reality, irreality dressed up as real and liable to implode soon, hopefully.][7]

#4: Theory listens to the objects and splits the rocks

'Praxis must respect the primacy of the object' without, though, adapting to it: the subject must not submit to the object but realize the fact that the subject him- or herself is mediated by the object. This is the difficulty of praxis: being a subject while neither flag-wavingly cockily lording it over the world of objects nor grovelling before it. True praxis is a thin, thorny path manoeuvring between these two versions of failure. Praxis 'well understood' means that the subject mediates that which the object wants: the true subject acts as the object's midwife, not its dominator, without becoming in turn dominated by heteronomy, that is, rule by a commandeering object. The object cannot tell us what it wants though, as its needs are already mediated by the societal totality. Sadly, the totality does not talk to us in plain, simple vernacular either: its strange abstract code can only be deciphered by theory. Praxis relies on theory therefore to know what the world asks the subject to do in the first place. Marx complained therefore not that the philosophers wasted so much precious time interpreting the world but that they *only* interpreted the world, without seeking to change it. As the world refuses to speak our language, interpretation is needed. The increasingly common hostility to theory is therefore really hostility to change. Desperately impatient praxis, too busy to stop, breathe and translate the world's fragmented cuneiform code, becomes delusional, starving, frenetic, naked, invoking fake-theory that has lost its connection to truth the moment it submitted to praxis's central command.

A well-calibrated quantum of delusion is what makes movements and collectives attractive to individuals who seek to get a grip on their personal insanity. Adorno references here the psychoanalyst Ernst Simmel:[8] collective paranoia gives meaning and direction to private paranoia, deprives the latter of its power to disintegrate the individual and neutralizes the subject's inability reflectively to accept real-world contradictions that refuse to be dissolved by the subject's visions of harmony. Projections of unity and its fierce defence are a Band-Aid for schizoid dissociation. The paranoid, collectively sanctioned delusion grants pleasure but threatens the subject; the fetishization of the subjective moment of the historical process, of spontaneity, is a (not entirely unreasonable) reaction to the fact that theory is indeed powerless in the administered world, and reinforces this powerlessness. Without the mediation by theory, though, praxis is unable to read the world's needs, and therefore runs on empty. The belief in the power of praxis in and of itself means the refusal to take proper account of how difficult the task really is in the face of an ever more closed totality. Only theory effects spontaneity.[9] Praxis can only win any battle at all by locating the vulnerable spots where the cracks caused by the pressures of petrification become visible. Such praxis, suffused by theoretical reflection, aims to hit the sweet spots like the quarry worker who will split a block of slate by hitting it at exactly the correct angle. Hammering it abstractly, without attention to the concrete shape of the object, feigning action because we need to be seen to be doing something, will not split the rock.

#5: When the spirit goes playing, we see hope

The existence of spirit presupposes material labour and can therefore not in fact be separated from it. Nevertheless, the separation of theory and praxis is still an indicator of historical progress that leads beyond the blind predominance of material praxis. The fact that there are people in society who can live without having to do any manual labour is an injustice but as such also conjures up the idea that this should be possible for everybody – that in fact it *is* possible given the enormously developed forces of production. Ordering spirit to return to the barracks and workplaces is reactionary. It does not lead to the reconciliation of theory and praxis but to the reversal of spirit's (as yet incomplete) emancipation, humanity's re-subordination under praxis and production in a positivist-technocratic regime that spirit by definition means to oppose. [Having said that, many if not most really-existing intellectuals are of course perfectly fine with

serving positivist technocracy]. Humans needed to gain sufficient distance from
the ongoing, ever-repeated business of self-preservation, labour, production, in
order to take sight of the goal, the abolition of domination in which the natural
history of self-preservation perpetuates itself. Enthusiastically but prematurely
moving to the synthesis of theory and praxis risks killing off the antithesis while
it is no match yet for the thesis. Meanwhile, the elements of moderation, well-
meaning, tenderness that can actually be found in praxis are already the first
buds of its reconciliation with spirit. Praxis and production are driven to take
on aspects of spirit by the difference and distance between them. Give up the
relative autonomy of the spirit, and self-preservation will snap back into its bad
old ways. Desublimation is the name, violence is the nature of the game.

#6: Theory rejects reform of the violent totality as much as violence against it

The sixth section begins with a sequence where Adorno seems to misquote a
passage in which Marx (supposedly in a letter to Kugelmann which Adorno here
probably quoted from memory, i.e. invented) warned against the 'relapse into
barbarism', presumably (judging from the context) resulting from the wrong
kind of revolution that could lead to the 'collapse' (presumably of civilization).
Adorno suggests here that Marx's (assumed) fear of a 'relapse into barbarism'
expresses the 'elective affinity between conservatism and revolution': Adorno
might have had in mind here Walter Benjamin's idea that revolution is the
'emergency brake' that stops the progress into barbarity,[10] a key idea of Critical
Theory (especially since *Dialectic of Enlightenment*) that rejects the liberal and
socialist belief in (automatic, predetermined, teleological) progress (and in this
specific sense could seem 'conservative'). The three sentences at the beginning of
section six in which this idea is expressed [without Adorno's customary clarity]
would seem to support the widespread notion of the anti-revolutionary, quasi
fatalistic character of Critical Theory after the Second World War, but they are
followed, and cashed in, by one of those trademark key sentences that begin
with a BUT: Adorno seems to be saying here that Marx may have been a bit
conservative because a liberal civilization worth defending from collapse still
existed in his time, but it does not anymore now. Auschwitz and Hiroshima
put paid to that: the relapse has happened, civilization has failed; end of.
There is no reason anymore for fearing the collapse. Hence Adorno counsels

we do not need any more to heed the pathetic consolation that things could be worse. We must not accept bad reality for fear of a worse one to come, but rather we need to 'work our way out of barbarism'. This is Adorno's version of the vaunted 'lesson' of Auschwitz: forget reformism. Liberal moderation or democratic reforms did not win the war on barbarism. The rub is, though, that in the next sentence – at the next turn of the dialectical rollercoaster – Adorno posits *violence* as the principal characteristic of the barbarous reality that needs to be undone. In a period in which accelerated history moves at hypersonic speed, barbarism has infected all resistance to it. Many contemporaries agree that the barbarous totality can only be fought by barbarous means (which is 'the lesson' an affirmative reading of WW2 must arrive at – it took a Stalin, amongst others, to defeat a Hitler). Adorno grants somewhat unenthusiastically that in the context of the revolutions at the end of WW1, violence might have appeared justified to the 'all too abstract' longing for total change; after National Socialism and Stalinism, though, violence *as such* is unequivocally part of what needs to be changed. Society's *Schuldzusammenhang* (the concatenation of guilt and blame) has become total; violence means submission to and participation in it when only rejection of the *Verblendungszusammenhang* (the blinding concatenation of ideologies and fetishisms) that maintains the totality can lead beyond the barbarous reality. Pseudo-radical praxis, that is praxis that partakes in the violent forms of practice exercised by the totality, only reboots the old horror. The philistine inanity that fascism and communism were the same thing has become true: bourgeois society, in whose political forms both partake, has made them the same (that is, elements of the same totality). This is not, though, an endorsement of the philistine celebration of the golden middle as a safe space: Adorno complains that whoever rejects raw and irrational violence (or violence as such, for that matter) will find him- or herself being pushed into the vicinity of that reformism that is equally responsible for the continued existence of the bad totality. No silver bullet exists that would provide a quick, explosive exit route from this quagmire, whereas 'was hilft, ist dicht zugehängt'[11]: there are ways out, but they are well hidden.

#7: Theory lives from the experience of open-ended discussion that is not instrumentalized

Actionism is part and parcel of a trend prevalent in bourgeois society: instrumentalism, the fetishization of means over ends. The bourgeois carriers of instrumental rationality and its fetish of means are unapproachable. They do not listen but in turn accuse their opponents and victims of failing to listen. One of the instruments of their authoritarianism is the discussion, a classic-bourgeois social form which they have reduced to the status of a tactical weapon applied in the fight to octroy false consensus. [The praxis-fetishists and 'issue entrepreneurs'[12] resemble in this the managers of modern businesses, including universities, who have also learned how to disguise the handing down of the marching orders as a brainstorming with foregone conclusions. Employees of regular businesses are more likely to see through this kind of spectacle, though, as they are less likely to believe in the moral value of the goals of the enterprise.] The activists' pseudo-discussions are matches between factions that aim to establish by combat which set of foregone conclusions will prevail, to the exclusion of any intellectual experiences of genuine, open-ended discussion.

#8: Major Tom is a cog in the ground-controlled machine

The administered societies of advanced industrial capitalism produce pseudo-activity as a form of opposition to themselves which they also celebrate. Similarly, they celebrate individuality, autonomy and personality at a point in time when they have all but falsified them. Pseudo-activity tends to take itself the more important the more removed it is from societal realities, having become unable even to perceive the proportion between itself and society at large. Fighting on the barricades is ridiculous when the enemy commands nuclear bombs; this is why they are permitted temporarily, from time to time, as games and spectacle. Personality cults grow the bigger the less personalities matter, and the less personality the leaders have. Oppositional pseudo-activity is condemned only for show: it is in fact welcome because it covers up the actual ineffectiveness of autonomous practice by individuals who struggle to form the independent wills that voluntarist politics would presuppose. The astronauts who circumnavigate the moon, as powerful an image of human achievement and agency as they come, can hardly be said to have been acting at all, as every movement they made was directed in minute detail by ground control: the image is one of collective, coordinated and hierarchical action in the context of a huge bureaucratic-technological machinery, not exactly one of free and autonomous will in the sense celebrated by nineteenth-century philosophy. This is our world; the ground-controlled astronaut is the latest human. The leaders of the protest movements mirror the characteristics of the administered world: they tend to be virtuosos of the rules of procedure, rulers of the agenda items. The supposed enemies of the state tend to fight for the institutional recognition of demands worked out and triangulated by a combination of committees. The overall societal process that makes the means colonize and marginalize the ends also makes instrumentalism usurp subjectivity (given that the latter is an end of sorts) and the particular characteristics of individuals: pseudo-activity and pseudo-revolution go together with pseudo-subjectivity.[13]

#9: Make my day, authority!

In section nine Adorno has some tough love for his students: the activism of the student movement is irrational when looked at in relation to the actual power in society which it hardly disturbs. Whence the seriousness with which such objectively irrational practice is pursued? Adorno asserts that many students are in fact desperately poor and thus do have a material interest in radical change, and also that the activists' commitment to creating a pseudo-reality is objectively caused by society's shutting down any other avenues to meaningful change. Mostly, though, he finds it must be explained psychologically: the dynamism of the drives ties down and makes effective in the individuals the ideologies which a brutal reality suggests. Adorno observes two psychological traits in the student activists: narcissism and authoritarianism. They have a huge interest in exploring their own emotional needs but are entirely affirmative about them, avoiding reflection and self-critique. Their own needs become the parameters of praxis, while they overestimate narcissistically their own societal relevance. At the same time they project an abstractly negative conception of authority onto the authorities, that is, their opponents, expecting them to be cold, distant and mechanical. When the authorities turn out not to be such (which might often have been the case in the more liberal spaces of 1960s Federal Republic, such as the Sociology Department of Frankfurt University where professors will have been nice, friendly and supportive), the student rebels react with spiteful anger, suggesting that they secretly wish the authorities to be properly authoritarian. Soft-mannered, liberal-minded authorities – like Adorno himself, one might surmise – are doubly despicable to the authoritarian character for not acting in the expected authoritarian manner. [The suicidal strategies of some militants subsequently in the 1970s to provoke the liberal state to show its true fascist colours could be seen as confirmation of Adorno's group-psychological speculation.]

#10: Reason, by being increasingly rational, drives the techniques of self-preservation to the point of transcending self-preservation

Reason, or rationality, must be directed at the self-preservation of the human species, on which that of the individuals depends. Only when the reasoned reflection on reason (the self-reflection of reason) arrives at this limit-point (the reflection on humanity as the end, or *telos*, of reason) is it able to transcend its commitment to self-preservation, because the self-preservation of humanity means the self-preservation of the possibility of transcendence (which is the end, or goal, of humanity). The self-preservation of humanity is therefore the transcendence of self-preservation in the concept of humanity. [Adorno inserted here a handy two-page summary of everything you ever need to know about Max Weber.] Reason, or rationality, understood as anything less than this material-idealist conception, leads to the unhappy dialectic of the Weberian position that doggedly defends rationality in its stripped-down understanding as means-end rationality while simultaneously deploring that in its most highly developed real-world manifestation, bureaucratic-industrial capitalism, it becomes that depressing 'casing hard as steel' ('stahlhartes Gehäuse', in English better known in Talcott Parsons' mistranslation as the 'iron cage'). Weber wilfully obstructed the way out of this tragic situation by insisting that ends, goals and values must be chosen by the individual without any interference by reason (let alone science), while means must be chosen rationally-scientifically in a value-free manner in order to serve those irrationally determined ends. [Weber had to do this mental acrobatics so as not to become – perish the thought! – a socialist of sorts. Also theory that is determined to avoid its own obvious and necessary conclusions is hard work.]

#11: Theory helps countering the force of gravity concretely, positively exerted by the totality

Always looking on the bright side is a feature of ego-weakness. The whistling individual cannot muster the strength to reflect on his or her own powerlessness.

Some actionists decry theory as abstract and therewith repressive, which is undeniably true: every discipline is by definition repressive. Unmediated breathless praxis is closer to oppression, though, than the thought that tries to take a breath. Only theory can determine what non-repressive praxis would look like, able to navigate between spontaneity and organization, resisting the bourgeois supremacy of means over ends. The technocratic reform of the university is not only the counterpunch to the student protests but also feeds on their logic: the conversion of academic freedom into customer service subjected to market-driven quality controls cunningly responds to the populist complaint that academics in their ivory towers produced abstract, out-of-touch, repressive and elitist theory that is little adapted to real-world problems. [If only...]

#12: Theory punctures the delusion that we are the good ones

Very few individuals ever genuinely make a conscious moral decision to sacrifice their lives for a cause that they must assume is likely to fail. Adorno gives as an example the 20 July 1944 conspirators, members of the German military elite who tried (and failed) to assassinate Hitler. They are famous because there were so few of them. There is a reason for this: Adorno suggests their heroism came from an immediacy that overcame the bourgeois coldness that is one of the normal defence mechanisms that allows individuals to survive the brutal reality of bourgeois society. Adorno illustrates the concept of bourgeois coldness by taking his own unheroic experience as a case in point: it *was* possible to bear the news about Auschwitz when and because one was tucked away safely in distant America. This experience of his own coldness leads Adorno to judge the moralistic demands of some of the student activists that one *could not* possibly sit back and watch the carnage in Vietnam without 'doing something' to be made in bad faith: one *can* watch these things. One can coldly analyse that one is powerless to materially influence (beyond simply protesting against) large-scale geopolitical events that play out as the local manifestations of the global dynamics of imperialism and the Cold War. Likewise, one must and can, against the impulses of justified moral outrage, acknowledge that the moral clarity of the Vietnamese cause is very different from the case of Auschwitz – in the post-Second World War world the globally accepted gold standard of genocide – as the Stalinist Vietcong was not exactly a textbook example of an innocent victim: its power was itself the reactionary result of brutal class struggle within Vietnamese society.[14] [Adorno would probably have agreed that solidarity properly understood can only be with human beings, not with assorted Leviathans and Behemoths – state, military, party organizations.][15]

No one can live in bourgeois society without a sufficient measure of bourgeois coldness, a key element of what Horkheimer termed 'the anthropology of the bourgeois epoch'.[16] To claim one lacked this coldness implies claiming one was already the humane being that can only be the result of revolutionary reformulation of what a human being is: humanity will be created by a reasonable form of society once it is achieved, by the absence of fear, if it will be at all. As things stand, our ability to identify with suffering strangers is low. [Talking of which: we hardly ever manage to acknowledge, let alone cope with, our own suffering. The ability to perceive actual strangers, be they suffering or in the pink, rather than what we project onto them, may not only depend on, but also increase, our ability to admit to ourselves our own suffering.] The misguided and arrogant claim to be so humane takes away from the necessity of revolutionary change: if *you* can be so good then *everybody* can. The reality is, though, that we cannot. Bourgeois society has constituted us such that we *can* live with the knowledge of all the evil for which we are fundamentally responsible. Therefore we make judgements and choices, and to make them well we need a theory or two rather than a sense of moral superiority and a strengthening of the dictatorship of conscience and superego. Our wish to be good must collide with our drive to self-preservation and happiness, and we better acknowledge this lest we become our own enemies. One cannot be too afraid of the world as it is; some will genuinely decide to sacrifice themselves but 'making sacrifice a demand is part of the fascist repertoire'.[17] Some will gain narcissistic pleasure from the commitment to a hopeless struggle but will find the rewards to be short-lived as the organizations that demand the sacrifice tend to give out different and opposing marching orders every so often. Adorno ends this section with a reference to Bertolt Brecht's admission (quoted by Walter Benjamin) that he enjoyed making theatre more than making politics. Adorno applauds Brecht's honesty and sarcastically contrasts it to the protest movements' efforts to turn politics into (not very good) street theatre.

#13: Theory loosens belonging

The praxis fetish facilitates belonging. More recent social movements replicate the disciplinary attitude that was pioneered by the communist parties at a time when the historical situation still seemed open enough to make them seem plausible. [Like above, Adorno again grants that Leninist politics – here the politics of discipline and belonging – at least might have been worth considering in their own historical context at the end of the First World War, but does not commit to a full endorsement.] Standardized slogans are handed down by leaders. One must jump into the melting pot in order to belong. One must sign up by constantly signing things. Ideas are critiqued and rejected as ideologies not because one has practically experienced their falseness but because they are linked to the wrong interests. Through the opium of collectivity, fetishized practice obscures its own impossibility. Responding to critique with the reflex-like demand to declare 'what is to be done' instead then is the equivalent of asking for a passport.

#14: Theory breaks through enemy lines because it is not designed for that purpose

Theory and praxis are neither the same nor totally different. There is no straight line leading from the one to the other: the discontinuity between them is marked by something extra, an '*addendum*' or jolt, something spontaneously encountered during the journey that had not already been in the hand luggage. Theory that simply summarized praxis would be ideology; praxis that simply enacted theory would be doctrinaire and untrue to theory. When Robespierre and St. Just attempted a practical application of Rousseau's concept of the 'general will', it did not turn out anything like Rousseau might have expected. [Then again, though, Rousseau's concept was not entirely innocent of its repressive Thermidorian interpretation.] Only the dialectical contradiction between theory and praxis can be fruitful. Theory as a moment of the totality can resist the latter's spell to an extent – as a constituent part it is more than merely a means or an expression of the totality. Theory and praxis are not gradually, step by step to be translated into each other: they are opposites that suddenly explode and become the other. The theory most likely to become praxis is that which does not want it so much: theory must not be designed with application in mind. In this it resembles basic research in the sciences. Marx's critique of political economy, the only theory that Marx fully developed, lacks any instructions on how to do what the eleventh thesis on Feuerbach claimed was its point: to change the world. Marx refused to provide theoretically grounded recipes for praxis or a positive outline of the classless society. *Das Kapital* contains plenty of polemics but no programme for action. One cannot derive from the theory of surplus value how to make the revolution (but it is essential to spotting and denouncing pseudo-revolutions). Marx was an anti-philosopher not least because he thought philosophy had no business giving instructions to revolutionaries; consequently, as an organizer and man of political praxis Marx did not deploy much complicated theory beyond the idea of the self-emancipation of the proletariat. (The latter means the same thing: the rejection of leadership by middle-class sophisticates and do-gooders). He kept his theory and his praxis at arm's length which allowed the one to be the other's *Kraftquelle* respectively – its source of energy. Reflecting on his own theoretical works, Adorno writes that their impact resulted from the fact that readers do not feel they were being sold a political programme. *Dialektik der Aufklärung* has no obvious practical purpose, and therefore does not provoke 'sale's resistance'. This is how it can work behind enemy lines like a Trojan horse,[18] or indeed, like 'the old mole', the revolution, mentioned by Marx.[19]

Adorno's final observation in this piece is revealingly weird: he asserts that the one thing in which theory and praxis are in fact identical is an obsessiveness that creates blind spots. Any critical theory must by necessity overestimate the importance of the particular object of its critique, as it can only work by obsessively focusing on a particular. This is the element of delusion in critical theory which warns against overdoing it. Yes, that is right: Adorno seems to be saying here, in the concluding section of one of his final texts, we should not get too obsessed with critical theory. [*Now he tells us!*]

Notes

1   Theodor W. Adorno, 'Marginalien zu Theorie und Praxis', in *Stichworte. Kritische Modelle* 2 (Frankfurt/M.: Suhrkamp, 1969), 169–91; Theodor W. Adorno, 'Marginalia to Theory and Praxis', in *Critical Models. Interventions and Catchwords*, translated by Henry W. Pickford, introduction by Lydia Goehr (New York: Columbia University Press, 2005), 259–78.

2   As in Samuel Beckett's play, *Krapp's Last Tape*, https://archive.org/details/gov.ntis. ava19372vnb1.

3   I thank Werner Bonefeld and Chris O'Kane for their numerous helpful suggestions and observations in the reviewing process.

4   'Idiot', as in the Greek word '*idiotes*', 'private person'. When idiots rule the world, they use private, selfish, subjective, instrumental reasoning as opposed to 'objective reason' that aims to work out the reasonable requirements of the object, the social world.

5   Adorno, 'Marginalien zu Theorie und Praxis', 172.

6   To counteract misunderstandings, it should be added that many other animals seem to be quite playful. Mandeville famously did not write 'The fable of the otters'.

7   The etymology gives some useful hints as to the meaning of the word *Wirklichkeit*: it was first introduced as the German translation of Latin *actualitas* (actuality), which contains *agere*, to act. *Actualitas* is in turn a translation of Greek *energeia* (which gives us the English word 'energy' and which derives from *ergon*, from which also 'work' derives. [The Indo-European root of *ergon* had a 'w'-sound at the beginning, a letter called 'digamma' which disappeared in classical Greek, so it was probably pronounced *wergon*]). *Wirklichkeit*, actuality, is not just anything that exists but it is what *wirkt*, what has effects, what works, what drives history forward. This brings us back to the theme of work, the process of civilization and (the critique of) labour.

8   Adorno refers to an essay by Simmel contained in a volume edited by Simmel himself, one of the key works of the classical theory of antisemitism (Ernst Simmel, 'Anti-Semitism and Mass Psychopathology', in *Anti-Semitism: A Social Disease*, edited by Ernst Simmel [New York: International Universities Press, 1946], 33–78).

9   'Spontaneity', from Latin, *spōns*, 'free will'. Spontaneity, consistent with Rosa Luxemburg's use of the word, depends on experience, reflection and learning. Being swayed and triggered by events without mediation by theoretical reflection is the opposite of spontaneity.

10 Walter Benjamin, *Gesammelte Schriften vol. I*, 3 (Frankfurt/Main: Suhrkamp, 1977), 1232.

11 Adorno 'Marginalien zu Theorie und Praxis', 180.

12 McCarthy and Zald talk about 'issue entrepreneurs' as well as 'entrepreneur[s] of the cause' (John D. McCarthy and Mayer N. Zald, 'Resource Mobilization and Social Movements: A Partial Theory', *American Journal of Sociology* 82, no. 6 (1977): 1212–41, here 1215 and 1226).

13 Adorno's theory might have given consolation to Tocqueville who took part in an actual revolution (albeit on the other side) and who admitted more than a century earlier to an embarrassing affliction for which, being a proper liberal, he failed to blame the totality, though: 'Every time that a person does not strike me by something rare in his mind or sentiments, I so to speak do not see him. I have always thought that mediocre men, as well as men of merit, have a nose, a mouth, and eyes, but I have never been able to fix in my memory the particular form of these features in each one of them. I am constantly asking the names of these unknowns whom I see every day, and I constantly forget them; yet I do not despise them, only I consort with them little, I treat them as commonplace. I honor them, for they lead the world, but they bore me profoundly' (Alexis de Tocqueville, quoted in Harvey C. Mansfield and Delba Winthrop, 'Editor's Introduction', in

Tocqueville, Alexis de, *Democracy in America* [Chicago: University of Chicago Press, 2002], xvii–lxxxvi, xxii).

14 Adorno could not have known *In the Crossfire* by Ngo Van, but he would have seen it as confirmation. Ngo Van, *In the Crossfire. Adventures of a Vietnamese Revolutionary*, edited by Hélène Fleury and Ken Knabb (Oakland and Edinburgh: AK Press, 2010 [2000]).

15 The concept of 'solidarity' (coined in the French Enlightenment context but as a political concept first developed in nineteenth-century Catholic social doctrine) refers to a kind of 'solid' interdependence or mutualism based on a sense of fundamental universal *equality* that makes the other's suffering and interests my own and vice versa. As an individual I cannot express solidarity with a state; states have their own forms of solidarity which are called treaties, alliances, pacts and so on. 'Solidarity with Vietnam', 'Solidarity with Israel', 'Solidarity with Palestine' (the names of two states and a state in the making) are meaningless phrases unless one imagines oneself to speak on behalf of a state.

16 Max Horkheimer, 'Egoismus und Freiheitsbewegung. Zur Anthropologie des bürgerlichen Zeitalters', *Zeitschrift für Sozialforschung* 5, no. 2 (1936): 161–234.

17 Adorno, 'Marginalien zu Theorie und Praxis', 188.

18 Monique Wittig, 'The Trojan Horse', *Feminist Issues* 4 (1984): 45–9.

19 Marx uses the phrase 'Brav gewühlt, alter Maulwurf!' in chapter 7 of the *18th Brumaire*. He seems to amalgamate here a formulation by Shakespeare, 'Well said, old mole…' (*Hamlet* Act 1, Scene 5) with its adaptation by Hegel: 'Brav gearbeitet, wackerer Maulwurf!' (in *Vorlesungen über die Geschichte der Philosophie*, Teil 3, Abschnitt 3, on one of the first pages of 'Resultat'; Georg Wilhelm Friedrich Hegel, *Werke in zwanzig Bänden. Band 20* [Frankfurt am Main: Suhrkamp, 1979], 455). Marx suggests here that Bonapartist counter-revolution will in the future reveal itself to have been a mere stepping stone on the overarching, methodical and dialectical trajectory of revolution.

Appendix

12

Introduction to 'Theodor W. Adorno on Marx and the basic concepts of sociological theory'
From a seminar transcript in the summer semester of 1962

Chris O'Kane

Introduction

In this introduction I outline the importance that Hans-Georg Backhaus's transcript of Adorno's 1962 seminar on 'Marx and the Basic Concepts of Sociological Theory' has for shedding light on the relationship between Adorno's critical theory and the critique of political economy. First, I provide a few preliminary remarks on the predominant Anglophone reception of Adorno, which are intended to show the importance of the seminar transcript for Anglophone scholarship on Adorno, Western Marxism and Frankfurt School Critical Theory. I then contextualize the seminar in the Adorno's work following his return to West Germany in the 1950s and 1960s. Then I turn to an overview of what the transcript tells us about Adorno's interpretation of Marx and the importance this interpretation held for Adorno's critical social theory. I then point to the influence Adorno's seminar had on the formation and development of the new readings of the critique of political economy as a critical social theory and to new Anglophone interpretations of Adorno's relationship to Marx that go against the predominant Anglophone interpretation of Adorno.

An earlier version of this introduction originally appeared in *Historical Materialism* (26)1, 137–53. It was intended to highlight the importance of the seminar for understanding Adorno's interpretation of Marx and the relationship between this interpretation, Adorno's critical theory, and the New Reading of Marx for the general readership of a Marxist Journal. What follows has been revised and updated to focus on the importance of the seminar for understanding the importance that Adorno's interpretation of Marx has for his critical theory and for the genesis and further development of the new readings of the critique of political economy as a critical social theory for a readership I assume will already be interested in these topics.

Anglophone reception

While a definitive account of the reception of Adorno's critical theory in the Anglophone world has yet to be written,[1] it is important to note that this reception was formulated beginning in the mid-1960s in the context of the development of the New Left. From our present vantage point it can be seen that this shifting constellation was undoubtedly influential in establishing a number of Anglophone shibboleths regarding the relationship between Adorno's critical theory of society, Marx, and Marxism. This can be seen by examining the two interpretations of Adorno's critical theory that have been most influential in establishing the predominant Anglophone reception: the Western-Marxist and Habermasian interpretations.

The construction of Western Marxism as a coherent historical lineage (a lineage canonized in the work of Martin Jay and Perry Anderson)[2] has meant that the development of Adorno's critical theory is often studied from the perspective of such a historical trajectory. Consequently, since this paradigm is generally thought to have terminated with Adorno, his thought has been interpreted by way of contrast to that of its purported founder, Georg Lukács. This meant that the question of the relationship between the critique of political economy and the critical theory of society in Adorno's thought was reduced to treating the latter in terms of how it deviated from Lukács's theory of reification. As Jay succinctly encapsulates it, Adorno's theory of reification was thus said to substitute the Marxian elements of Lukács's theory of reification – including the labour-theory of value and economics – for the trans-historical notion of the 'exchange principle'.[3]

The emergence of the Habermasian paradigm of critical theory was no doubt also influential in the construction of the historical lineage of Frankfurt School Critical Theory. In this discourse's treatment of Adorno's late work as the culmination of the first generation of Frankfurt School Critical Theory we see the mirror image of the Western-Marxist interpretation. Authoritative historians of critical theory, such as Ralf Wiggershaus (and also Martin Jay),[4] thus contend that Adorno held 'precisely the same Hegelian-Marxist position which Lukács had developed in *History and Class Consciousness* – but he supported it independent of class considerations and as unashamed speculation'.[5] Moreover, the recent work of Anita Chari characterizes the widespread view that, following *Dialectic of Enlightenment*, 'the critique of reification is detached from its basis in the Marxian analysis of the historically specific commodity form and instead is deployed in the service of a critique of reason as such, which is now identified with instrumental rationality'.[6]

As a whole, these interpretations have led to the pervasive view not only that Adorno lacked a unique interpretation of the critique of political economy integral to his critical theory of society but also that Adorno's late work abandoned his modification of Lukács's theory of reification for a totalizing and trans-historical theory of instrumental reason that failed to grasp the emancipatory aspects of modern society. This consequently led to the political 'cul-de-sac'[7] that marked the end of Western Marxism and the obsolescence of the critical theory of the first generation of the Frankfurt School. Such a reception conveniently legitimated the persistence of Anderson (and others) traditional Marxism and the necessity of the Habermasian turn of the so-called second-generation of Frankfurt School Critical Theory, which are said to overcome these pitfalls.[8] Yet it misses the importance that Adorno's distinctive interpretation of Marx had on his late work as well as its influence on the development of a new strand of 'Western Marxism' and a second generation of critical theory that further developed Adorno's interpretation of the critique of political economy: the new readings of the critique of political economy as a critical social theory. The transcript of Adorno's 1962 seminar on Marx casts light on both of these matters.

Context

Adorno returned to Frankfurt from the United States in 1949 with the intent of resuming the post of *Privatdozent* of philosophy at the University of Frankfurt from which he had been expelled by the process of Nazification in 1933. These modest ambitions were wildly exceeded. The 1951 publication of *Minima Moralia* was unexpectedly a best-seller. Coupled with numerous radio and print appearances, Adorno became a prominent public intellectual. He was appointed professor of philosophy and sociology in 1957, sole director of the Institute for Social Research in 1958, and head of the German Sociological Association (the DSA) from 1963 to 1968. Consequently, it was for a critical social theory that encompasses sociology and philosophy that Adorno became a well-known and influential thinker.

As this suggests, Adorno fused his teaching in sociology and philosophy with his research and writing, the institutional roles he played, and his overall public prominence to further develop and promulgate his critical theory of society. Adorno's elaboration of the relations between critical theory and the critique of political economy was at the heart of this effort. The subjects he discussed in his weekly seminars on sociological theory from the mid-1950s onwards were thus crystallized in a number of academic contributions he made during this period, such as 'The Present State of Empirical Research' as well as two textbooks that were intended to showcase what was becoming known as the Frankfurt School's approach to sociology.[9] This distinct critical-theoretical Marxian approach to sociology was also publicly promulgated in Adorno's contributions to what became known as the Positivist Dispute, ranging from the 1957 'Sociology and Empirical Research', to his 1969 introduction to *The Positivist Dispute in German Sociology* (which assembled the contributions to the debate), to 'Late Capitalism or Industrial Society?' – his final address as president of the DSA. In addition, this sociological aspect of his thought informed his philosophy courses, which focused on figures such as Kant and Hegel and topics like history and freedom, as well as his philosophical masterpiece, *Negative Dialectics*.[10]

Yet while Adorno's critique of positivism, his relationship with continental philosophy and *Negative Dialectics* are widely discussed in the secondary literature on him,[11] with the exception of the work discussed below, the predominant Anglophone reception of Adorno outlined above, coupled with his typically elliptical and enigmatic references to Marx in the works he published at the time, have caused the integral link between Adorno's critical social theory and his interpretation of the critique of political economy to be overlooked. The contours of this relationship are signalled in one of Adorno's discussions of the main concerns of sociology *qua* critical social theory in 'The Present State of Empirical Research', wherein the primary interests of sociology are cast in an avowedly critical theoretical Marxian light:

> Sociology is not one of the humanities. The questions it is concerned with are not primarily and essentially those of the conscious or even the unconscious nature of human beings of which society is composed. Its questions are concerned primarily with the interaction between man and nature and with the objective forms of societalization that cannot be reduced to mind in the sense of the inner constitution of men. The task of empirical social research in Germany is to clarify strictly and without any transfiguration the objective nature of what is socially the case, an objective reality that is largely hidden from individuals and even the collective consciousness.[12]

Such a conception of society is also evident in passages from 'Sociology and Empirical Research' (1957) and *Negative Dialectics*, where the social constitution of the objective and subjective forms of socialization referred to above are derived from the Marxian notion of 'exchange'. For instance, a passage from 'Sociology and Empirical Research' (widely quoted in value-form literature) states that 'exchange' is 'not merely the constitutive conceptuality of the knowing subject but also a conceptuality which holds sway in reality [*Sache*] itself'. Thus, '[t]his conceptuality is independent both of the consciousness of the human beings subjected to it and of the consciousness of the scientists... It is not an illusion to which organizing science sublimates reality but rather it is imminent to reality'.[13]

Yet as is often the case in Adorno's published writings, despite his statement that 'The law which determines how the fatality of mankind unfolds itself is the law of exchange',[14] his explication of 'exchange' could do more to establish its genesis, its social objectivity, and indeed its relationship to the critique of political economy. For here, whilst Adorno links this supraindividual conceptuality to the commodity's fetish-character, the ability of exchange-value to dominate reality, and the 'exchange relationship' itself, the exact nature of the link between these ideas is left somewhat unclear.[15]

Hans-Georg Backhaus's transcript of one of these aforementioned sociology seminars is therefore significant, because in it we find Adorno's most extensive and thorough discussion of his interpretation of Marx, and because it demonstrates its significance for Adorno's critical theory.

Adorno's interpretation of the critique of political economy

As I will now show, Adorno's interpretation of these aspects of Marx's thought and their central import for his critical theory of society are rendered more substantive in the 1962 Seminar than in his extant writings or published lectures.

Adorno introduces this interpretation at the start of the seminar and unpacks the aforementioned elements of 'On the Current Position of Empirical Research' and 'Sociology and Empirical Research'. He states, contra Popper, that 'Exchange itself is a process of abstraction' created by the activity of 'relating the same to the same' that grants 'the conceptuality in the relationship of exchange... a kind of facticity', which possess the 'power/violence [*Gewalt*]' of social objectivity. In order to substantiate this, Adorno moves to his account of the critique of political economy, which centres on his interpretation of Marx's theory of value *qua* the fetish-character of the commodities.

Yet, as I have indicated, the 'familiar' Anglophone view of Adorno disregards or misconstrues the relationship between Adorno's critical theory and the critique of political economy. For example, Martin Jay draws on Gillian Rose's statement that Adorno's theory of reification 'was based on commodity fetishism in a way which depended not on work or the labour-process (alienation) but on Marx's theory of value, especially on the distinction between exchange-value and use-value'.[16] This odd distinction leads Rose to argue that Adorno's notion of reification 'is grounded in Marx's theory of value in a highly selective fashion' that 'does not mobilize Marx's distinction between abstract and concrete labour, nor does it lead to any theory of the extraction of surplus value;'[17] rather, 'it is the way unlike things appear to be identical or equal, and the mode of thinking which can only consider them as equal, which is reification as a social phenomenon and as a process of thinking for Adorno'.[18] This leads Jay to conclude that 'the labour theory of value was never... as central' to Adorno's thought, 'because he saw it as an aesthetic reflection of the bourgeois world'.[19]

However, in this seminar, Adorno provides an interpretation of the critique of political economy that cuts against these interpretations. As Adorno states in the seminar, in his view the critique of political economy consists in a double-faceted, immanent critique of the social constitution and autonomization of society as a 'comprehensive totality' and of the deficient science of political economy. Drawing on the Hegelian terminology used to describe exchange in 'Sociology and Empirical Research', Adorno holds that the task of such a critique is to 'account for the conditions that result in the becoming-independent of conceptual relations', whilst '[t]he transition to independence itself is to be deduced from [the] social dynamics' of the class relation. Consequently, Adorno's interpretation of the critique of political economy does not eschew or distinguish between the labour process and Marx's theory of value but brings them together as a critique of the social constitution and reproduction of social objectivity. In contrast to Rose and Jay's interpretation, in Adorno's view, the critique of political economy is thus concerned with accounting for the genesis and reproduction of the autonomous supraindividual inverted real abstraction of exchange in the dynamic of the antagonistic capital-relation premised on production for exchange-value, which abstracts from need and has become an end in itself. In this regard, Adorno states:

> What makes commodities exchangeable is the unity of socially necessary abstract labour-time [*Arbeitszeit*]. Abstract labour, because through a reduction to unity one abstracts from use-values, from needs. When a businessman calculates, he can recur neither to conditions under which a commodity came about nor to whatever a commodity is good for, but focuses on labour-time, profit, material. This is what a commodity is composed of, but this is what makes it a kind of sum of something solid, thing-like [*dinglichem*]. Through abstract labour-time one abstracts from living opponents. On the face of it, this abstraction makes

what is exchanged a thing-in-itself. What is in fact a social relation appears as if [*erscheint als ob*] it were the sum of objective qualities of an object. The concept of commodity-fetishism is nothing but this necessary process of abstraction. By performing the operation of abstraction, the commodity no longer appears as a social relation but it seems as if value were a thing- in-itself.

Consequently, this social process of real abstraction grants commodities fetishistic forms, which Adorno characterizes in terms of their autonomous properties created by the necessary displaced appearance of the historically specific antagonistic social relations of production for exchange. For it is

> characteristic of a commodity economy [*Warenwirtschaft*] that what characterises exchange – i.e. that it is a relation between human beings – disappears and presents itself as if it were a quality of the things themselves that are to be exchanged. It is not the exchange that is fetishised but the commodity. That which is a congealed social relation within commodities is regarded as if it were a natural quality, a being-in-itself of things. The illusion [*der Schein*] is not the exchange, because exchange really takes place. The illusion [*Schein*] in the process of exchange lies in the concept of surplus-value.

Therefore, as Adorno further enumerates, the fetish-form of the exchange abstraction is socially objective, not a 'merely... subjective category' or psychological. Rather '[i]n a society in which exchange-value is the dominant principle, this fetishising is realised necessarily'.

This is because the dominant principle of exchange-value realizes itself necessarily in an inverted and autonomous form of compulsion: the end-of-itself of capitalist accumulation. Therefore, both sides of the class relation are forced to take on the function of 'character-masks', which are 'derived from objective conditions' wherein 'the role [...] [is] imposed on the subject by the structure'. Workers are compelled to sell their labour-power in order to survive. Capitalists are compelled to valorize value to prevent themselves from going broke. For Adorno, the late Marx is thus concerned with the domination and dehumanization rendered by society, rather than a merely idealist, anthropological or psychological account of these phenomena. For it is ultimately the conceptuality of value itself as a real abstraction that transforms individuals into character-masks compelling them to reproduce society.

As can be seen, in contrast to prevalent interpretations among Anglophone scholars, Adorno's comments in this seminar thus adumbrate a distinctive interpretation of the critique of political economy that draws on the categories of abstract labour and surplus-value to align class antagonism and exchange (what Rose calls the labour process and Marx's theory of value). In his view, Marx is concerned with deciphering the social constitution of the autonomous fetishistic form of the exchange abstraction, which inverts to compel individuals to reproduce the very same antagonistic relations of production for exchange that constitute it. Moreover, in further contrast to this perspective, as well as that exemplified by Chari, the importance of this interpretation of Marx's account of the fetishistic form of the exchange abstraction for Adorno's critical theory of society is also evident in the seminar transcript. For, as Adorno puts it, such a concept is still 'key to society' and thus 'distinguishes' the Frankfurt School from Popper and 'all other traditions of sociology'. This can be seen by quickly aligning Adorno's interpretation of the critique of political economy with the account of the fetish-form of the exchange abstraction provided throughout his later 'sociological' and 'philosophical' work.

Adorno's interpretation of the critique of political economy and his critical theory of society

Before undertaking this alignment, it should first be noted, following his designation of exchange as pertaining to commodity economies, that Adorno provides a historically-specific account of the emergence of the exchange abstraction in *Negative Dialectics*.[20] Here, in contrast to Chari and the Habermasian reading, rather than a trans-historical account that ties the exchange principle to 'instrumental rationality', Adorno describes the exchange abstraction as having emerged historically from the 'dissolution of all products and activities into exchange values'. The exchange principle is thus 'presupposed' by the capitalist social form of production, which was constituted by 'the dissolution of all solidified personal (historical) relationships of dependency in production, as much as the all-round dependency of the producers on each other'. Due to this development, a contradictory form of atomized dependence arose in which 'the production of every individual is dependent on the production of all others; as much as (also) the transformation of one's products into food has become dependent on the consumption of all others'. What Adorno refers to as 'this reciprocal dependency' is 'expressed in the constant necessity of exchange and in exchange-value as an all-round mediator'.[21]

Such an account of the social constitution of capitalist society thus sets the basis for Adorno's elucidation of 'exchange' in his critical theory of capitalist society, which, as I will now show, draws on his interpretation of the critique of political economy and can be found in his sociological and philosophical work. For such an antagonistic relation of atomized dependence constitutes the exchange abstraction, which lies in 'society itself' and 'becomes constitutive of society'. The objective and subjective moments of society are thus reproduced by the supraindividual mediation of the exchange abstraction on an objective and subjective pole in Adorno's dialectical social theory of capitalist society as a negative totality.

The objective pole of Adorno's dialectical social theory of domination is thus characterized by the abstract and autonomous aspects of his interpretation of the fetish-form of the exchange abstraction. In *Negative Dialectics* and 'Late Capitalism or Industrial Society?', and his contributions to *The Positivist Dispute*, the mediating conceptuality of the fetish-form of the exchange abstraction is utilized to account for the internal relation between the state, the household and the economy. This is encapsulated in the theoretical statements Adorno provides that describe the abstract and inverted characteristics of the fetish-form of the exchange abstraction, and which present them as constitutive of the social domination of totality. This can be seen in Adorno's characterization of this 'mediating conceptuality' as 'the essence of society', a 'negative totality' that is anything

> but ethereal, but on the contrary an *ens realissimum* [Latin: that which is most-real, materially existent]. Insofar as it is abstractly veiled, the fault of its abstraction is not to be blamed on a solipsistic and reality-distant thinking, but on the exchange-relationships, the objective abstractions, which belongs to the social life-process. The power of that abstraction over humanity is far more corporeal than that of any single institution, which silently constitutes itself in advance according to the scheme of things and beats itself into human beings.[22]

The fetishistic 'power' of the exchange abstraction is further reflected in Adorno's characterization of its autonomous and dominating properties as 'the objectively valid model for all essential social events', such that 'society obeys this conceptuality *tel quel*'.[23] Finally, it is evident in his statement on the inverted status of society in which 'the fetish character of commodities [...] historically has become the *prius* of what according to its concept would have to be *posterius*'.[24] For Adorno, this indicates the general predicament of constitutive social inversion *qua* abstraction, where 'while we imagine that we act as ourselves, in reality we act to a great extent as the agents of our own functions'.[25]

Consequently, an inverted form of supra-individual domination and powerlessness that Adorno characterizes as 'free-floating angst' or 'fate' characterizes the subjective pole of his social theory. Here, 'Individuals are subsumed under social production, which exists as a doom outside of them; but social production is not subsumed under individuals, who operate it as their capacity in common.'[26] Such a state of affairs reflects the fetish-form of the exchange abstraction in which 'the abstraction of exchange value is *a priori* allied with the domination of the general over the particular, of society over its captive membership'.[27] This means that '[t]he concrete form of the total system requires everyone to respect the law of exchange if he does not wish to be destroyed, irrespective of whether profit is his subjective motivation or not'.[28] As a result, classes and the individuals in these classes are dominated by the 'negative universality' of late-capitalist totality, so that 'economic processes continue to perpetuate domination over human beings, the objects of such are no longer merely the masses, but also the administrators and their hangers-on' who as 'appendages of machines' have become 'the function of their own apparatus'.[29] As in Adorno's interpretation of Marx, this means that individuals 'are compelled to carry out the functions of "character-masks", which in turn leads to regressive character formation wherein individuals "compelled to as-sume the roles of the social mechanism" now "model themselves on such, without reservation, on the level of their most intimate impulses"'.[30]

This relationship between Adorno's critical social theory of the negative totality of capitalist society and the critique of political economy is summarized in *Negative Dialectics:*

> [T]he economic process, which reduces individual interests to the common denominator of a totality, which remains negative, because it distances itself by means of its constitutive abstraction from the individual interests, out of which it is nevertheless simultaneously composed. The universality, which reproduces the preservation of life, simultaneously endangers it, on constantly more threatening levels. The violence of the self-realizing universal is not, as Hegel thought, identical to the essence of individuals, but always also contrary. They are not merely character-masks, agents of value, in some presumed special sphere of the economy. Even where they think they have escaped the primacy of the economy, all the way down to their psychology, the *maison tolère* [French: universal home], of what is unknowably individual, they react under the compulsion of the generality; the more identical they are with it, the more un-identical they are with it in turn as defenceless followers. What is expressed in the individuals themselves, is that the whole preserves itself along with them only by and through the antagonism.[31]

Finally, in opposition to this present state of things, as the introduction to *The Positivist Dispute* indicates, Adorno's critique of capitalist society draws on the critique of political economy, deriving these objective and subjective types of domination from antagonistic class-relations. For

> the Critique of Political Economy… attempts to derive the whole that is to be criticized in terms of its right to existence from exchange, commodity form and its immanent 'logical' contradictory nature. The assertion of the equivalence of what is exchanged, the basis of all exchange, is repudiated by its consequences. As the principle of exchange, by virtue of its immanent dynamics, extends to the living labours of human beings it changes compulsively into objective inequality, namely that of social classes. Forcibly stated, the contradiction is that exchange takes place justly and unjustly. Logical critique and the emphatically practical critique that society must be changed simply to prevent a relapse into barbarism are moments of the same movement of the concept.[32]

Critical theory, in turn, does not accept the law-like nature of this dynamic nor the relapse into barbarism as inevitable. Rather it points out its contradictory character and ultimately its irrationality whilst pointing to its origins: the antagonistic class-relations constitutive of the capitalist form of the domination of external and internal nature. In so doing, it moves to break the spell of second nature and negate these relations, including the exchange dynamic that issues from and reproduces them and their miserable persistence.

From this perspective, it is not surprising to hear that 'shortly before his death, Adorno described Marx's value theory as the "most holy estate" of Critical Theory'. Adorno's dialectical critical social theory uses the theory of the fetish-form of the exchange abstraction to theorize the constitution of supra-individual forms of social domination. He thereby articulates the ways in which these forms invert to compel the reproduction of the antagonistic class-relations that cause individuals to become reliant on the very forms that oppress them, thus demystifying and critiquing the reproduction of capitalist society as a negative totality in hope of negating it.

The new readings of the critique of political economy as a critical theory of society

Moreover, although the Habermasian construction of the lineage of critical theory often puts weight on Habermas's time in Frankfurt to establish institutional continuity in his reformulation of critical theory, the case can be made that Adorno was theoretically closer to a number of students he worked with following his return to Germany, including Alfred Schmidt, Hans-Georg Backhaus and Helmut Reichelt. Not only did Adorno (and Horkheimer) supervise Alfred Schmidt's work on the concept of nature in Marx, he later drew on it in the chapter on natural history in *Negative Dialectics*.[33] In addition, while Hans-Georg Backhaus and Helmut Reichelt credit this very seminar – which Backhaus recorded in shorthand[34] – as inspiring their work on the critique of political economy, Adorno also invited the former to lead a seminar on his work in 1965.[35] As this indicates, although they are of the same 'generation' as Habermas, Schmidt, Backhaus and Reichelt construed the relationship between their work and Adorno's in a very different way. Whereas Habermas renounced what he saw as a totalizing social theory of instrumental reason, the latter group of students tried to better ground the relationship Adorno demarcated between critical theory and the critique of political economy. Bonefeld's characterization of the early *Neue Marx-Lektüre* as developing 'the critical theory of the early Frankfurt school, especially Adorno's account' through the 'sustained effort at a critical reconstruction of the critique of political economy as a critical social theory', provides a good characterization of this relationship.[36]

For, as Bellofiore and Redolfi Riva and Bonefeld point out, the interpretation of Marx Adorno presents in the seminar is also important for grasping the interpretation of Marx that motivated the research questions of Schmidt, Backhaus, and Reichelt's New Reading of Marx and much of the *Nueue Marx Lektüre*.[37] Indeed, the seminar's discussion of topics such as critique, social constitution, autonomization, inversion, personification, the social objectivity of the exchange abstraction and positivism, as well as the relationship between the critique of political economy and Hegel's system, was taken up in Schmidt, Backhaus and Reichelt's pioneering work on the critique of political economy as a critical social theory. For instance, Schmidt's 'On the Concept of Knowledge in the Critique of Political Economy' stresses the double-character of the critique of political economy as an immanent critique of 'real political-economic conditions as they necessarily arise from capitalist forms of production and distribution, and secondly, as a criticism of political economy'.[38] In addition, Reichelt's thesis and first book, *On the Logical Structure of Marx's Concept of Capital* attempts to reconstruct the esoteric dialectical structure of *Capital* as that of the unfolding of value as the autonomous inverted supraindividual overgrasping subject'. Finally, Backhaus's 'On the Dialectic of the Value-Form' moved to decipher Marx's theory of value as a monetary theory of value. In so doing, it built on Adorno's analysis of the fetishistic form of the exchange abstraction, even going so far as to argue that Adorno was 'the only author to have thematised what Marx terms the "objective illusion" of economic categories'.[39] Indeed, as Backhaus's publication of the seminar as an afterword in a collection of his work on the critique of political economy indicates, he would later go so far as to state that Adorno's 'posing of the constitution problem in the Seminar is a common thread that permeates his work',[40] while signalling that the importance of Adorno's interpretation of fetishism holds for his own work by making the claim that his interpretation of Marx's theory of value has been fundamentally concerned with uncovering the aspects of the critique of political economy Adorno points to in this seminar.[41] As these comments indicate, the seminar is thus important for understanding the *germinus* of a subterranean lineage of Frankfurt School Critical Theory and 'Western Marxism' that has been occluded by a pervasive Anglophone reception.

This is no doubt why the seminar has been utilized in notable recent scholarship that has contested this reception and further developed the critique of political economy as a critical social theory. Originally intended for publication in issue 24 of *Common Sense* (before it ceased publication), the seminar has been repeatedly cited in Werner Bonefeld's work, playing an important role in his *Critical Theory and the Critique of Political Economy*. Christian Lotz's *Capitalist Schema*[42] also draws on it, as does Josh Robinson's introduction to *Marxism and The Critique of Value*,[43] Riccardo Bellofiore and Tommaso Redolfi Riva's *Neue Marx-Lektüre*, and Patrick Murray's 'Critical Theory and the Critique of Political Economy: From Critical Political Economy to the Critique of Political Economy'. Finally, recent work by a new generation of scholars, including Frederick Harry Pitts, Fabian Arzuaga and Charles Prusik have drawn on it.[44]

In the hope that it will lead to the proliferation of scholarship on Adorno and Marx that goes against the grain of the prevalent Anglophone reception of Adorno and to the further development of the critique of political economy as a critical social theory, we offer it here.

Notes

1   Two recent works – Robert Zwarg, 'Half a Heart and Double Zeal: Critical Theory's Afterlife in the United States', *New German Critique* 43, no. 3 (2017): 225–40 and Howard Prosser, *Dialectic of Enlightenment in the Anglosphere: Horkheimer and Adorno's Remnants of Freedom* (London: Springer, 2020) – come closest. However,

Zwarg's article, which adapts the arguments of his German book, focuses on the development of a distinct North American approach to critical theory. Moreover, Prosser solely focuses on the reception of *Dialectic of Enlightenment* from a position that mirrors the Western Marxist and Habermasian interpretation of the book.

2   Perry Anderson, *Considerations on Western Marxism* (London: Verso, 1979).; Martin Jay *Marxism and Totality: The Adventures of a Concept from Lukács to Habermas* (Berkeley: University of California Press, 1984). For a dissenting view that nonetheless uses the category of Western Marxism see Russell Jacoby, *Dialectic of Defeat: Contours of Western Marxism* (Cambridge: Cambridge University Press, 2002).

3   Jay, *Marxism*, 268–70.

4   Martin Jay, *The Dialectical Imagination: A History of the Frankfurt School and the Institute of Social Research, 1923–1959* (London: Heinemann, 1973); Ralf Wiggershaus, *The Frankfurt School: It's History, Theory and Political Significance*, New ed. (Cambridge: Polity Press, 1995).

5   Wiggershaus, *Frankfurt School*, 95.

6   Anita Chari, *A Political Economy of the Senses* (New York: Columbia University Press, 2016), 72.

7   Jay, *Marxism*, 274.

8   Jay and Wiggershaus, among others, put forward such a narrative.

9   One of these textbooks has been translated as Frankfurt Institute for Social Research, *Aspects of Sociology* (Boston: Beacon Press: 1972).

10 A number of these lecture courses have been translated into English by Polity. Dirk Braunstein has also edited a four volume collection of Adorno's seminar protocols from 1949 to 1969 that will hopefully be translated into English at some point.

11 See, for instance, Vincenzo Mele (ed.), 'What Is Living and What Is Dead of the Positivist Dispute? Fifty Years Later', *Journal of Classical Sociology* 15, no. 2 (2015). Paul Giladi (ed.), *Hegel and the Frankfurt School* (London: Routledge, 2021); Peter E. Gordon, *Adorno and Existence* (Cambridge MA: Harvard University Press, 2016): Timo Juetten, 'Adorno on Kant, Freedom and Determinism', *European Journal of Philosophy* 20, no. 4 (2012): 548–74; Brian O'Connor, *Adorno's Negative Dialectic: Philosophy and the Possibility of Critical Rationality* (Cambridge, MA: MIT Press, 2005).

12 Adorno, 'Zur gegenwärtigen Stellung der empirischen Sozialforschung in Deutschland', *Gesammelte Schriften*, vol. 8, pp. 481ff., cited in Stefan Müller-Doohm, *Adorno: a Biography* (Cambridge: Polity Press, 2005), 337.

13 Theodor W. Adorno, *The Positivist Dispute in German Sociology*, 80 (Farnham: Ashgate, 1981). That such an idea was central to Adorno's thought during this period is confirmed in his 1968 lectures on sociology (published as *Introduction to Sociology*), where it is repeated practically verbatim.

14 Adorno, *Positivist Dispute*, 80.

15 Ibid.

16 Gillian Rose, *The Melancholy Science* (New York: Columbia University Press, 1988), 47.

17 Rose, *Melancholy Science*, 47.

18 Rose, *The Melancholy Science* (New York: Columbia University Press, 1988), 47.

19 Jay, *Marxism*, 270.

20 As Werner Bonefeld, *Critical Theory and the Critique of Political Economy* (London: Bloomsbury, 2014) points out, such an interpretation of *Dialectic of Enlightenment* neglects that, for Adorno, following Marx's notion that 'the key to the anatomy of the human is the anatomy of the ape', history can only be written from the perspective of the present moment. Moreover, such an interpretation also neglects the qualitative difference Adorno and Horkheimer posit between pre-capitalist and capitalist domination. From this perspective, contra neo-Romanticism, the history they sketch delineates the development of historical presuppositions that had contributed to the predicament of capitalist society in 1944, not a trans-historical negative teleology of instrumental reason. See also Massimiliano Tomba, Adorno's Account of the Anthropological Crisis and the New Type of Human, in *(Mis) Readings of Marx in Continental Philosophy*, edited by Jernej Habjan and Jessica Whyte (Basingstoke: Palgrave, 2014); Marcel Stoetzler, 'Dialectic of Enlightenment', in *The SAGE Handbook of Frankfurt School Critical Theory*, edited by Werner Bonefeld, Beverley Best and Chris O'Kane (London: SAGE, 2018).

21 Theodor W. Adorno, *Negative Dialectics*, translated by Dennis Redmond. Available at https://libcom.org/library/negative-dialectics-theodor-adorno. 'Interruption of the Dialectic in Hegel'.

22 Adorno, *Negative Dialectics*.

23 Adorno, *Positivist*, 80.

24 Ibid.

25 Theodor W. Adorno, *History and Freedom: Lectures 1964–1965*, 1st ed. (Cambridge: Polity, 2006), 80.

26 Theodor W. Adorno, 'Late Capitalism or Industrial Society?' translated by Dennis Redmond. Available at https://www.marxists.org/reference/archive/adorno/1968/late-capitalism.htm

27 Adorno, *Positivist*, 14.

28 Ibid.

29 Adorno, 'Late Capitalism'

30 Ibid.

31 Adorno, *Negative Dialectics*, 'Law and Fairness'.

32 Adorno, *Positivist*, 25.

33 Endnotes, 'Communisation and Value-Form Theory' *Endnotes 2* 2010 also claims that Schmidt provided Adorno with the passages from the *Grundrisse* cited in

Negative Dialectics. This would seem to be confirmed by Reichelt's statement in 'From the Frankfurt School to Value-Form Analysis', *Thesis Eleven* 4, no. 1 (1980): 166–9 that Adorno only took some interest in the *Grundrisse*, but this is countered by Adorno's use of the introduction to the *Grundrisse* in *Minima Moralia*.

34 Private communication from Helmut Reichelt to the author following a conversation with Backhaus. The author neglected to ascertain whether Adorno delivered this lecture in a windbreaker, as Detlev Clausen, Theodor W. Adorno, *One Last Genius* (Cambridge: Belknap Press, 2008) states he often did.

35 As stated in Riccardo Belloriore and Tommaso Redolfi Riva, 'The Neue Marx-Lektüre: Putting the Critique of Political Economy Back into the Critique of Society', *Radical Philosophy* 189 (2015). Available at: https://www.radicalphilosophy.com/article/the-neu-marx-lekture

36 Bonefeld, *Critical Theory*, 5.

37 See also Jan Hoff, *Marx Worldwide* (Leiden: Brill, 2016).

38 Alfred Schmidt, 'On the Concept of Knowledge in the Criticism of Political Economy', in *Karl Marx, 1818–1968*, edited by Golo Mann (Bad Godesberg: Inter Nationes, 1968), 95 (translation of the title modified by the author).

39 Hans-Georg Backhaus, Hans-Georg, 'Between Philosophy and Science: Marxian Social Economy as Critical Theory', in *Open Marxism. Volume 1: Dialectics and History*, edited by Werner Bonefeld, Richard Gunn and Kosmas Psychopedis (London: Pluto Press, 1992).

40 Hans-Georg Backhaus, Hans-Georg, *Dialektik der Wertform. Untersuchungen zur marxschen Ökonomiekritik* (Freiburg: ça ira-Verlag, 1997), 29 (translated by the author).

41 'The subject of my work is basically only one thing: the problem of fetishism. It presents itself in three ways: as the objectivity of the economic object, then as the problem of its contradictory structure, i.e. as the problem of unity and difference, and finally as the basis of the analysis of non-empirical theories.' Backhaus, *Dialektik* 34 (translated by the author).

42 Christian Lotz, *The Capitalist Schema: Time, Money and the Culture of Abstraction* (Lexington Book, 2016).

43 Josh Robinson, 'Introduction' in *Marxism and the Critique of Value*, edited by Neil Larsen, Mathias Nilges and Josh Robinson (Chicago: Mcmprime, 2014), IX–Li.

44 Frederick Harry Pitts, *Critiquing Capitalism Today: Ways of Reading Marx* (London: Palgrave, 2018) Fabian Arzuaga, 'Socially Necessary Superfluity: Adorno and Marx on the Crises of Labor and the Individual', *Philosophy and Social Criticism* 45, no. 7 (2018): 819–43; Charles Prusik, *Adorno and Neoliberalism: The Critique of Exchange Society* (London: Bloomsbury, 2020).

13

Theodor W. Adorno on 'Marx and the basic concepts of sociological theory'
From a seminar transcript in the summer semester of 1962

On Popper's 'social nominalism': In Popper, the concept of law is implicitly identified with the regularity of repeated occurrences. In truth, the concept of law is concerned with codifying a particular procedure/event [*Ablauf*] in its structure.[1] It is essential for positivism to hypostatize the division of labour in the sciences, thereby also rejecting this concept of law – when Popper argues, for instance, that historiography cannot verify the concept of law. Here, historiography is being isolated. Marx is accused of 'economism'. There are intellectual [*geistige*] relations that take on a life of their own such that, if they are offhandedly reduced to economic causes, one makes a mess of Marx. Instead, what matters – and this is our task – is to account for the conditions that result in the becoming-independent of conceptual relations. The transition to independence itself is to be deduced from social dynamics.

Popper accuses Marx of 'essentialism'. Marx would have sneered and commended himself as a nominalist (to turn Hegel on his head). Nevertheless, I would say that Popper is right insofar as, in Marx, structural concepts are autonomous, without which social diversity cannot be thought, whereas Popper is essentially hostile to theory. Once the element of the autonomy of the concept is given up, the possibility of theory is denied. Then theory is replaced with the demand that sociology, understood as a kind of agency [*Agentur*] of society, provide well-ordered facts which are used in the respectively dominant praxis.

An earlier translation of this seminar appeared in *Historical Materialism*, 26(1) 154–64 (2018). The translation that follows has been revised.

From where does Popper take his demand for an open society? After all, this is itself a general concept which appears like a shot. Here, a general concept is introduced rather naively and without thought [*unreflektiert*]. 'Humanity' [*Humanitär*] is already a general concept with respect to individual human beings [*Menschen*].

On the problem of social nominalism: Enlightenment recognizes more and more general concepts as fabricated by us. It wants to see through [*durchschauen*] the semblance of autonomy of that which is made by us. It is the human being who produces everything that appears as autonomous-in-itself, it is *thesei* and not *physei*. Popper accuses Marx and Hegel of antiquated conceptual fetishism, but there is no consciousness [*Bewusstsein*] of any fact which is not mediated by consciousness.

It is prohibited to speak of general concepts in the belief that external determination/heteronomy [*Fremdbestimmtheit*] is thereby overcome [*aufgehoben*]. The image of society is reduced to facts, which are said to be products of individual human beings [*Menschen*] in order for them to be conceivable as facts. At the same time, human beings [*die Menschen*] form associations which transcend individual, concrete actions such that these facts, which supposedly are primary, in actuality are themselves mediated. They are taken to present themselves to us immediately as if they were absolutely primary (what is most real), even though they contain a totality which is immediate/ unmediated. Popper would not object to the empirical study of institutions. When I speak of essence [*Wesen*], however, he [Popper] would denounce this as conceptual mythology. When I speak of the structure of our society as a comprehensive totality, the positivists would say: capitalist society does not exist, our society is pluralist. So I ask: Is it really the case that the concept is something the knowing subject adds to the material, or is there something like a concept in the object with which we are dealing?

I here raise the central problem. Our answer on this issue distinguishes our Frankfurt School from all other traditions of sociology. Exchange itself is a process of abstraction. Whether human beings [*die Menschen*] know it or not, by entering into a relationship of exchange and reducing different use-values to labour-value they actualize a real conceptual operation socially. This is the objectivity of the concept in practice. It shows that conceptuality lies not only in the minds of the philosophers but also in the reality of the object itself such that, when we speak of essence [*Wesen*], we refer precisely to that which society, without knowing it, already has in itself. If we stick to the facts, then we ourselves encounter the concept. We are forced to recur to the concept in the object itself instead of retroactively subsuming the object under ordering concepts. When Popper speaks about alienation, abstraction, he comes close to this moment: that the relations between human beings [are] of an abstract kind. The concept is not to be fetishized but instead is embedded within a dialectic with facts. The conceptual structure is itself a fact.

Natural science has objects that do not have consciousness. If it were not for subjects who realize abstraction, that is, if subjects were not also thinking subjects, objective conceptuality would not come into existence. Objects are not immediately subjects, but there is something subjective within objects in the sense of what is necessary for abstraction. The object is nothing self-sufficient [*nichts Autarkes*]. However, one should not posit it as absolute because there is the moment of second nature, which, towards us, tends to harden into something opaque. The superiority of the social is so strong that society appears as if it really were first nature. Positivism is so blinded by society that it regards second nature as first nature and identifies the data of society with the data of natural science. In these questions, our school is in opposition to all sociological traditions of the world.

When we say that a moment of conceptuality [*Begrifflichkeit*] lies in the object, this should not be taken to mean that society is based on something conceptual [*auf etwas Begrifflichem*]. One cannot arrive at relationships of exchange without a moment of conceptuality. It is a process of abstraction, which relates the same with the same to the same. Otherwise, irrationality would reign in society. It is the moment of calculatory equation which has founded the difference between bourgeois society and feudalism. Even if a single human being [*Mensch*] had not had the idea of this absolute exchange, there would objectively still be a process of abstraction in the objective reduction to the same, a process of abstraction which amounts to the objectivity of the conceptual moment, regardless of whether human beings [*Menschen*] reflect on it or not. On the contrary, the greater the power/violence [*Gewalt*] of this conceptual moment, the less it is thought by human beings but lies within the object itself. Therefore, the concept is the object itself and not the subjective unity of features [*Merkmalseinheit*] of the object comprehended under it.

This kind of objectivity of the concept is something else entirely than the kind of objectivity that is taught by mythological conceptual realism, instead containing nominalism as a whole. The conceptuality in the relationship of exchange is itself a kind of facticity. Yet there is something like a primacy of the object over the concept, and likewise there is a primacy of the nominalist over the realist motive. When we say that concept and fact are both moments, this does not mean that both have the same dignity. There is the predominance of the impenetrable over the other [*Es gibt das Übergewicht des Undurchdringlichen gegenüber dem Anderen*]. This way, we do not get into a kind of mythology.

Marx accuses Hegel of making the predicate, that is, the operations and functions, the subject. Marx was a pure nominalist, according to his own understanding, but not according to his objective structure.

Hegel says, to be sure, that the concept of the state is historically prior to the concept of society. Human beings would have first encountered society as the state. Then again, the method [*Weg*] in *The Philosophy of Right* is to develop [the argument] that society necessarily strives towards the state by force of its own dialectic, that is, that the state is the product of society.

Marx was extremely anti-anthropological, anti-psychological. His real interest is in the institutions which dehumanize human beings [*den Menschen*]. He does not provide an analysis of humanity [*des Menschen*]; this would be superficial with regard to historical being.

Marx's understanding of Hegel is very problematic. The mature Marx, however, resumed the objectivity of the concept, particularly in contrast to the Left-Hegelians.

The human being [*der Mensch*] is that living being [*Lebewesen*] that reproduces itself. The human being becomes a human being through itself, through social labour. Only through the phases of social labour does the human attain to the concept of humanity [*des Menschen*], that is real, free humanity.

Marx imputes a concept of spirit to Hegel which is separate from the material sphere of being. In Hegel, spirit is described as totality; the determinations of labour [*Arbeit*] are by no means of a separate intellectual principle. Hegel thinks of a contestation of humanity [*des Menschen*] with nature, but interprets the total movement as a spiritual one. However, the moments in labour [*Arbeit*] are equally material moments and not activities of an isolated spirit. The slave [*Knecht*] is not an intellectual. The spiritual lies only in the general relation which unfolds between master [*Herr*] and slave [*Knecht*]. Objectivity [*Gegenständlichkeit*] has, in a certain sense, a more conclusive meaning in Hegel than in Marx because an unresolved remnant of the institutional vis-à- vis a free society remains.

(Adorno: it is the core theoretical lecture of the seminar.) What does critique of political economy mean in Marx? (1). Critique of the classical theory of liberalism. (2). Critique of the economy itself. That is, critique of the self-understanding of liberalism (in particular in Volume 4, the *Theories of Surplus Value*) as well as a [critique] of liberalism itself. Marx is concerned with an immanent critique of liberalism. In the East, Marx serves the interests of power relations; this Marx belongs to the sphere of pulp literature. In the West, the accusation is made that Marx's theory is premised on subjective-proletarian class consciousness. This is precisely what is not meant. Liberal theory is confronted with its own claim with regard to the act of exchange. 'You say that equivalents are exchanged, that there is a free and just exchange, I take your word, now we shall see how this turns out!' This is immanent critique. That the human [*Mensch*] becomes a commodity has been perceived by others. Marx: 'These petrified conditions must be made to dance by singing to them their own melody' ('Contribution to the Critique of Hegel's *Philosophy of Right*'). Not: to confront capitalist society with a different one, but: to ask if society conforms to its own rules, if society functions according to laws which it claims as its own. Now, Marx does not just say, no, this is wrong, but he takes the dialectic seriously and does not just flirt with its terminology. In an exchange, something is both equal and unequal; it is and at the same time is not above-board. The theory of liberalism conforms to its own concept and by conforming it also contradicts its own concept. The exchange-relation is, in reality, preformed by class relations: that there is an unequal control of the means of production: that is the heart of the theory. This question is of almost no importance in today's discussion of Marx. Critique tests claim by confronting them with the object and by deducing tendencies of development out of this contradiction. The late Marx would say that this method is still too abstract.

The stages of development are developed as qualitatively different from each other. As in Hegel. Nodal points of development. Rostow, by contrast, does not recognize any qualitatively different fundamental structures. For him, two different stages are a more-or-less [*ein Mehr oder Weniger*], there are no qualitative differences. Marx is not simply an economic historian; for him, historical and systematic moments are mediated, the historical process itself is regarded as the logical, necessary transition from one structure to another. Marx differentiates himself from static doctrines as well as from the mere historian [*vom bloßen Historiker*] who only describes different stages. The concept is entirely historicized. The process is formally idealist, it is the self-actualization of the concept, in the case of Marx the modes of production. Double rejection: with regard to invariant idealism and descriptive positivism.

The commodity is characterized by its exchange-value. It is precisely not need that constitutes the commodity. Commodity value is not derived from need but from objective conditions of production of which need is an element but only in the last instance, that is, mediated by the interest to get rid of the stuff. It is characteristic of objective theory that it starts from institutions rather than needs, from actual relations of power, relations of disposal/control [*Verfügungsverhältnissen*]. 'You always talk about explaining the economy out of needs, but the *mechanism/business keeping* [*Getriebe*] does not primarily serve the needs; rather these are satisfied at great cost and under the terrible grinding of the system.' Need is only dragged along and this is why the economy must not start from needs – because the world does not turn according to our needs. The latter are only an epiphenomenon.

What is decisive is the primacy of the apparatus of production over needs. This must be maintained against the objection that the phenomena described by Marx could be represented subjectively.

Marx's method consists of subsequently correcting abstractions by way of very extensive differentiations. Here, I want to give notice of the problem of whether this is reconcilable with dialectics or whether Marx may have violated the principles of dialectics.

What makes commodities exchangeable is the unity of socially necessary abstract labour-time [*Arbeitszeit*]. Abstract labour, because through a reduction to unity one abstracts from use-values, from needs. When a businessman calculates, he can recur neither to conditions under which a commodity came about nor to whatever a commodity is good for, but focuses on labour-time, profit, material. This is what a commodity is composed of, but this is what makes it a kind of sum of something solid, thing-like [*Dinglichem*]. Through abstract labour-time one abstracts from living opponents. On the face of it, this abstraction makes what is exchanged a thing-in-itself. What is in fact a social relation appears as if [*erscheint als ob*] it were the sum of objective qualities of an object. The concept of commodity-fetishism is nothing but this necessary process of abstraction. By performing the operation of abstraction, the commodity no longer appears as a social relation but it seems as if value were a thing-in-itself.

Exchange is still the key to society. It is characteristic of the commodity economy [*Warenwirtschaft*] that what characterizes exchange – i.e. that it is a relation between human beings – disappears and presents itself as if it were a quality of the things themselves that are to be exchanged. It is not the exchange that is fetishized, but the commodity. That which is a congealed social relation [*ein geronnenes gesellschaftliches Verhältnis*] within commodities is regarded as if it were a natural quality, a being-in-itself of things. The illusion [*der Schein*] is not the exchange, because exchange really takes place. The illusion in the process of exchange lies in the concept of surplus-value.

However, fetishized perceptions are not an illusion either, because insofar as human beings in fact become dependent on those objectivities, which are obscure to them, reification [*Verdinglichung*] is not only false consciousness, but also simultaneously reality, insofar as commodities really are alienated [*entfremdet*] from human beings. We really are dependent on the world of commodities [*Warenwelt*]. On the one hand, commodity fetishism is an illusion; on the other, it is utmost/ultimate reality – and the superiority of the reified commodity [*der verdinglichten Ware*] over humanity stands as testament to this. That the categories of illusion are in truth also categories of reality, this is dialectic.

Concepts like the fetish-character of commodities can only be understood when one does not merely transform them into subjective categories. Here, I do not mean the appeal to today's human beings [*Menschen*], which emanates from commodities in a store. It is not about the psychological fetishizing of individual commodities but about the objective structure of the commodity economy [*Warenwirtschaft*]. In a society in which exchange-value is the dominant principle, this fetishizing is realized necessarily. What is essential is that the commodity disappears as a social relation; all other reactions of reified consciousness [*des verdinglichten Bewusstseins*] are secondary.

To be sure, the commodity is the archetype [*Urform*] of ideology; yet the commodity itself is not simply false consciousness but results from the structure of political economy. This is the actual reason why consciousness is determined by being. What is decisive is that the objective structure of economic form realizes from within itself fetishization. This is the objective process of ideology – independent of the consciousness of individuals and their will. The theory of ideology [*Ideologielehre*] has its seriousness [*Ernst*] only in the fact that false consciousness itself appears as a necessary form of the objective process that holds society together. Socialization itself takes place through this ideology. Here, the issue of the problem of ideology becomes very serious.

Even if we see through illusion, this does not change the fetish-character of the commodity: every businessman who calculates has to act according to this fetish. If he does not calculate in this way, he goes broke.

Money is also only a symbol of congealed labour [*geronnene Arbeit*] and not a thing-in-itself, such that the processes in finance are not primary; rather, financial relations have to be derived from political economy.

When exchange-value becomes independent, then I can strive for it as a thing-in-itself. And this reification of exchange-value is what is meant by the formula M–C–M'.

Crucial question: Where does surplus-value come from? The sphere of circulation is secondary. Surplus-value is already contained in it. In the sphere of circulation, entrepreneurs scramble for surplus-value, which is, however, already produced.

Labour power [*Arbeitskraft*] is the source of surplus-value because it is at the same time use-value and exchange-value. This is the crux of the matter. The worker is free insofar as he can move from one branch to another.

Value itself is defined as social labour. For this reason, machines cannot produce value. What they do refers back to labour because machines themselves are produced by human beings. Entrepreneurs strive for absolute surplus-value – but not because they are bad people. Psychology is as alien to Marx as it is to Hegel.

Marx's theory of 'character mask' contains the concept of role [*Rollenbegriff*]. Only that it is here derived from objective conditions; the role is imposed on the subject by the structure. Today – as in Parsons – there is no reflection on, but instead an absolutization of the concept of role itself. The real reason why I am sceptical of the concept of role is that it is not understood as a necessary moment in a process, but that it is instead isolated and singled out.

Essence of dialectics: Capitalists are forced to try to accumulate surplus-value. For this purpose, they are impelled to develop machines in order to replace living with dead labour. If not, then they are in competition. Here, a moment of the sphere of circulation impacts on the sphere of production. However, because they are forced, capitalists create the conditions of productive forces that do not need the chains of capitalist economy. Second, they thereby create a dynamic which turns against themselves; more and more labour is set free, thereby creating the conditions of crisis and the continuously increasing threat to the system itself. In order to maintain itself, the system must produce precisely such moments through which it increasingly undermines [*untergräbt*] its own possibility. The purpose of spontaneity is to get this process under control, which is otherwise headed for the destruction of the whole, so as to transform [*aufheben*] the whole to a higher mode of production. Whereas dialectic itself, insofar as it is blind, also creates the conditions for the other [*für das Andere*]. If there is no moment of freedom, that is, if the whole is left to itself, then it goes under.

Eternal uncertainty is one of the reasons for the backwards-oriented desire for agrarian and artisanal [*handwerklichen*] relations. This is the authentic moment in it. The other, the transfiguration, is false: these relations cannot be restored.

In order to understand the concept of surplus-value, two time-spans have to be compared: the time which is necessary for the production of labour-power and the time that the worker gives in labour. One must not start with the commodity produced by the worker, rather it is a matter of an exchange process: the worker sells his labour-time [*Arbeitszeit*] for which he receives his equivalent. But the time he gives and the time that is needed for the reproduction of his labour-power are different. On the one hand, exchange takes place in the form of equivalents: the worker gives his labour-time and receives what is required for the reproduction of his labour-power in return. Here lies the source of surplus-value without having to consider the commodity produced. One exchanges the same for the same [*Gleiches mit Gleichem*] and simultaneously the same for the not-same [*Gleiches mit Nicht-Gleichem*]. Behind this lies the entirety of class relations. Only because the worker has nothing else but his labour-power does he accept these conditions. Behind this strange exchange lies the question of class relations.

It would probably be flawed to say that subjective theory is unable to explain the entire mechanism of the economy in terms of needs. It can certainly also be done in terms of subjective categories – if one settles for outlining a formalistic scheme for economic processes. However, in doing so one abstracts from the moment of social power and impotence [*Macht und Ohnmacht*]. It is not as if it is only today that consumption is controlled. Today there is only a new quality, which prevails in the regulation of consumption. But in this society the consumption of subjects is not the key for the economy because the subjects' own possibilities of consumption depend on (1). the overall economic system as a whole; one can consume only as much as social status permits; (2). consumption depends on the contemporary overall economic situation.

The actual controversy does not concern which of the two directions economic processes can be represented more smoothly, but rather what theory more adequately portrays the reality in which economic relationships of human beings take place. An approach that does not account for the consumer's dependence on the overall system is inadequate to reality. One can demonstrate that the changes in the customs of consumption [*Konsumsitten*] do not spring from the subject but that they are objective processes which have their roots in the structure of society. This is why Marx does not start with consumption but with production – production understood as dominance [*Vorherrschaft*] of the proprietors [*der Verfügenden*]. This approach is more in line with reality.

The choice of coordinate system is not neutral with regard to the issue. That system is better in which more of the real relations appear. If relations are antagonistic (class system), then antagonisms must also be expressed in theory.

Subjective economics is essentially an analysis of market processes in which established market relations are already presupposed. Engels rightly invokes the heritage of German philosophy: the question was concerned with constitutive moments through which surplus-value comes about, with immanent conditions through which the system comes about, while subjective doctrine attempts to elegantly formalize already-established processes.

By contrast, Marx is not concerned with the description of market society but instead enquires about the constituents of experience and provides a critique of these categories of economic activity. This approach, which proceeds from the problem of constitution [*vom Konstitutionsproblem*], is deeper; it enables more of reality to be expressed. The point is whether constituents of totality can be seized. The question of constitution is already present in the ostensible discretion concerning where to cut through reality for the purpose of abstraction. Subjective doctrine is essentially apology. The analysis of the question of price is an epiphenomenon in contrast to the questions of constitution.

On critique: One cannot stop at the phenomena of alienation [*Entfremdungsphänomenen*]; in principle, alienation is an idealist category. However, alienation results from the commodity character of the economy [*der Ökonomie*]. Nor can one speak in abstractions about power, for the question of power asserts itself by virtue of the reproduction of the material life of man. If it were only about questions of alienation and power, Marx would not have anything to tell us; then all that would remain of Marx would be Left-Hegelianism. But Marx wanted to criticize how power and alienation play out in concrete society.

The concept of relative immiseration [*Verelendung*] is diabolically amusing [*urkomisch*]. When no worker knows anymore that he is [pauperized] – as Schelsky claims – where, then, lies the possibility to draw on the concept of class?

The concept of technology [*Technik*] is not clear in Marx. This concept is inherited from Saint-Simon without the latter having thought through his position concerning relationships of production. These are, on the one hand, shackling; on the other, they are constantly changing and become productive forces. This is the problematic nature of this concept.

We can see that the utmost difficulties are inherent in the system. Marx is burdened with a whole string of questions. The bleakness of our situation consists in the fact that these aspects are not developed further but instead criticized from outside without confronting the theory with its own immanent difficulties. On the one hand, the theory is defamed – in the West – on the other hand, it is fetishized – in the East. In the East, the theory is placed under a taboo; in the West it is considered a cardinal sin to concern oneself with it. The future of thinking about society depends on whether we can solve these problems. The genius of Marx consisted precisely in the fact that, filled with disgust, he tackled exactly that which he found disgusting: the economy [*Ökonomie*].

To the objection that socialism leads to massification, one must reply that the latter will disappear only when individuals are no longer determined by relations of exchange.

Translated by Verena Erlenbusch-Anderson[2] *and Chris O'Kane*[3]

Notes

1   Translators' Note: The German original is included in brackets for technical and difficult-to-translate terms and when words or phrases were added for clarification.
2   Department of Philosophy, Syracuse University.
3   Department of Political Science, University of Texas Rio Grande Valley. The translators would like to thank Patrick Murray and Jeanne Schuler for their comments on an earlier version of the translation and Lars Fischer for his comments on this translation of the seminar.

Index

Printed in Great Britain
by Amazon

37555814R00152